WIRRAL

From Old Photographs

IAN COLLARD

AMBERLEY

First published 2018

Amberley Publishing
The Hill, Stroud
Gloucestershire, GL5 4EP

www.amberley-books.com

British Library Cataloguing in Publication Data.

A catalogue record for this book is available from the British Library.

ISBN 978 1 4456 7803 0 (print)
ISBN 978 1 4456 7804 7 (ebook)

Origination by Amberley Publishing.
Printed in the UK.

Introduction

The Metropolitan Borough of Wirral was created by the 1972 Local Government Act, which combined the areas of Birkenhead, Wallasey, Bebington, Heswall, Hoylake and West Kirkby under one authority. It is bordered by the River Mersey to the east, the Irish Sea to the north and the River Dee to the west. Cheshire West and Chester occupy the southern section of the Wirral Peninsular.

In 1150 a Benedictine priory was established on the Wirral Peninsular on a headland of birch trees when Hamon de Mascy granted lands to the order of St Benedict. A group of Black Monks became the first inhabitants of Birkenhead when they moved from Chester. The monks were renowned for their hospitality to travellers and a priory was established near a landing stage at Woodside. In 1284 the road was diverted away from the ferry as the monks could not cope with the number of travellers using the facilities at the priory.

The travellers were then accommodated in houses that were built in 1318, and in the charter of 1330 Edward III granted the prior and priory of Birkenhead and their successors forever the passage over this arm of the sea and the rights to charge for their services. However, the monks were forced to leave the priory following the Dissolution of the Monasteries in 1536. Their lands were confiscated by the king and sold to Ralph Worsley, who became lord of the manor.

In the sixteenth and seventeenth centuries the Powell family owned the Woodside ferry. The estate was sold in 1694 and a boathouse and quay was built at Woodside. The land was purchased by the Price family in 1716 and the ferry was leased to a succession of tenants. In the early years of the nineteenth century new houses were built and the number of passengers travelling on the ferry increased. The chapter house and priory were replaced by a new church, which was dedicated to St Mary. The population of Birkenhead continued to increase and the new ferry services to Liverpool encouraged people and merchants to move to the town. The population of 200 in 1821 doubled in the following two years.

William Laird moved to Liverpool in 1810, became director of two shipping companies and acquired land near the Wallasey Pool at Vittoria Wharf. The railway companies were interested in gaining access to the Mersey at this time and purchased land to build a port on the Wirral side of the river. The census of 1831 showed a population of 2,569 inhabitants in Birkenhead and two years later an Act of Parliament was approved. Improvement Commissioners were established to appoint police and firemen, purchase fire engines and to build a market. William Laird's son John joined the company in 1828, and they made the decision to build ships of iron at Birkenhead.

The Improvement Commissioners became responsible for the Woodside ferry in 1842 and plans were drawn up to build a dock system at Birkenhead, which received royal assent in Parliament in 1844. Egerton and Morpeth docks were opened on 5 April 1847, followed by the Great Float, which was later divided into the East and West Floats. On 1 January 1858 the Mersey Docks and Harbour Board became responsible for the operation of the docks at Liverpool and Birkenhead.

Birkenhead Park, designed by Joseph Paxton, was also opened on 5 April 1847. It was the first town to ask Parliament for the powers to build a public park and the opening was attended by over 10,000 people. The Birkenhead Tramway was established in 1860 and ran from Woodside ferry to Birkenhead Park. It was the first tramway to operate in Europe. On 13 August 1877 a charter was granted to the mayor, alderman and the burgesses of the borough. By 1878 the population was 77,260, and under the Local Government Act of 1888 the town was created a county borough. The town included Bidston, Claughton with Grange, Oxton, Tranmere and part of Bebington (later known as Rock Ferry), Landican, Prenton and Thingwall, followed by Noctorum, Upton and Woodchurch in 1933.

The Foreign Animals Wharves were established at Wallasey and Woodside in 1878 and later came to handle half a million animals a year. Cattle were also shipped onwards or were slaughtered at the lairage and chilled meat was shipped from the wharf. Grain was imported to Birkenhead docks from European and Black Sea ports and later North and South America, India and Baltic ports. Chemicals and minerals were imported and factories set up around the dock estate to manufacture copper, steel, chemicals, cement, fertilizer, oils and bricks. Iron ore was imported through Birkenhead for onward shipment to the steelworks in North Wales and special cranes and handling equipment were provided at Bidston Dock. By 1954 the iron ore trade had increased to 1 million tons and two years later it had doubled to 2 million tons a year.

The Queensway road tunnel was completed in 1934, linking Birkenhead with Liverpool. It was opened by George V and Queen Mary on 18 July 1934 and by the early 1960s traffic had increased and plans were drawn up for the construction of another tunnel between Liverpool and Wallasey. Work began in 1966 and the first tube of the new tunnel was opened by Her Majesty the Queen on 24 June 1971. Oil is imported through the Tranmere Oil Terminal, which was opened in 1960 and is discharged and transferred through a 15-mile pipeline to Stanlow in Cheshire.

In the early 1970s a new dock system was opened at Seaforth and many of the goods and materials shipped through Birkenhead docks were transferred to the new facilities at Liverpool where specialist container, meat and grain handling terminals were built. This led to a dramatic reduction in the amount of goods and cargo shipped through the docks and there are now only a few operational berths at Birkenhead. However, a new roll on/roll off river terminal was built near Morpeth Dock, which brought new life and activity to an area that had been run down and out of use for many years. The terminal provides facilities for passengers and cargo services between the port and Belfast and Douglas, Isle of Man, in the winter months.

The name Wallasey comes from the Germanic word *Walha*, which is translated as stranger or foreigner, and is also the origin of the name Wales. Wallasey is bounded by the Irish Sea to the north, to the east by the mouth of the River Mersey and to the south-west by the inlet of a river. The Domesday Book of 1086 states that the Saxon landowner Ulstred had been dispossessed of his lands, which were awarded by William I to the Earl of Chester, and then held by Robert de Rhuddlan.

The development of Wallasey was greatly influenced by the fact that the area consists of new red sandstone from sea level to nearly 200 feet. The sandstone rock extends from the Red Noses in the north down to another ridge at Seacombe. These ridges and the deposited clay made the area fertile and ideal for farming and associated activities. Around AD 74, when the Romans arrived they found a Celtic tribe, the Cornovii, in charge of the area. The Anglo-Saxons controlled Wirral around AD 613 and they occupied areas such as West Kirby, Frankby and Irby. In the sixteenth and seventeenth centuries, horse races took place on Leasowe sands and these were organised by the Earls of Derby, and were regarded as the forerunners of the Derby races.

In the reign of Edward II the manor of Wallasey became part of Halton as Robert de Rhuddlan died without heirs. Liscard was held by the Astons and lands at Pulton paid rents in 1816 to Halton. The lordships and manor of Liscard was advertised for sale by public auction on 20 August 1800 and sold to John Penkett for £2,513. He was agent to the gunpowder magazine in Liscard and lived at Rose Mount in Egremont. The manor of Wallasey passed to his daughter Mary Ann, who married John Dennil Maddock, and she held the title of lady of the manor until her death in 1888.

Fort Perch Rock was completed in 1829 and the lighthouse the following year. The parish church of St Hilary was established in 1857 to replace the church built in 1730. A church had existed on the site since the fifth century and three of these had been destroyed by fire. The accounts for the parish date back to 1658, and the church registers to 1574.

James Atherton, a local merchant, purchased around 170 acres of land at Rock Point in 1830. He planned to develop a 'favourite and fashionable Watering Place' with residential homes, a church, hotel and ferry and establish packets between that place and Liverpool. The gunpowder magazine was closed in 1851, and houses were built with views of Liverpool and the River Mersey. Atherton founded the New Brighton ferry with his son-in-law William Rowson and a pier was constructed. The ferry was acquired by the Coulbournes in1850 and it was purchased by the Local Board ten years later. Work was completed in 1867 on an extended pier at New Brighton. The ferry operating from Egremont was transferred to the Local Board in 1861. A floating stage had been built at Seacombe in 1840 and by 1876 the annual passenger traffic had reached nearly 2 million, so a decision was made to build a new terminal.

The construction of the first stage of a new promenade was completed in 1891, and this was extended to New Brighton by the end of the century. Parliamentary sanction was granted in 1906 for the construction of the promenade from New Brighton ferry to the Marine Park and the Wallasey Corporation Act of 1927 approved the extension of the promenade to Harrison Drive. The development of the Mersey Railway and the improvements to the ferry services enabled more people to move to the Wirral, and New Brighton developed as a popular seaside resort. A tower and ballroom was opened at New Brighton in 1900.

With the increase in housing developments at the beginning of the twentieth century, Egremont, Liscard, New Brighton, Poulton, Seacombe and Wallasey village gradually merged together to become the town of Wallasey. The Local Government Act of 1894 created the Urban District Council, dividing Wallasey into eight wards, and a petition was lodged in 1902 for application as a borough to appoint a mayor, alderman and town clerk, and to establish a police force. A royal charter was granted in 1910 by George V with county borough status being granted in 1913. The district of Moreton was added to the borough in 1928, and in 1974, as part of local government reorganisation, Wallasey became part of the Metropolitan District of Wirral.

In the 1960s the popularity and attraction of New Brighton as a seaside resort began to decline and the bathing pool, pier and Tower Grounds have since disappeared. Victoria Road shops, cafés, cinemas and amusement arcades have been replaced by a housing development. The local authority commissioned a study on the viability of building an Ocean Dome at New Brighton, similar to one at Miyazaki in Japan. This was the world's largest all-weather indoor water park with a retractable roof and artificial lagoon. The building at New Brighton would have catered for 10,000 visitors and included restaurants, bars, cinemas and speciality shopping as well as hotels and a conference centre, a golf course and many other attractions.

It was proposed that the Dome would be the centrepiece of a wider development, which included a multipurpose observation tower, a new tidal lake and marina, a new jetty for ferries and hovercraft and a major Millennium Botanic Garden. It was claimed that there were 36 million people within a two-hour drive from the Dome and that 68 million day visits were made each year to leisure attractions in the United Kingdom. There were 24.5 million visits made to Merseyside each year and tourism contributed an estimated £41 million a year to the Wirral economy. It was estimated that the Dome would cost around £150 million and the cost of the whole project to develop the resort would have been £400 million, and this would have provided work for 2,000 people.

It was an ambitious plan for a new dynamic New Brighton redefining itself for the twenty-first century and would have required a substantial investment by the private sector and local authority. When it became apparent that the investment would not be found the plan did not get any further than the feasibility study conducted by the consultants Deloitte & Touche. However, a new development has brought a supermarket, shops, pubs, hotel, restaurants and a cinema to the town. New Brighton is experiencing a renaissance and is becoming very popular with visitors and local people, especially during the summer months.

Peel Ports acquired the Mersey Docks and Harbour Co. in 2005 and announced that they would give priority towards the redevelopment and regeneration of the Liverpool and Birkenhead dock estates. The Wirral Waters scheme involves a £4.5 billion investment and is a sister project to Liverpool Waters on the other side of the river. The object of the project is to regenerate a largely unused series of dock spaces and will see the creation of 5 million square feet of modern office space at the East Float and Vittoria Dock. This will also include the building of hotels, bars, restaurants and apartments. In addition to this provision the former Bidston Dock will be developed to include office, retail and leisure facilities.

The Wirral is now one of the six constituent districts of the new Liverpool City Region Combined Authority. A number of the borough's responsibilities have been pooled with neighbouring authorities within the metropolitan area and the combined authority has become the top-tier administrative body for the local governance of the city region. A city region mayor has been elected and negotiations are taking place between the central government and the region regarding its role and responsibilities in the future. Burton, Great Sutton, Ness, Parkgate, Capenhurst, Hooton, Neston Puddington, Ellesmere Port, Little Sutton, Overpool, Shotwick, Willaston and Little Neston are also located on the Wirral Peninsular. However, these are now administered by Cheshire West and Chester Council.

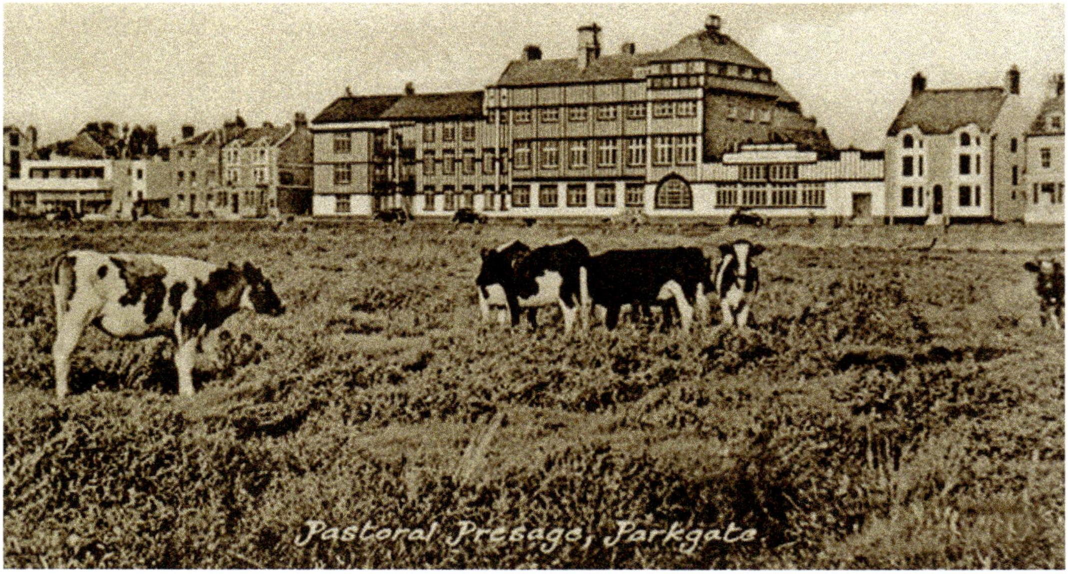

Parkgate.

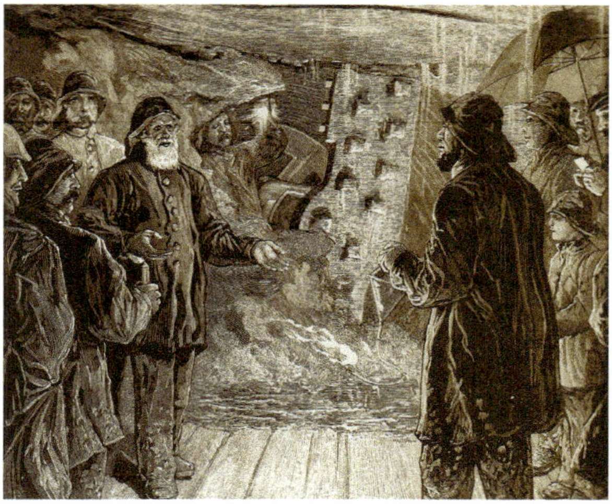

Parliamentary authority was obtained in 1871 for the construction of a double-track railway from Liverpool to the Wirral. However, it then took nine further years for funds to be obtained to begin the project. When the initial contractor experienced financial difficulties the project was given to Major Samuel Isaac, who made his fortune from work carried out during the Crimean War. Colonel Beaumont of the Royal Engineers devised a boring machine and picks and shovels were used in the construction of the main tunnel.

The Prince of Wales opened the line from James Street in Liverpool to Hamilton Square and Green Lane in 1886. The track was extended to Birkenhead Park, West Kirby, New Brighton in 1888, Rock Ferry in 1891, and the following year Central Station, in Liverpool city centre, was opened. The trains were propelled by steam engines initially, with the steam and smoke polluting the underground stations. The railway was on the verge of bankruptcy due to the low patronage caused by the choking atmosphere created by the steam engines. However, in 1903 the system was electrified becoming the world's first electric railway.

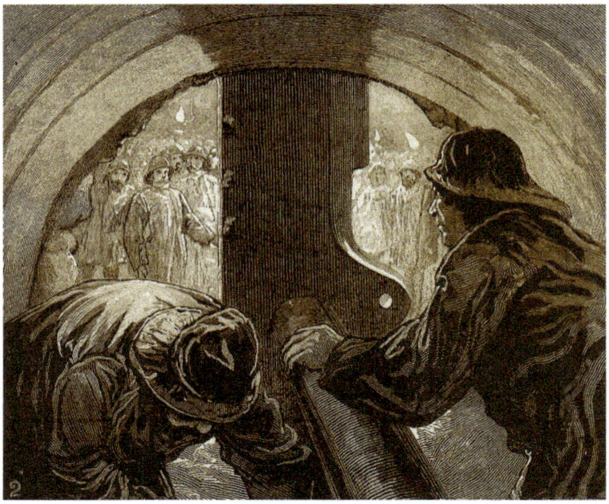

In the 1920s it became clear that the vehicular ferries operating across the river were having difficulty in coping with the level of traffic. A parliamentary bill was passed and Edmund Nuttal was appointed as the main contractor for the building of a tunnel from Liverpool to Birkenhead. By 1928 the two pilot tunnels met, and on completion of the project the tunnel was opened by George V and Queen Mary on 18 July 1934.

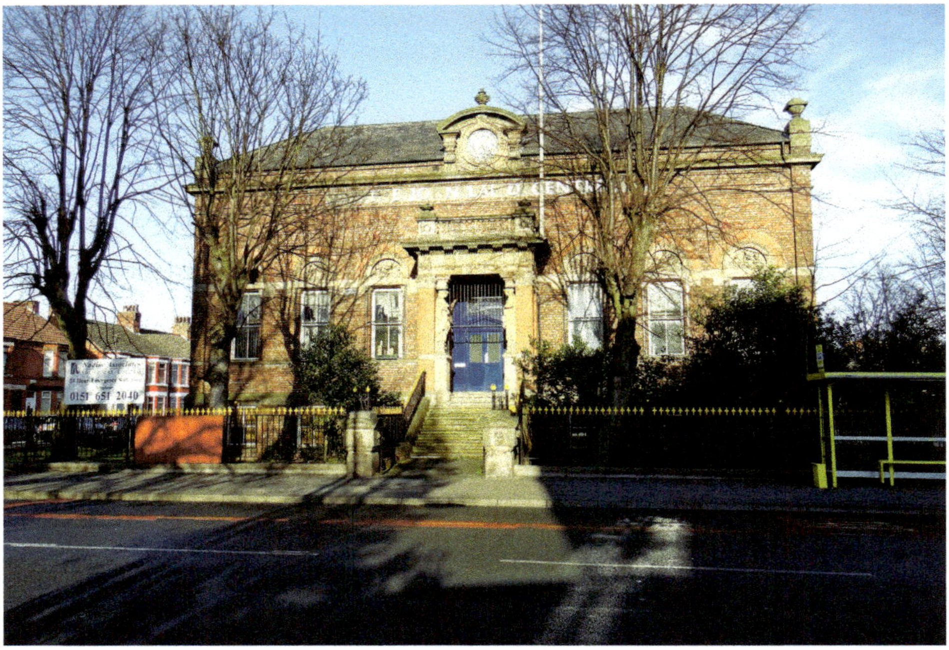

Laird School of Art in Park Road North was opened on 27 September 1871 and was the first public school of art outside London. It was given to the town by John Laird and operated until 1979, when it merged with the Birkenhead College of Technology in Borough Road.

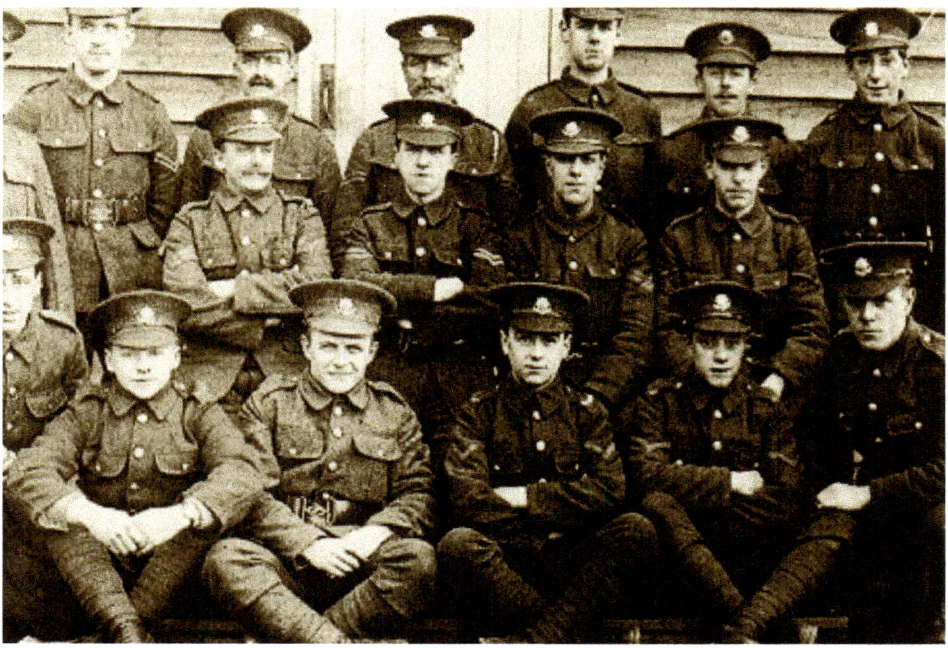

Birkenhead Bantams, Cheshire Regiment, 1914. The Bantams recruited volunteers at Birkenhead Town Hall at the beginning of the First World War in November 1914. Mr Alfred Bigland was responsible for persuading Lord Kitchener to allow smaller men under the regulation height to sign on for the Bantam Battalions.

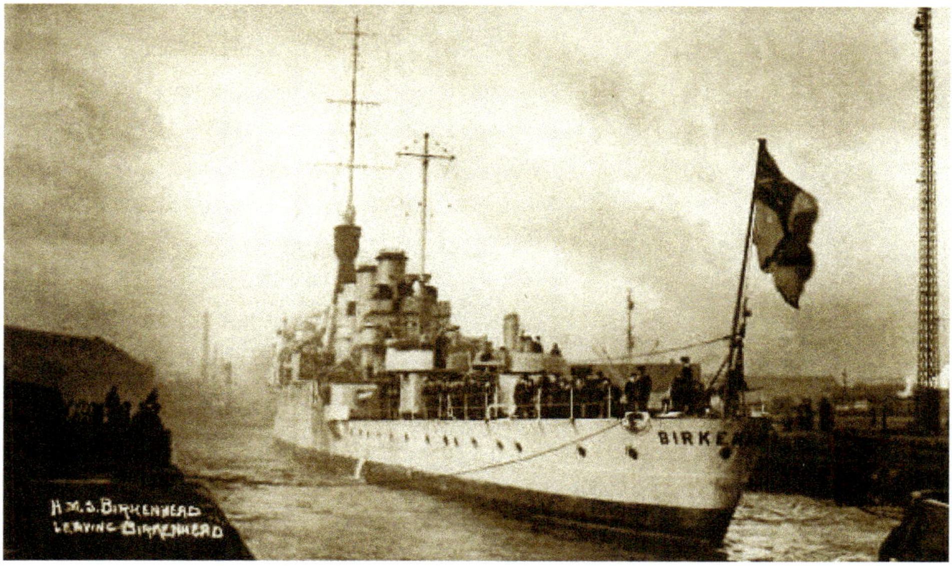

HMS *Birkenhead* arriving at Birkenhead docks. She was one of two Town class light cruisers originally ordered for the Greek Navy in 1914. She was to be named Antinavarchos Kountourotis but at the outbreak of the First World War both ships were purchased by the British government. Her sister became HMS *Chester* and they were assigned to the 3rd Light Cruiser Squadron of the Grand Fleet. On 31 May to 1 June 1916 *Birkenhead* and *Chester* took part in the Battle of Jutland. Birkenhead survived the war and was sold to John Cashmore in 1921 and was broken up at Newport after a very short career with the Royal Navy.

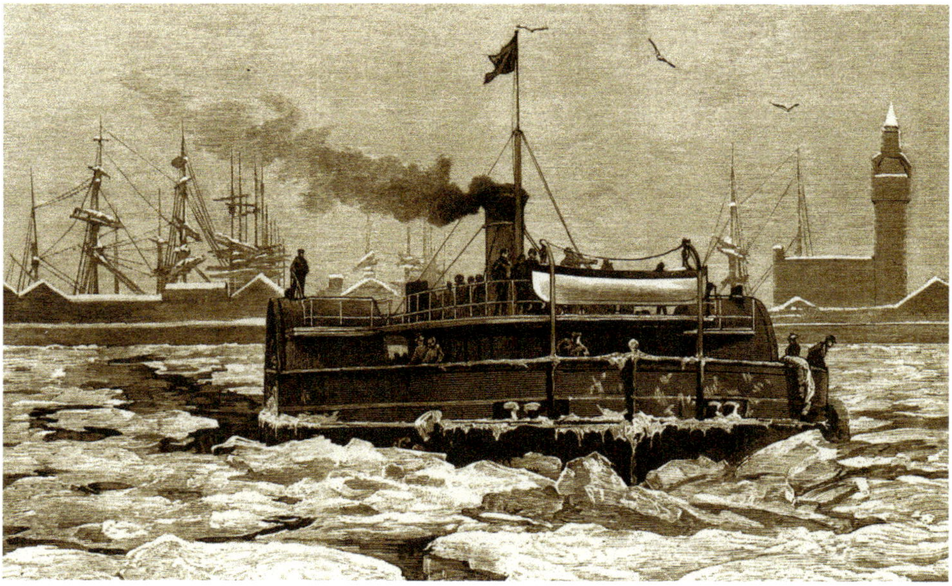

The ferry from Birkenhead to Liverpool ploughs through the ice in the winter of 1881. On 18 January 1881, a low pressure system developed in the English Channel and gale-force winds with heavy blizzards and drifting snow moved over the British Isles. The extreme weather paralysed transport, communication, trade and industries. It was claimed that over 100 people died as a result of the blizzard.

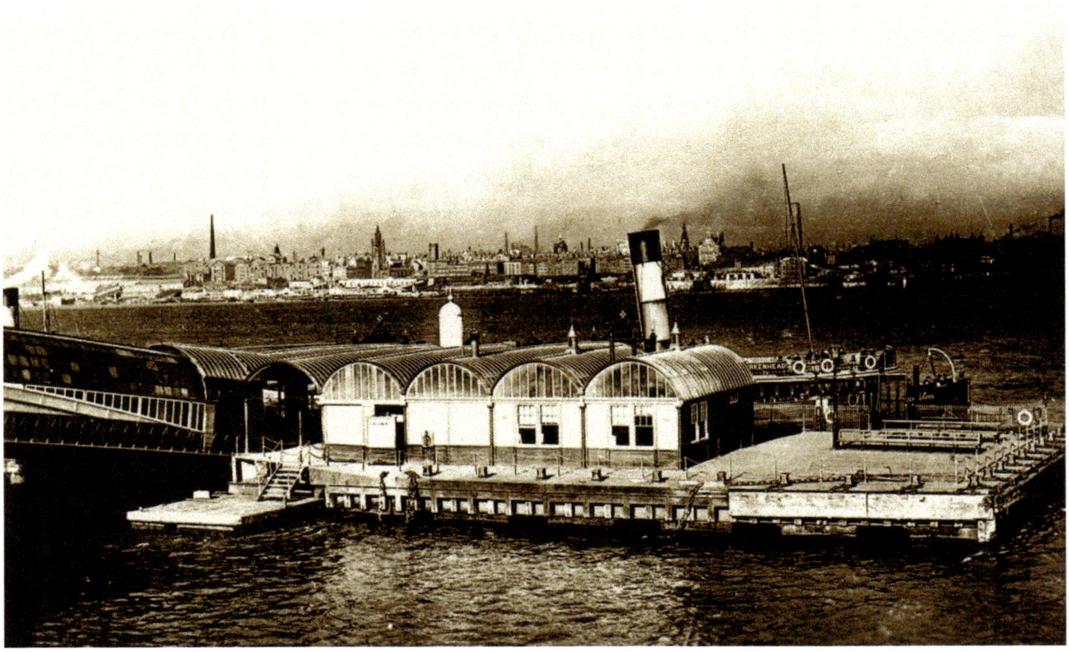

The Birkenhead ferry at Woodside at the beginning of the twentieth century. The photograph is clearly taken in the early years of the century as the Royal Liver Building, Cunard Headquarters and Dock Offices have not yet been built at the Pier Head.

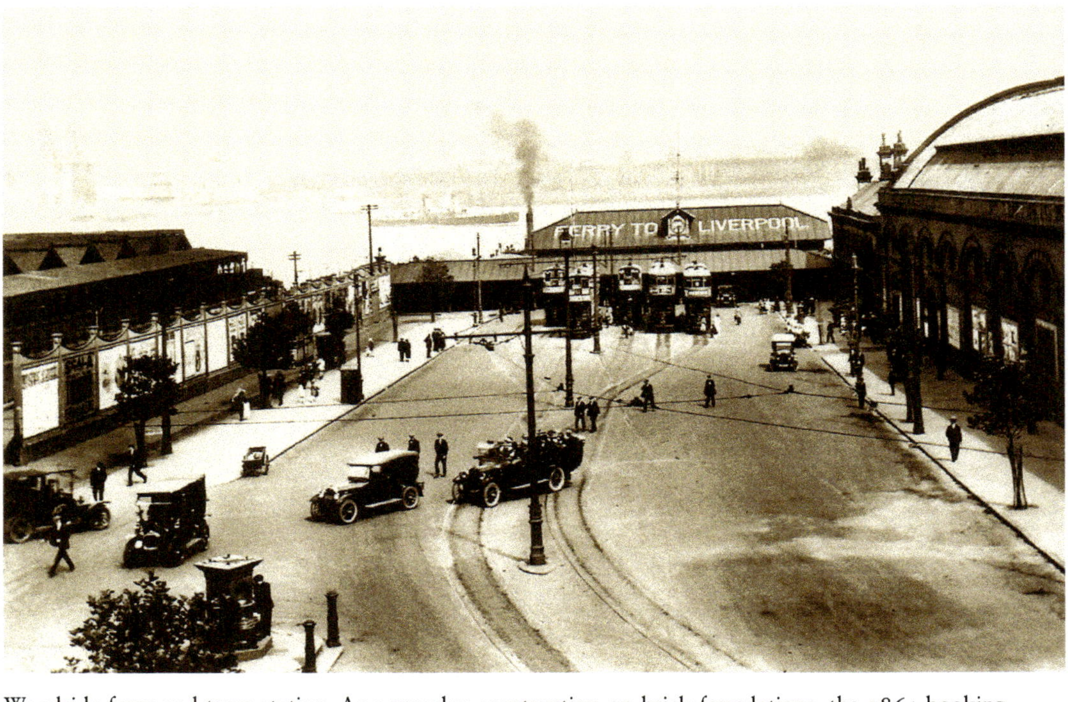

Woodside ferry and tram station. As a wooden construction on brick foundations, the 1864 booking hall is a listed building. It remains unaltered, and was refurbished from 1985 in the original style, with many of the original timbers being replaced. The building houses a booking hall and café.

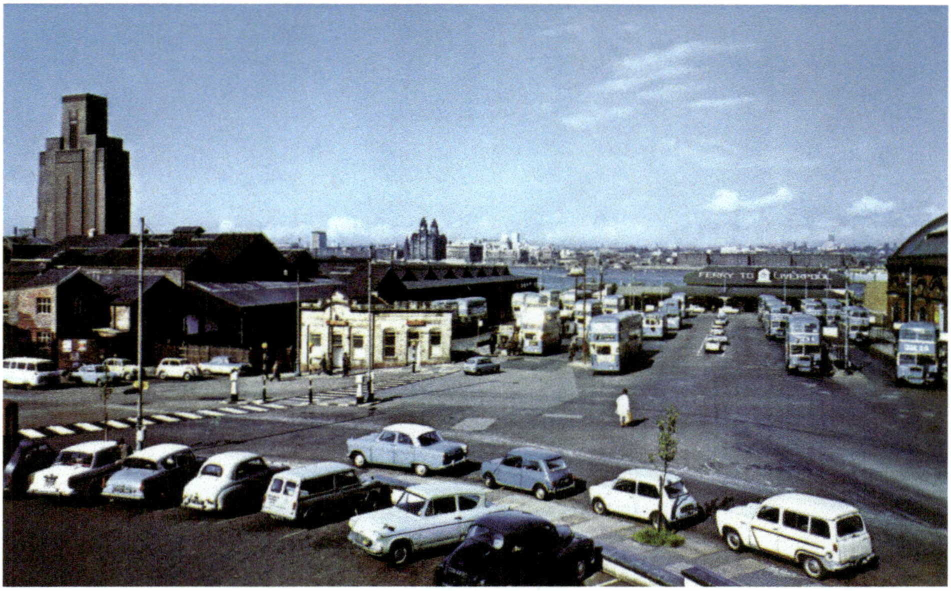

Woodside ferry and bus station in the 1960s. The Three Graces at Liverpool Pier Head can be seen across the River Mersey and the ventilation tower of the Mersey road tunnel is on the left. The photograph is taken from the front of the Woodside Hotel, which was built in 1834 to replace an earlier building of the same name. It was damaged by fire on 4 June 2008 and 13 August 2008 and was declared structurally unsafe. The hotel was then demolished without planning permission in October that year.

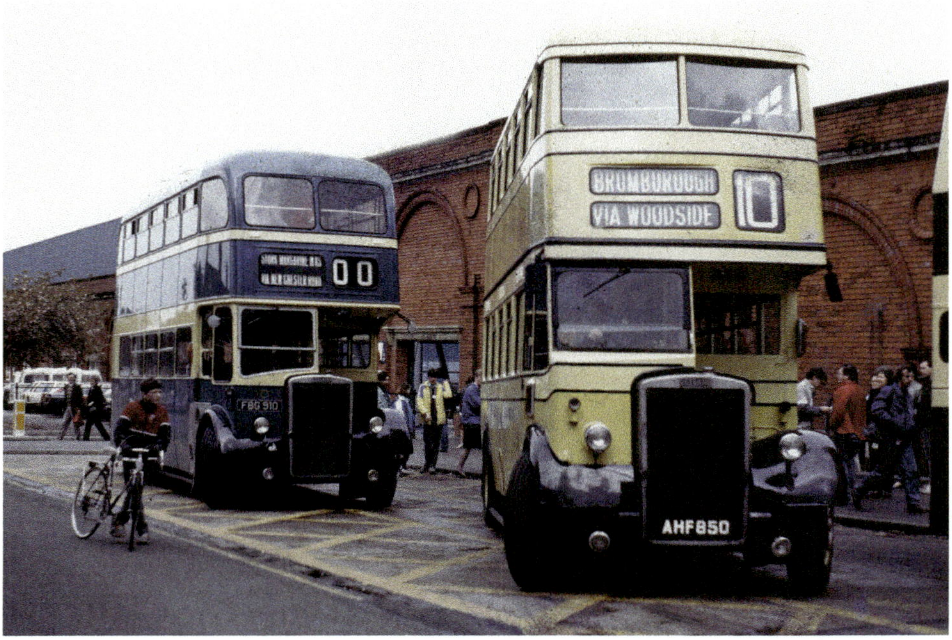

Birkenhead and Wallasey Corporation buses. The Birkenhead Corporation Transport No. 58 is shown picking up passengers at Woodside, next to Birkenhead Woodside railway station. The No. 58 shows a destination of Lower Bebington but would also continue to Clatterbridge.

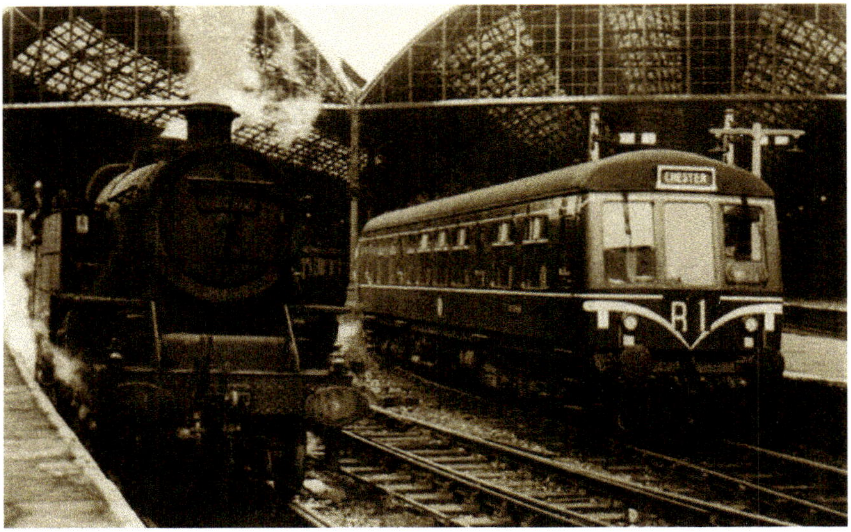

Birkenhead Woodside station. The station at Monks Ferry was closed in 1878 and the passenger services were transferred to Woodside station. The station was opened on 1 April that year when it became the terminus for the Birkenhead to Chester line. Work on the Chester & Birkenhead Railway began in 1838 and a single line was opened in September 1840. The Birkenhead terminal was built in Grange Lane, which was an equal distance from Woodside, Monks Ferry and Woodside ferries. Woodside railway station survived until 6 November 1967, when it was closed. A section of the site is now a car park for buses.

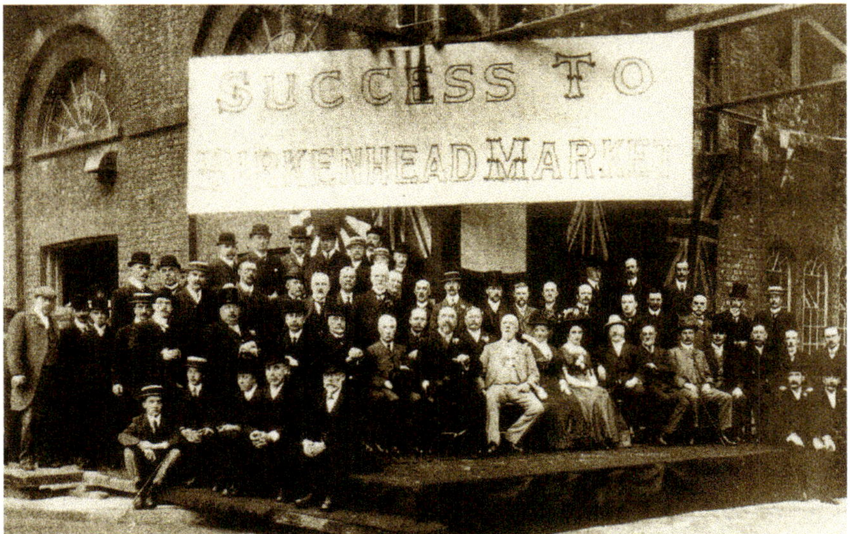

A group pose outside Birkenhead Market in 1890. The market was opened on 12 July 1845, replacing one built ten years earlier. The work was completed by Fox, Henderson & Co., who later worked on the Crystal Palace. The building was 430 feet long and 131 feet wide, and was situated between Hamilton and Albion Street. The market housed forty-two shops and eighty stalls, and was constructed of brick, glass and iron with a wrought-iron roof supported by cast-iron columns. The building was extended in 1909 and was partly destroyed by fire in 1974. A new market was later erected in 1977 near the shopping centre at Grange Road.

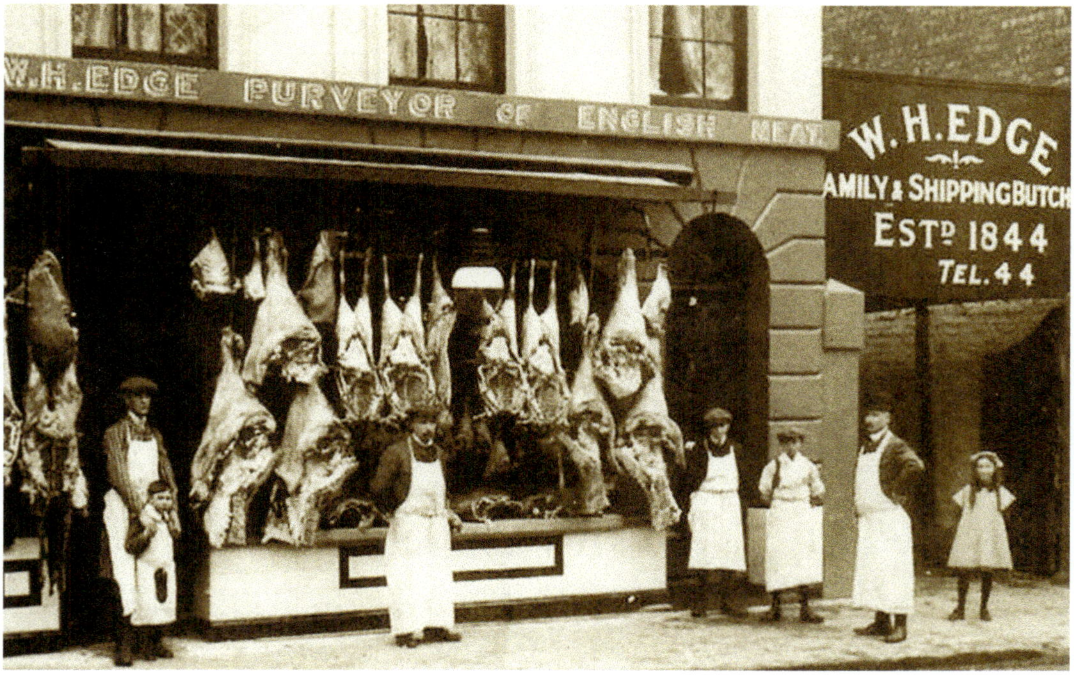

W. H. Edge, family butchers at New Ferry.

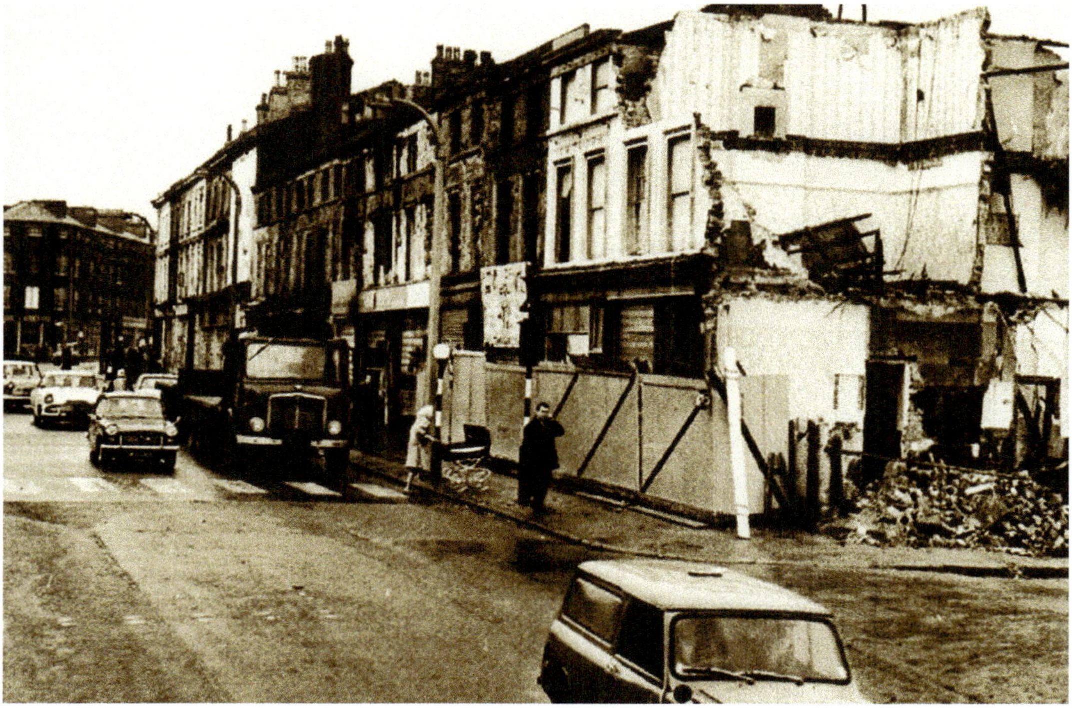

Part of Chester Street at Birkenhead was demolished in the 1960s. The Woodside ferry was connected to the road to Chester by Chester Street. The Birkenhead Arms was located in Chester Street on the corner of Grange Street.

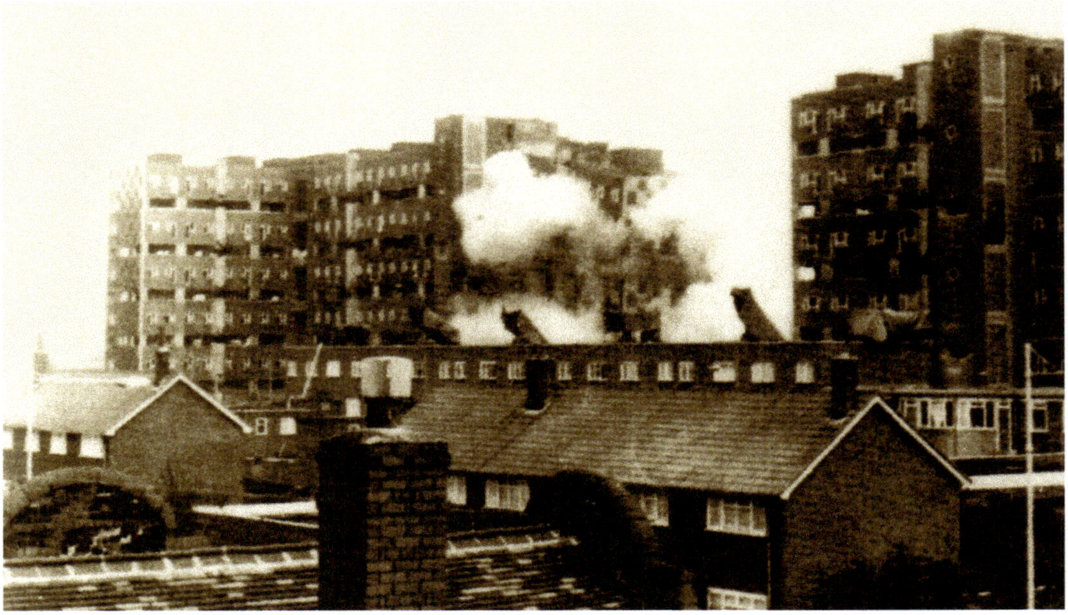

Oak and Eldon Gardens were opened in April 1958 but only survived for twenty years when they were demolished on 30 September 1979. The flats had been built on land that was previously Oak Street and Eldon Place, and a small community was broken up and housed elsewhere in the borough.

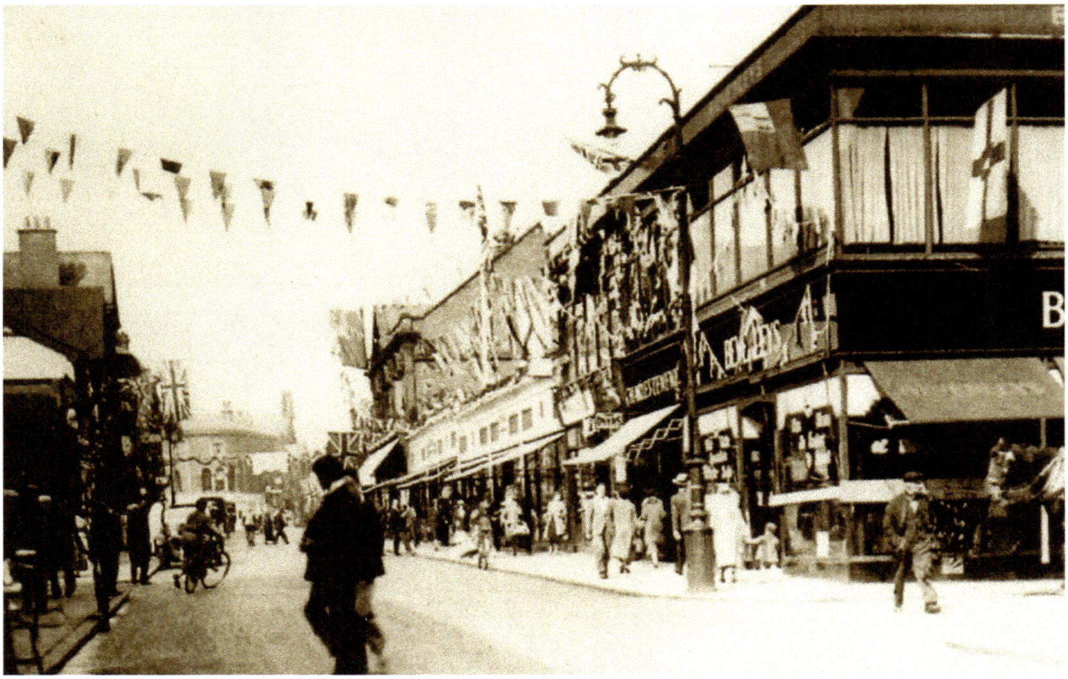

Grange Road, looking towards Charing Cross, is decorated for the coronation of George VI. The home furnishing shop Beverley's is on the right at the junction with Catherine Street with Robb Brothers Drapers in the distance. A large Asda supermarket has been built at the corner of Catherine Street and Grange Road.

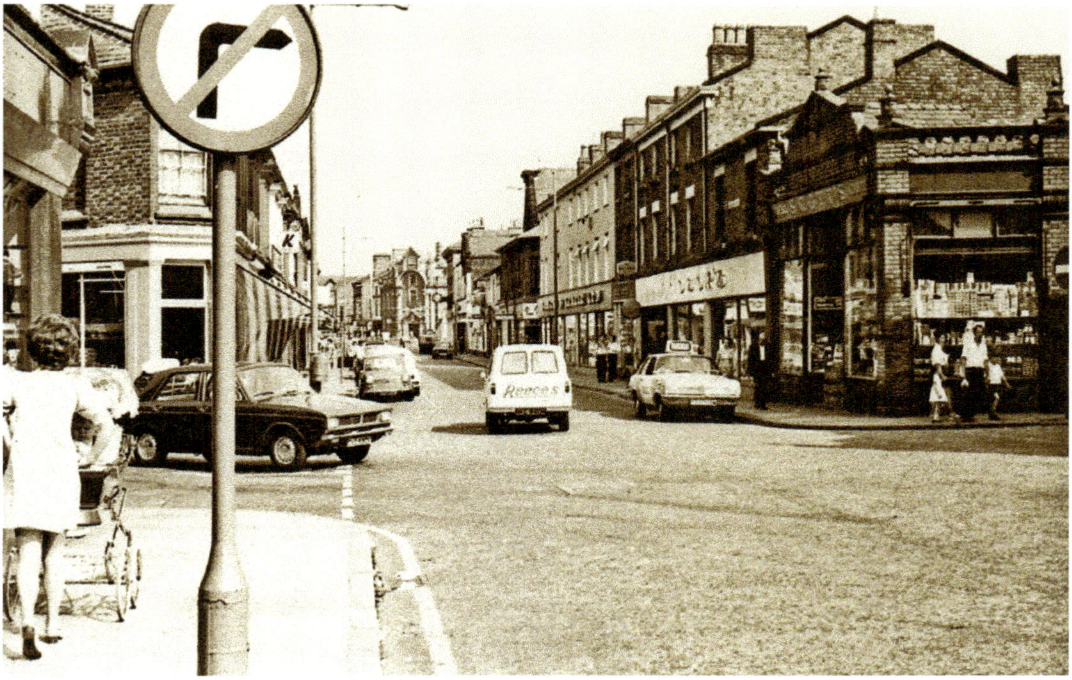

Grange Road West. The monks at Birkenhead Priory farmed the land and their nearest farm was at The Grange at Claughton. Grange Road, Grange Mount and Grange Road West led to the farm. A Reece's delivery van passes a police car parked outside Scott's food store.

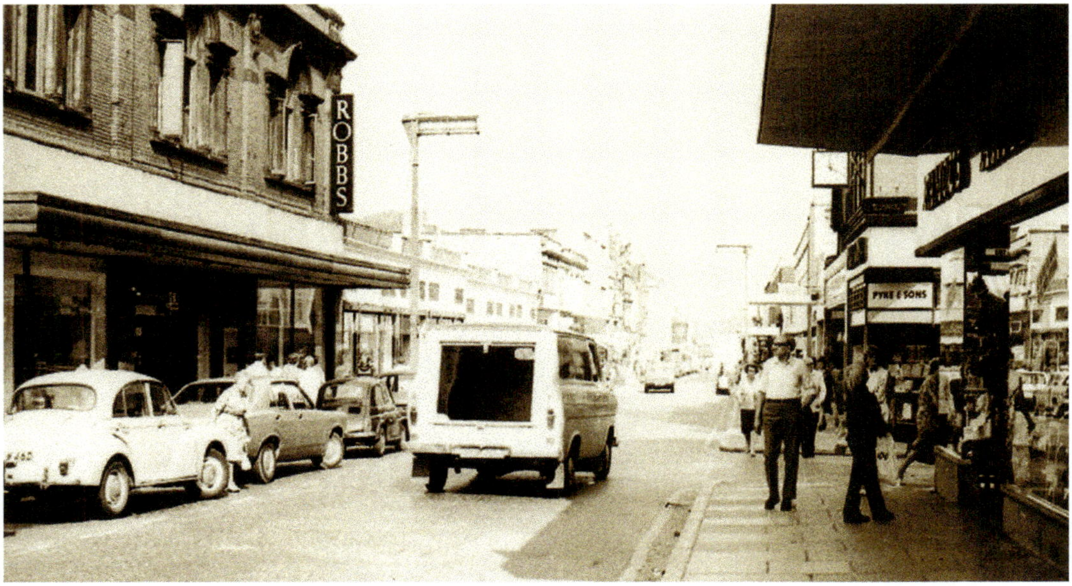

Robbs store on Grange Road, Birkenhead. Robbs advertised that they had 'Everything for the Family and the Home', where 'personal service and courteous attention are household words, and where value for money is the supreme consideration at all times'. The store included a ladies hairdressing and beauty salon and the Oakroom restaurant, which offered morning coffee, morning tea and daily luncheons at *2s 9d*, *3s 9d* and *5s*.

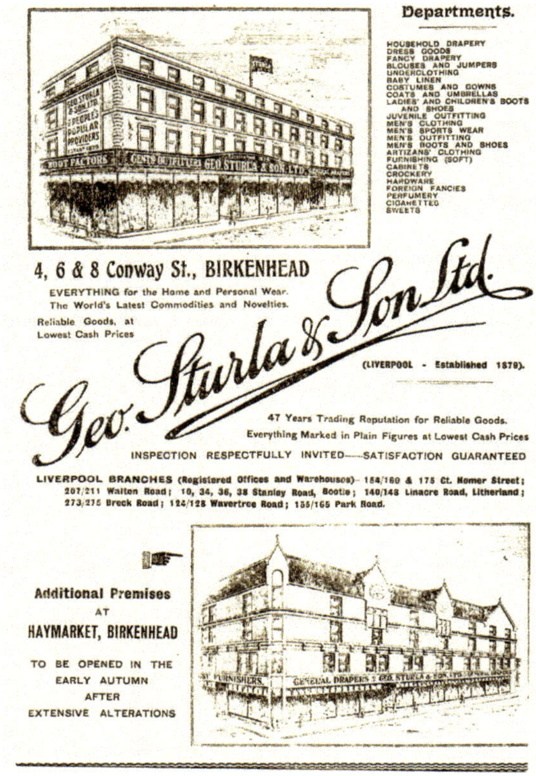

Left: Geo Sturla & Son Ltd of Nos 4, 6 and 8 Conway Street. The advertisement offers 'Everything for the home and Personal ware. The world's latest commodities and Novelties. Reliable goods at lowest cash prices.'

Below: Tutty's store in Oxton Road, Birkenhead, looking down towards Charing Cross. Tutty's operated in Oxton Road from 1904 to 1937, when they were taken over by Rostances, who survived on the site until 1977.

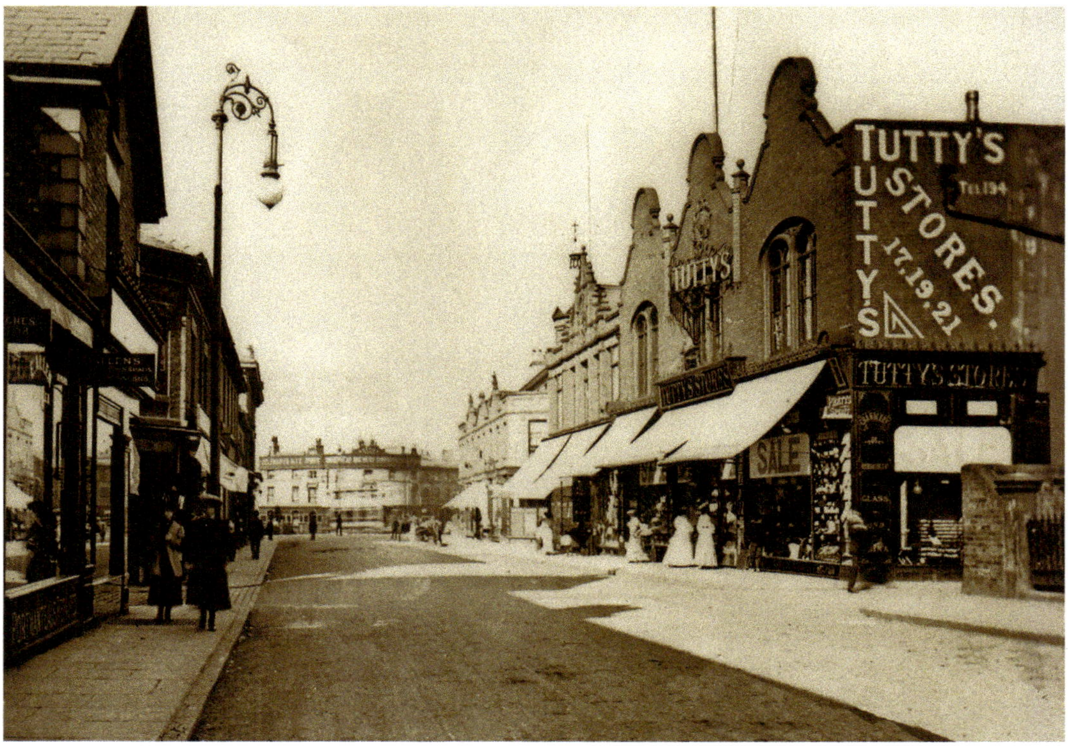

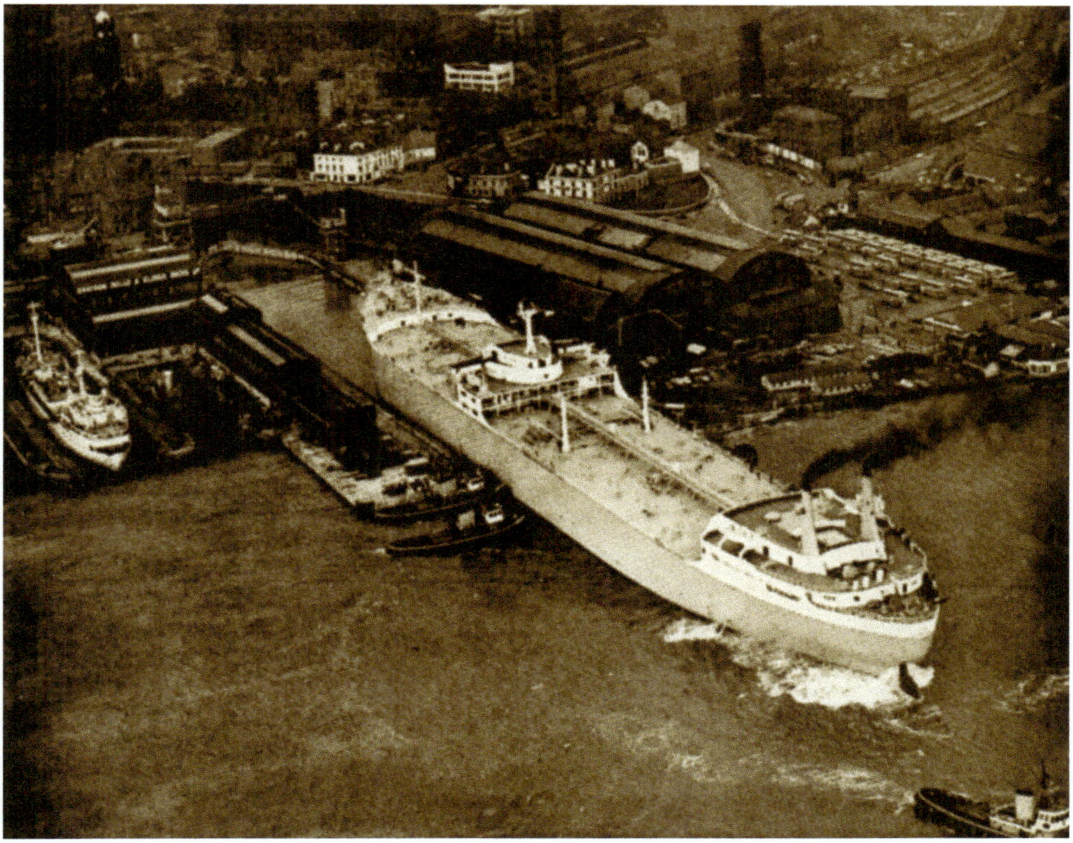

The Shell tanker *Sepia* enters the dry dock at Grayson Rollo & Clover's yard at Woodside, which was one of the largest in the United Kingdom. Grayson Rollo & Clover owned five private dry docks, which were all entered direct from the River Mersey. The dry dock was opened on 5 October 1960, and the firm was taken over by Western Ship Repairers Ltd in the 1970s. The workshops were demolished and the dry docks were filled in following the closure of the yard. *Inset:* A Grayson, Rollo & Clover advertisement from 1938.

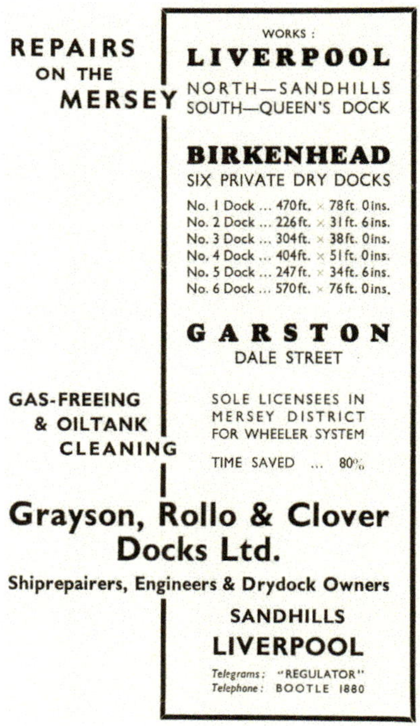

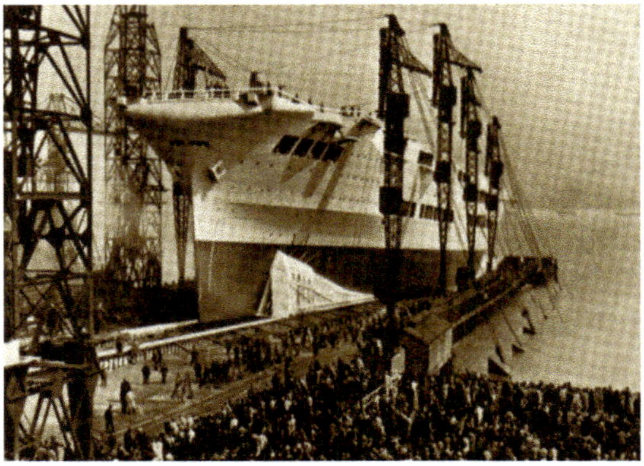

HMS *Ark Royal* was launched at the yard of Cammell Laird & Co. on 13 April 1937 and completed in November the following year. She was the first British naval vessel to be designed and constructed as an aircraft carrier. She was built to carry sixty aircraft, was armed with sixteen 4.5 inch guns, thirty-two 2 pounders and thirty-two 0.5 inch guns, and had a crew of 1,600 men. On 14 November 1941 the German U-81 torpedoed *Ark Royal* and a single torpedo hit the vessel on the starboard side. As the hit was amidships it caused four main compartments and over 30 metres of the ship's starboard bilge to flood. The torpedo made a hole 40 metres long by 10 metres deep, causing the starboard boiler room, air spaces, the main switchboard, oil tanks and the lower steering position to flood. She soon started to list, and the list increased from 10 degrees to 18 degrees in twenty minutes. The captain decided to evacuate the ship as she continued to take on water. The engineers who remained on board fought to reopen the ship's power plant and after five hours the plant was operating again. However, the list increased and the water spread across the whole width of the ship. Eleven hours after the torpedo struck the ship *Ark Royal* was listing by 20 degrees, and an hour later this had increased to 27 degrees and the captain gave the order to abandon the vessel. When the list reached 45 degrees HMS *Ark Royal* capsized and sank.

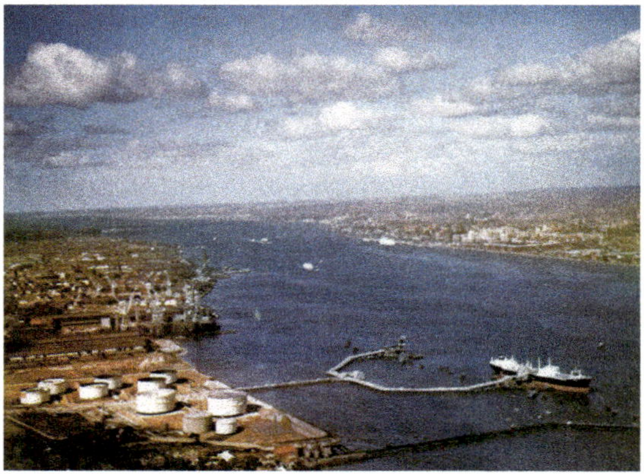

The oil terminal at Tranmere was inaugurated on 8 June 1960 with the arrival of the Shell tanker *Zenatia*, which discharged her initial cargo of crude oil. The oil facility was built to cater for the growing oil trade to the port as prior to this, petroleum fuel oil and other refined products were discharged at the Dingle Tanker Buoy, where four moorings could accommodate tankers up to 18,000 tons deadweight. Crude oil is pumped ashore at Tranmere and transferred through a 15-mile pipeline to storage facilities at the Stanlow Refinery in Cheshire. The terminal's first 200,000-ton tanker, *Melo*, arrived on 21 February 1970. She had been lightened, with some of her cargo being transferred into a smaller vessel to enable her to navigate the channel and up the River Mersey.

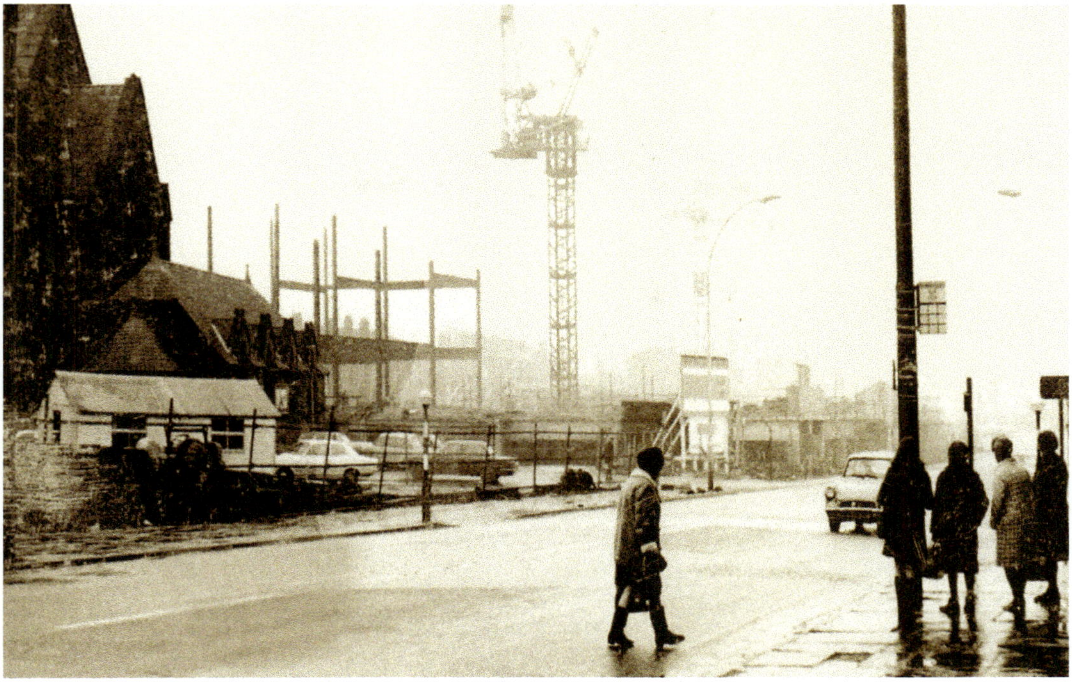

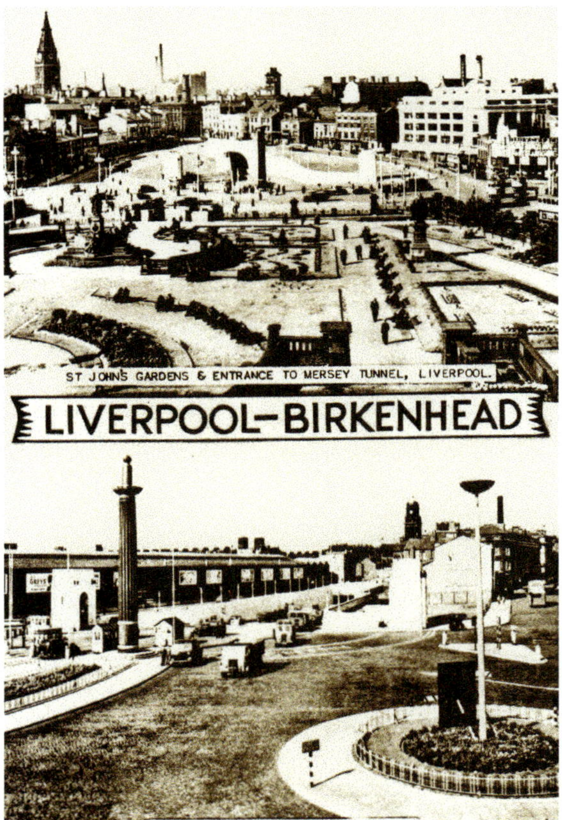

Above: Borough Road with the Pyramids Shopping Centre under construction. One of the courses of the ward and old township boundary follows the old stream, which was more or less on the line of the present Borough Road. In the 1870s Birkenhead became a borough and the new status was marked with the naming of one of the main roads as Borough Road.

Right: A postcard showing the Mersey Road Tunnel entrances at Liverpool and Birkenhead.

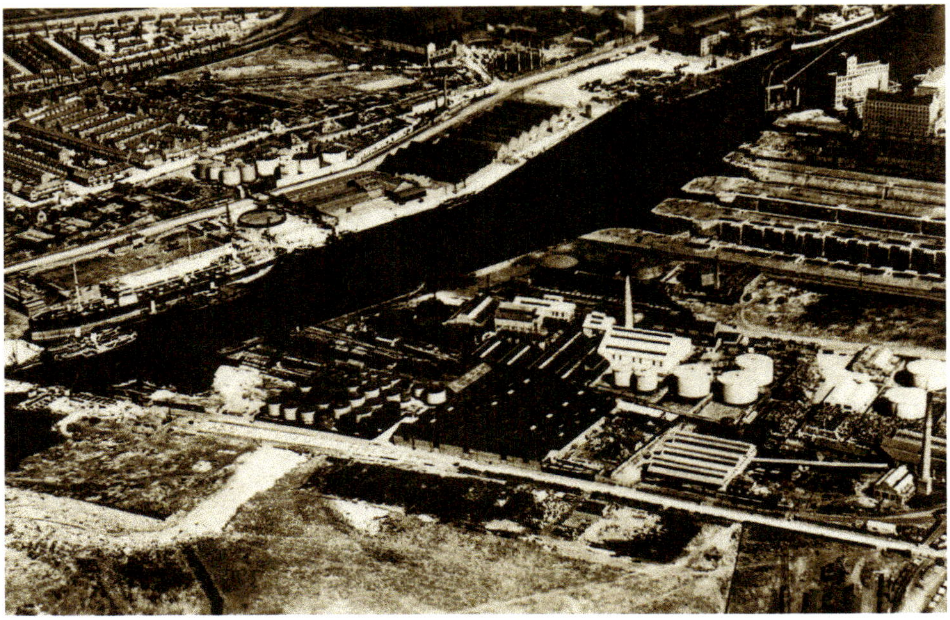

The West Float at Birkenhead showing the Penny Bridge, dry docks and Mobil Oil Co. This section of the port has changed dramatically in recent years. The dry dock's are no longer used, and the Mobil Oil buildings and storage tanks have been demolished.

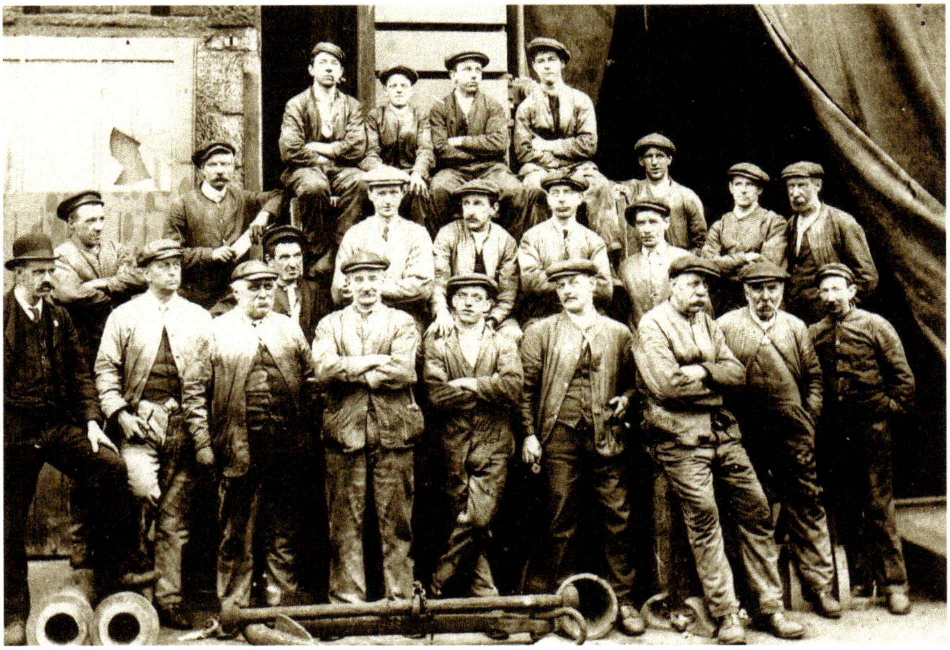

Workers at the Grayson Rollo and Clover yard. The shipyard was a repair and dry-dock facility situated on the river front at Woodside. It became Western Ship Repairers Ltd in the 1970s and was closed ten years later. The area has since been redeveloped with residential apartments, offices and small business units. A pedestrian walkway enables people to walk from Woodside to Monk's Ferry and evidence of the ship-repair facilities are still visible.

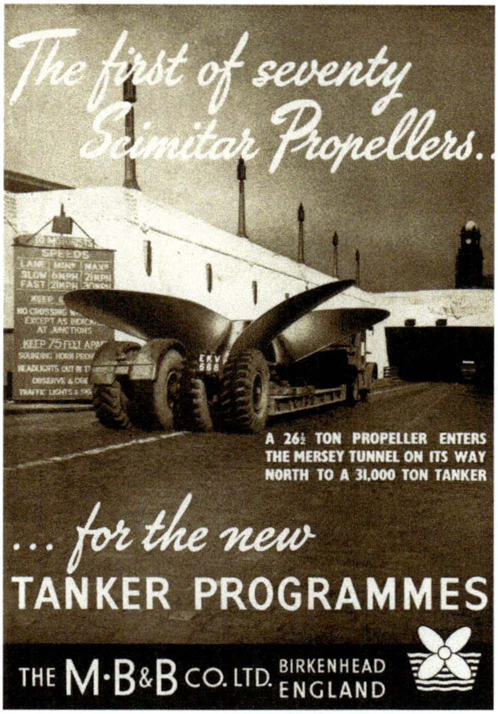

A 1952 advertisement for the Manganese Bronze Bearings Ltd.

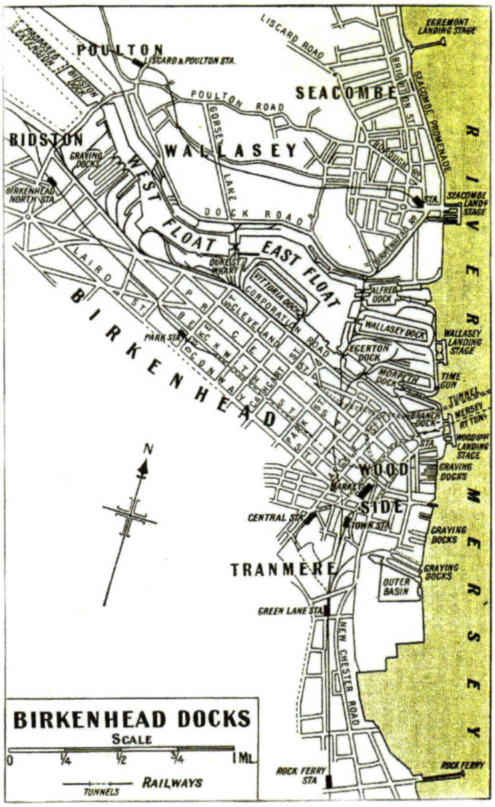

Map of Birkenhead docks.

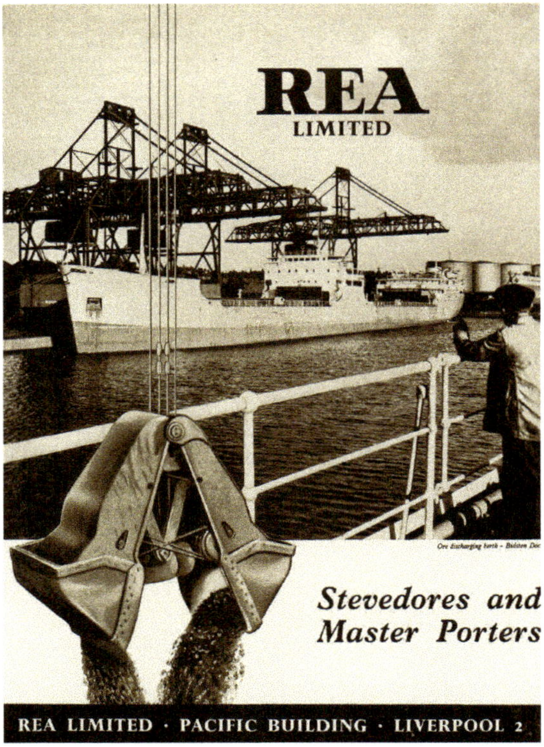

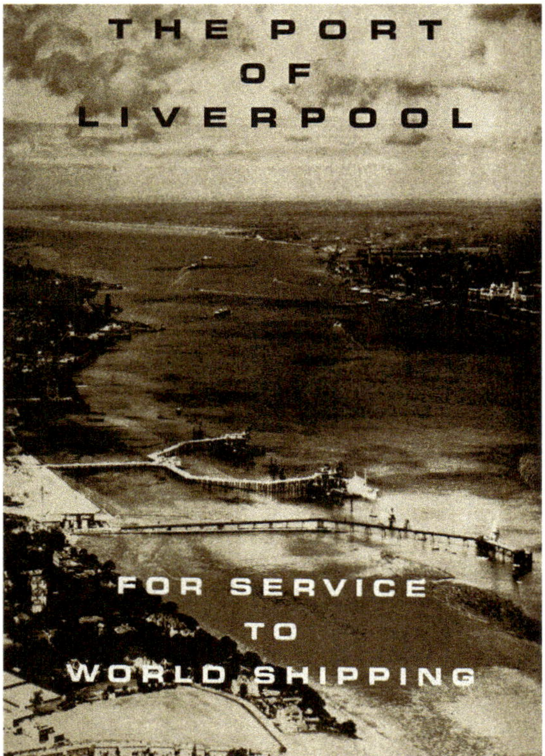

Rea and Port of Liverpool advertisements.

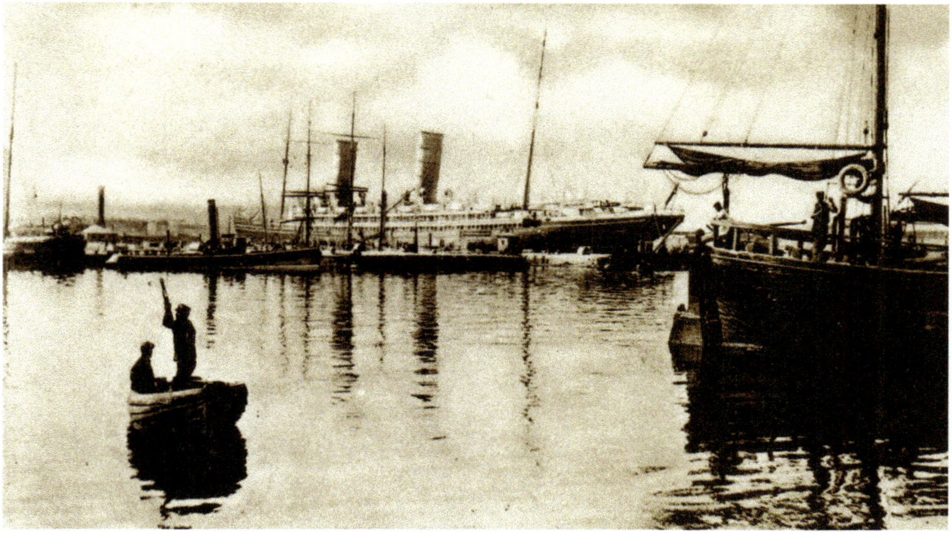

Cunard Lines Campania in the dry dock at the West Float, Birkenhead. She was built on the Clyde in 1893 for service between Liverpool and New York. Campania completed her last voyage for the Cunard Line in April 1914 and was chartered to the Anchor Line for five sailings. However, as *Aquitania* was requisitioned as a troopship, she was replaced on the Atlantic passenger service by Campania for several voyages, before she was sold to be broken up in October that year. The following month she was acquired by the British Admiralty and converted into a seaplane carrier by Cammell Laird at Birkenhead. On 4 November 1918 she dragged her anchor at Burntisland Roads in the Firth of Forth and collided with the British warship *Revenge*, gashed her hull open and sank by the stern.

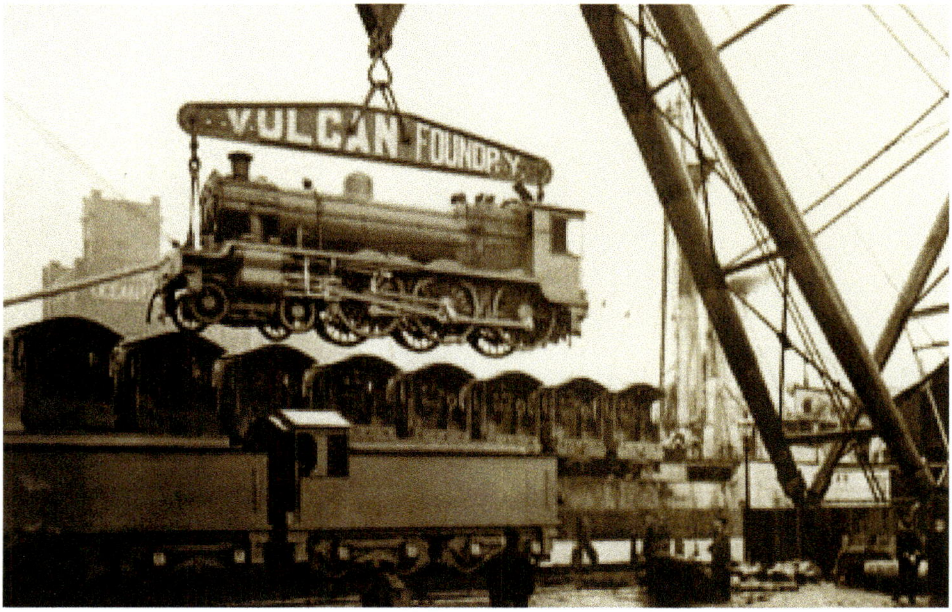

A steam locomotive being loaded onto a ship in the West Float in Birkenhead docks. New British manufactured locomotives were brought to the berth at Cavendish Wharf by road and transhipped onto floating cranes, and loaded onto vessels and shipped to Africa, India and the Far East.

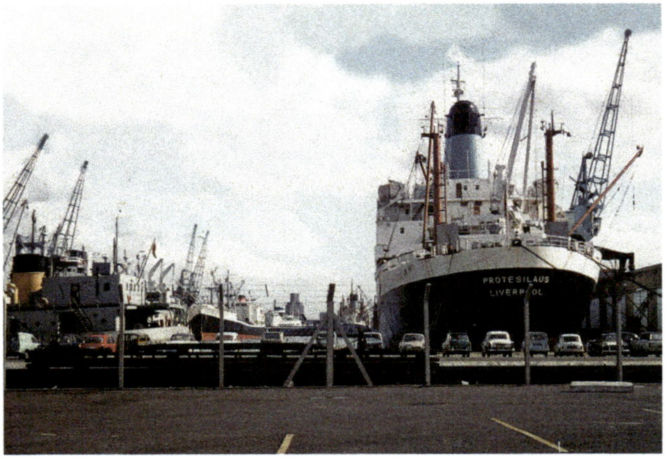

Clan and Blue Funnel Line cargo vessels loading at Vittoria Dock, Birkenhead, in the 1960s. The Blue Funnel Line *Protesilaus* was built in 1967 and operated from Birkenhead dock's until she was sold in 1978 and renamed *Oriental Importer*. The following year she was converted to a cellular container ship. On 1 June 1985, she was hit by two rockets on a voyage from Damman to Kuwait, and was scrapped at Kaohsiung later that year.

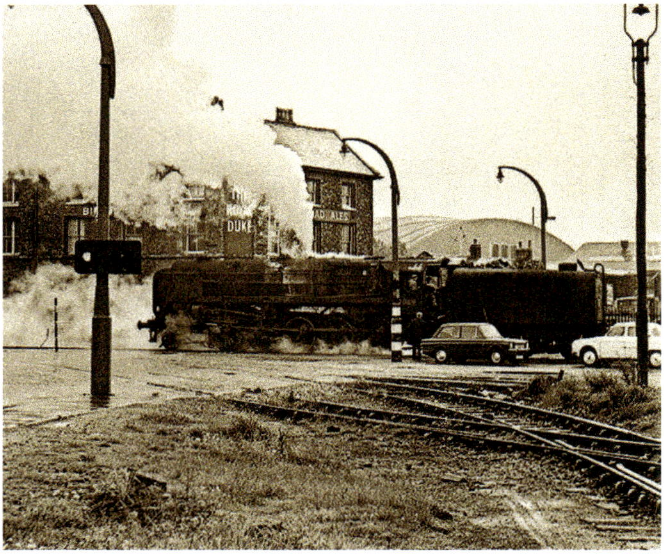

A steam engine at the Duke Street/Corporation Road junction at Birkenhead docks.

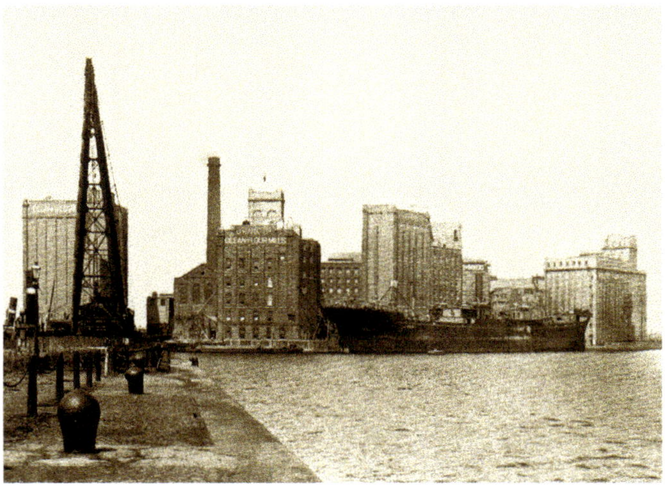

The flour mills in the West Float at Birkenhead. Following the opening of the new Royal Seaforth Dock in 1970, many of the traditional items shipped through Birkenhead docks were transferred to the new facilities at Liverpool where specialist grain handling terminals were provided. Several years later the mills at Birkenhead were demolished.

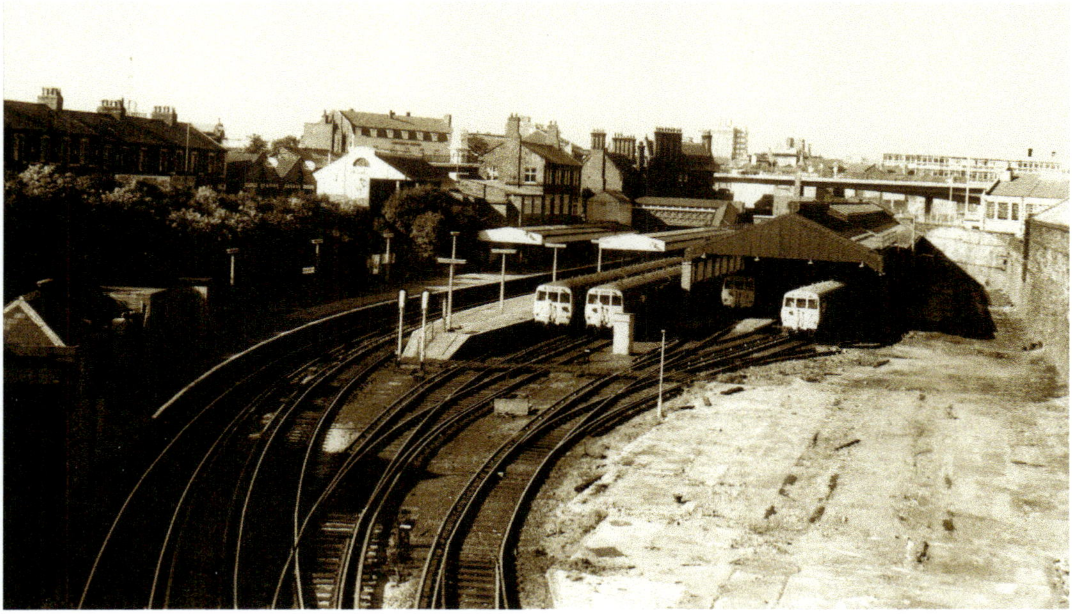

Liverpool and Rock Ferry trains at Birkenhead Central station. The station is on the Rock Ferry, Chester & Ellesmere Port line and is the nearest Merseyrail station to Birkenhead town centre and the Pyramids Shopping Centre.

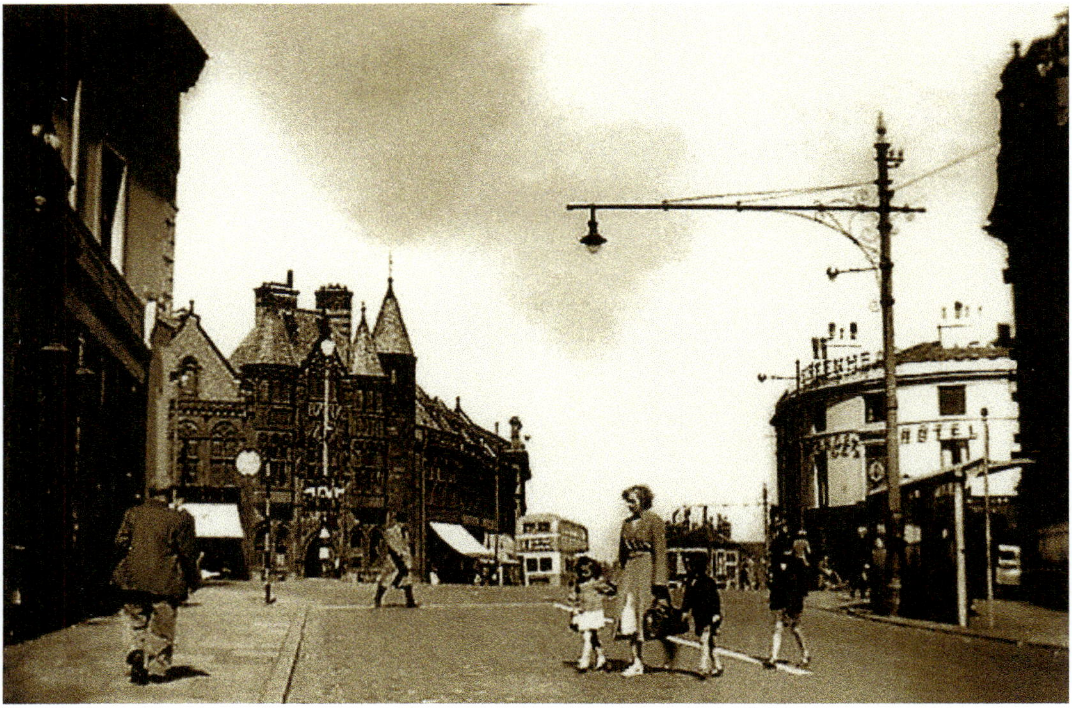

A mother guides her children across the road at Charing Cross. The road is one of the busiest junctions in Birkenhead. At one time there was a roundabout at the junction but it is now controlled by a series of phased traffic lights.

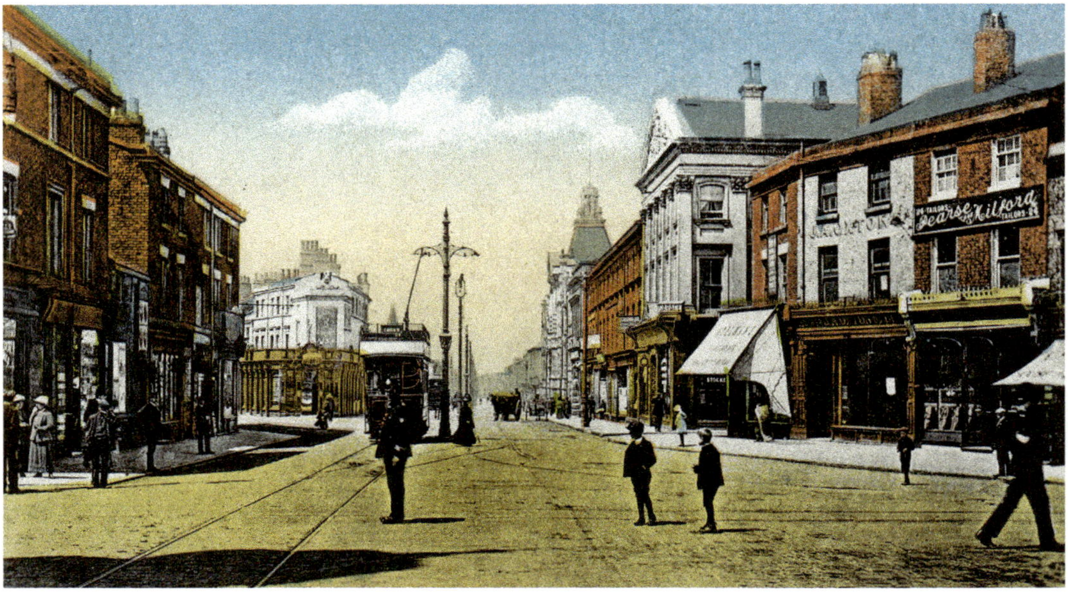

A tram approaches the junction between Conway Street and Argyle Street. The high building on the right was once the Empire Picture House and became Birkenhead's last cinema when it closed in January 1991. The building on the same side of the road was once the post office and later became the Super Cinema. The white building on the left at the corner of Claughton Road was the Conway Arms, which was demolished in the 1960s for the tunnel approach road flyover to be built.

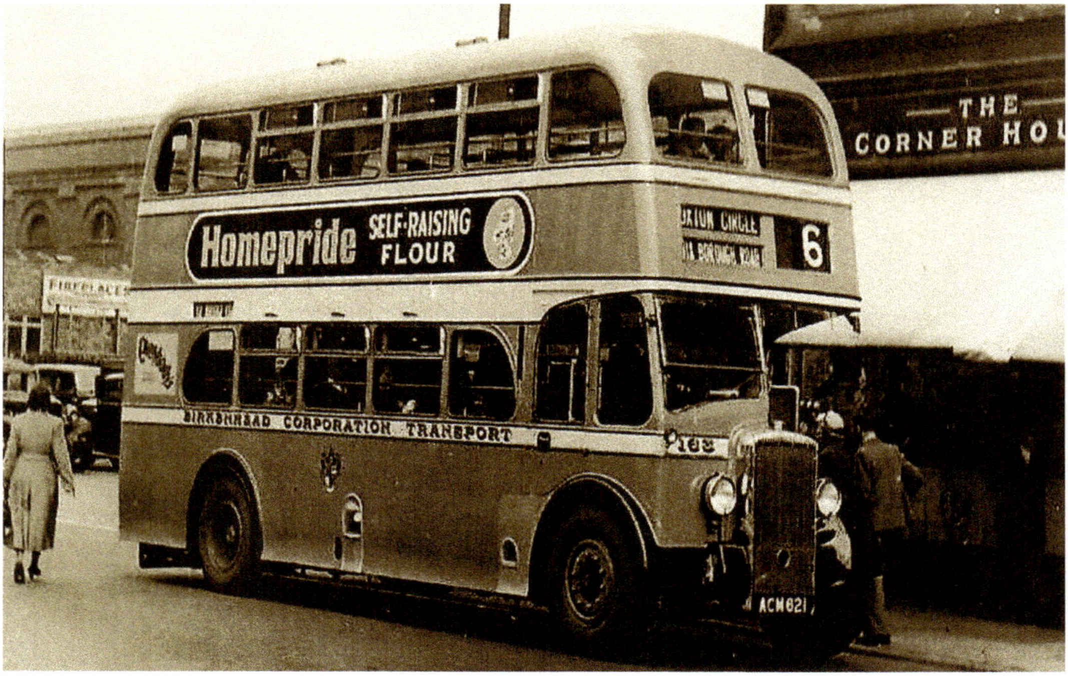

Birkenhead Corporation Transport No. 6 bus, 165 registered ACM 621, on the Oxton Circle via Borough Road service. She was a Daimler CVG6 type, with a Massey body, introduced into the fleet in 1949 and was withdrawn in the mid-sixties.

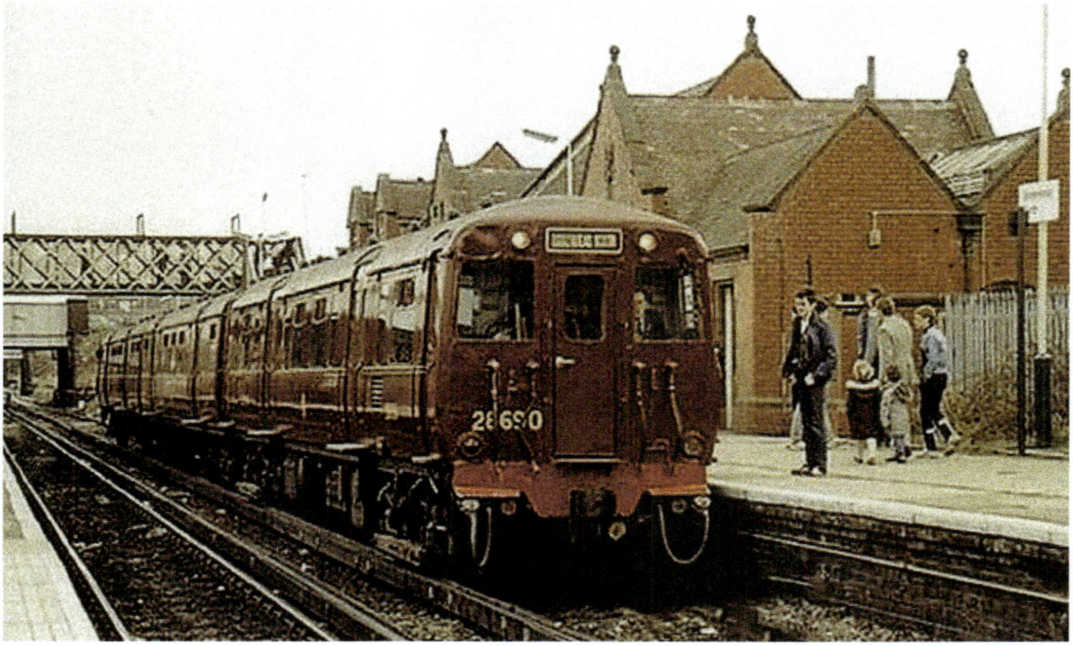

A Merseyrail train arrives at Birkenhead North from Liverpool Central. Trains from Liverpool Central to New Brighton and West Kirby pass through Birkenhead North station. Lifts and facilities for elderly and disabled people have recently been installed at the station.

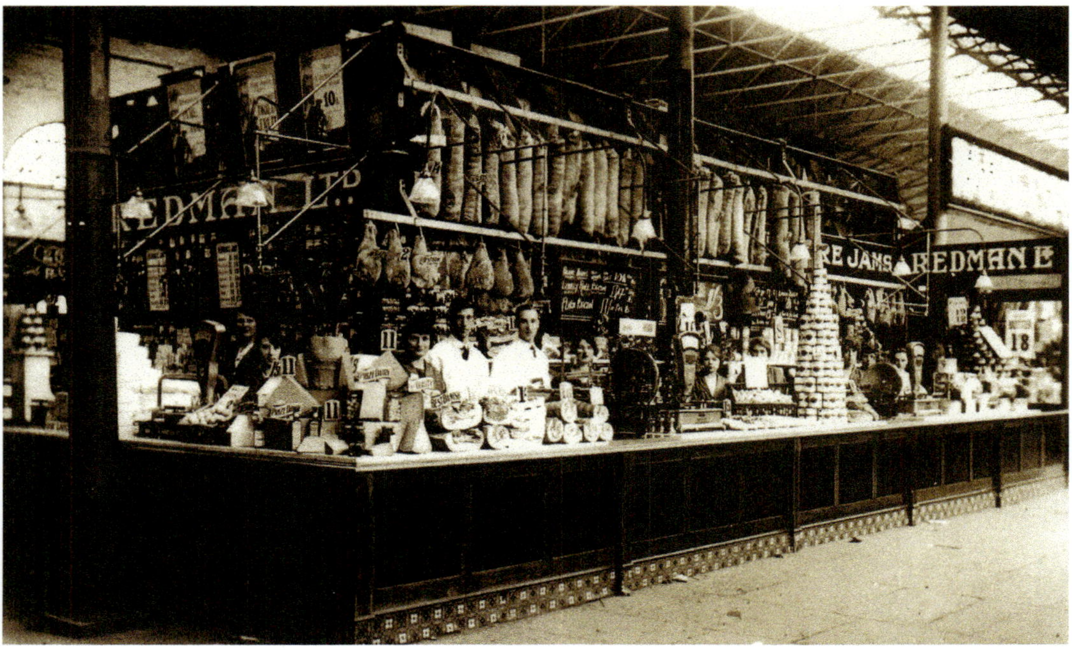

One of two Redman Ltd shops in Birkenhead Market, which was opened in 1845 and covered an area of 6,244 square yards. It contained three main avenues of shops and stalls and in the basement there were twenty-two large vaults and forty-three smaller ones. The Corporation enjoyed the sole market rights of the borough.

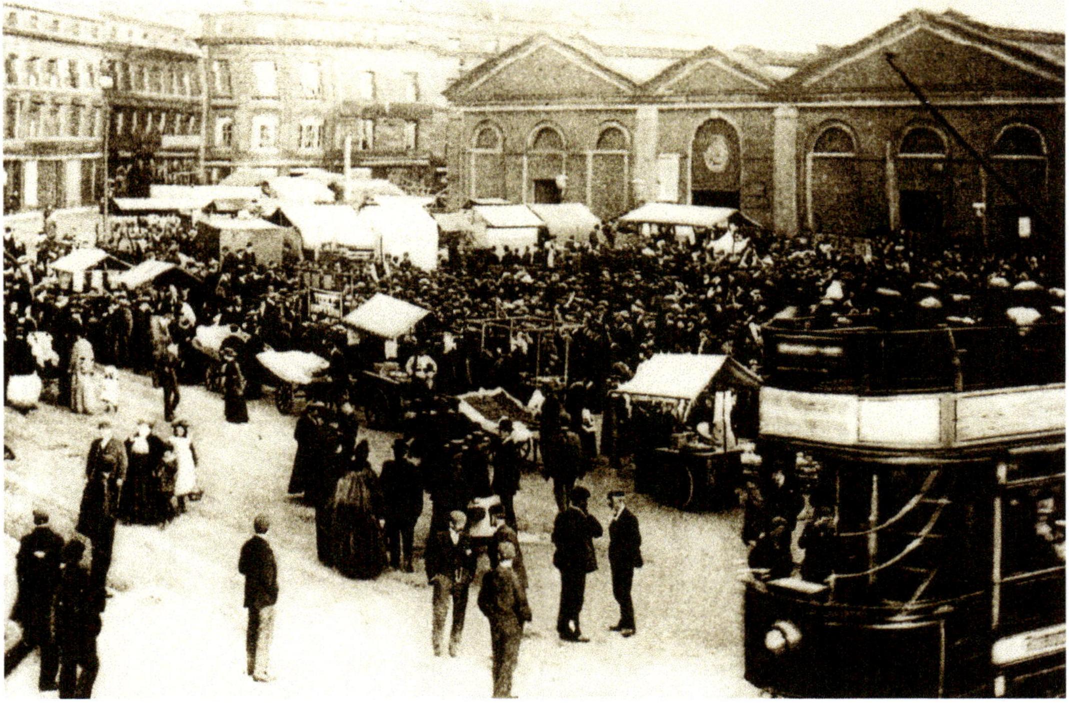

Outdoor stalls at Birkenhead Market.

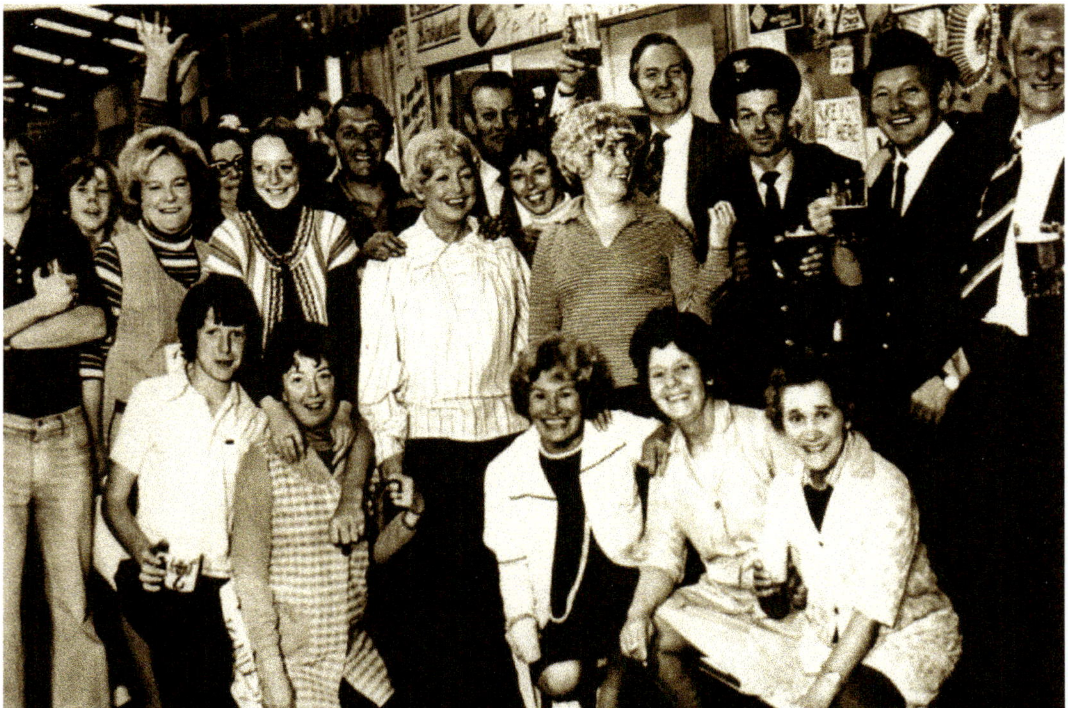

Christmas celebrations by staff at Birkenhead Market.

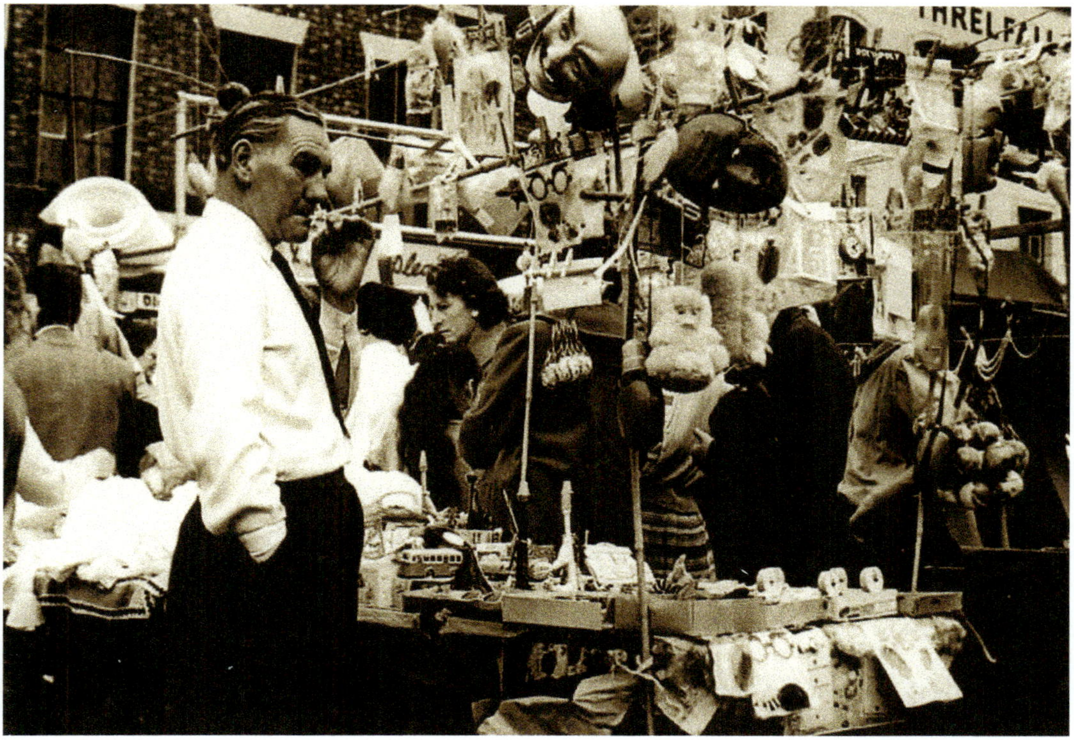

A toy and novelty stall at Birkenhead Market.

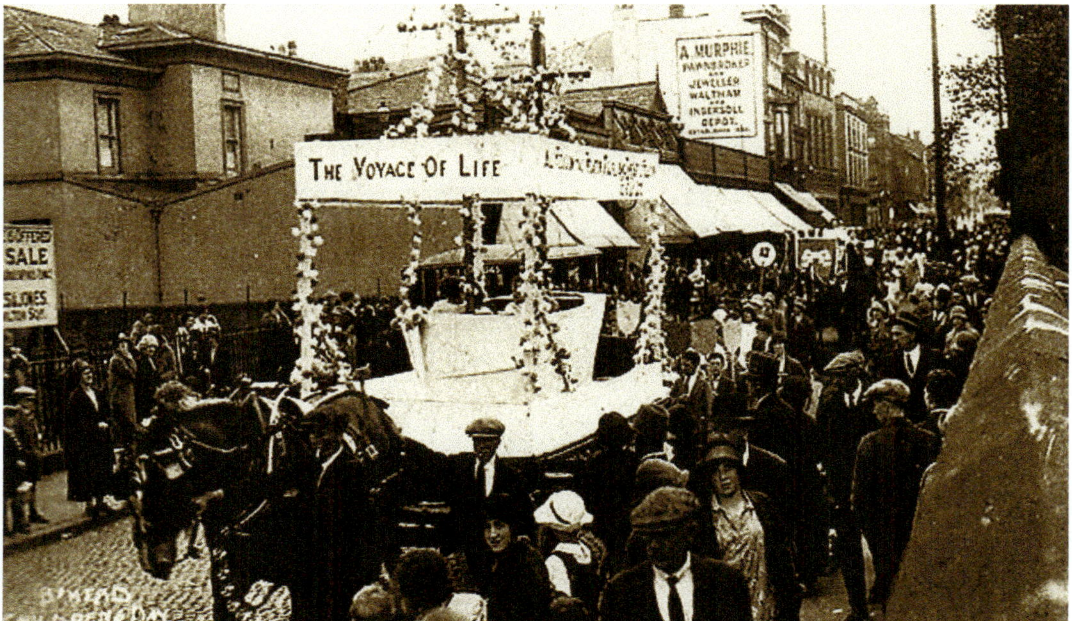

The Children's Day procession in 1926. The Voyage of Life is transported by a horse-driven cart supplied by James Crutchley, a local coal merchant. The building behind the procession was owned by A. Murphie, who were pawnbrokers and jeweller's and acted as a Waltham and Ingersoll Depot.

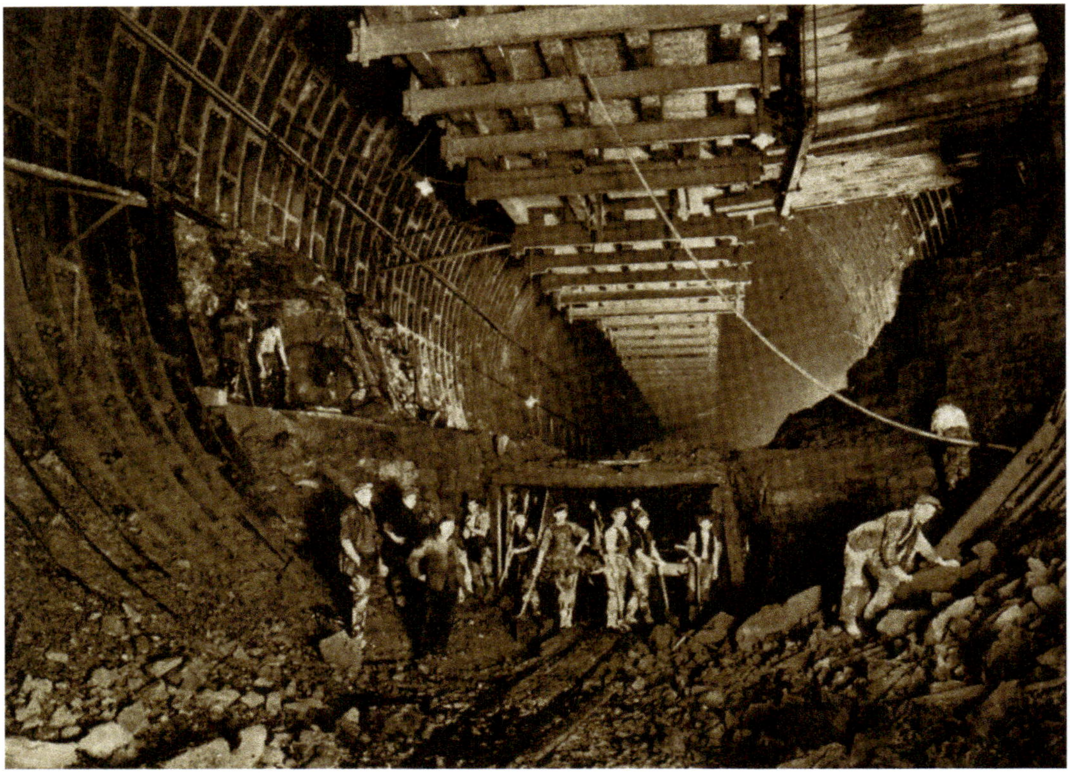

The construction of the Mersey Road Tunnel in the early 1930s.

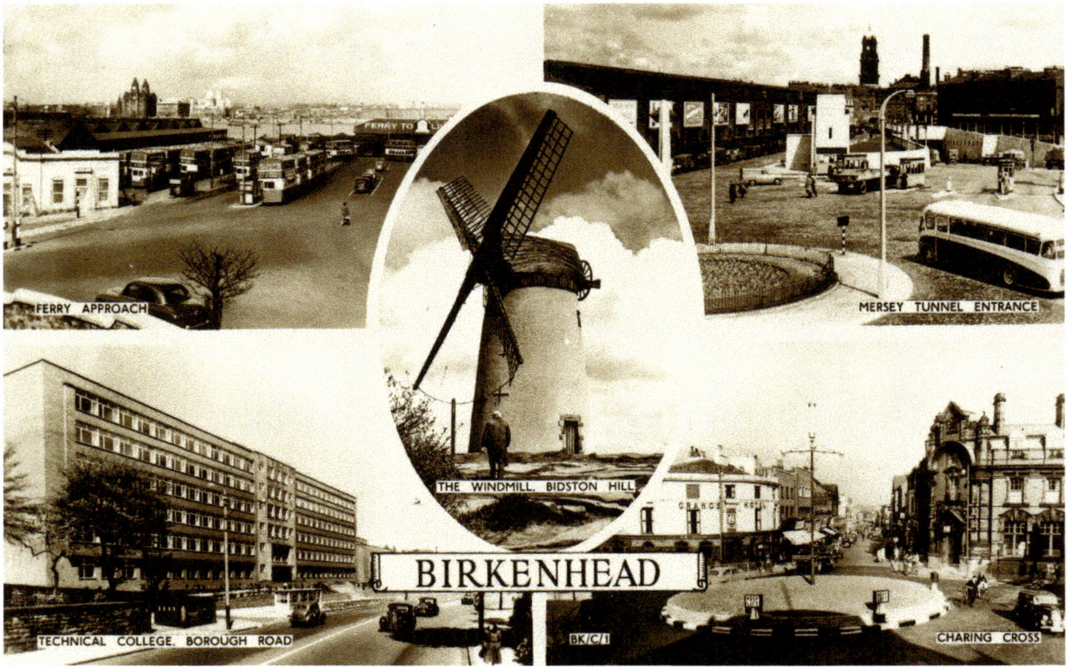

A postcard showing Woodside, Mersey Tunnel, Birkenhead Technical College and Charing Cross.

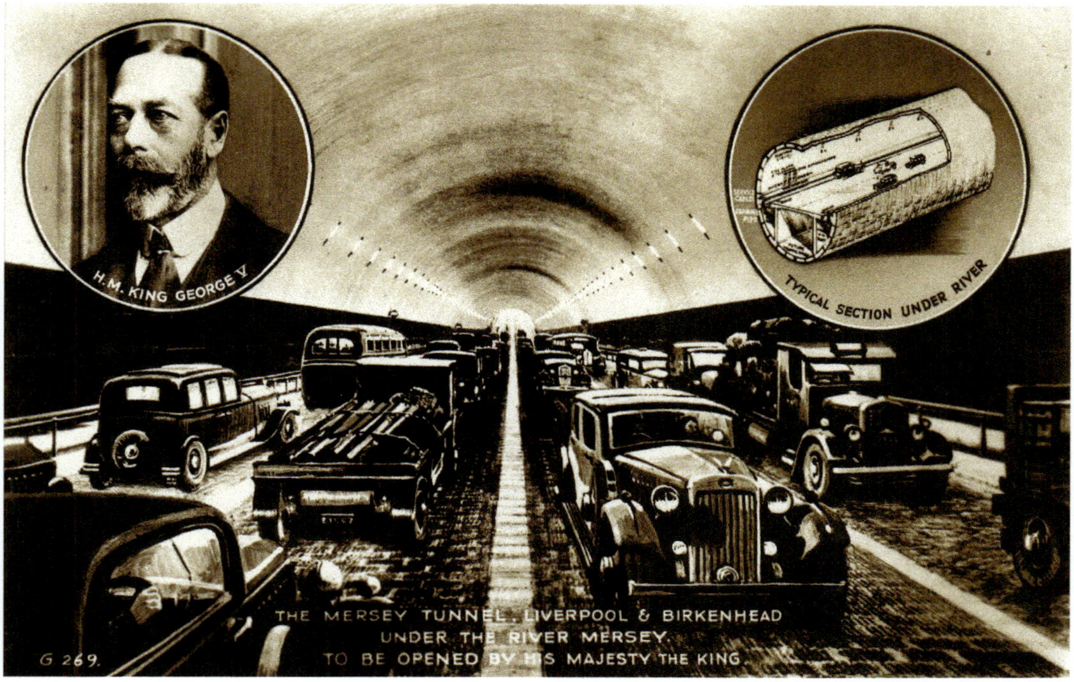

A postcard showing the Mersey Road Tunnel between Birkenhead and Liverpool. *Inset:* Queensway Mersey Tunnel advertisement from 1938.

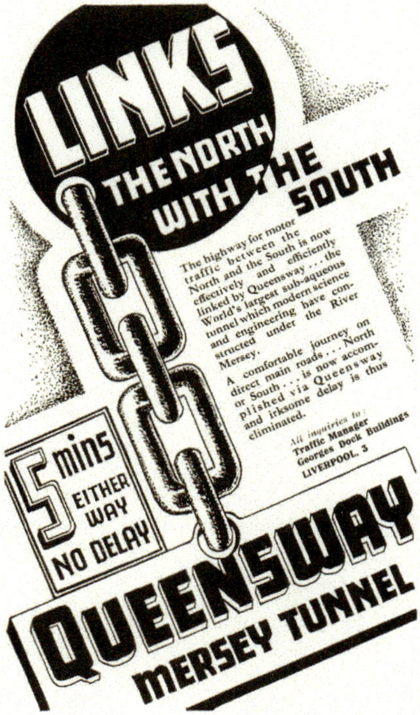

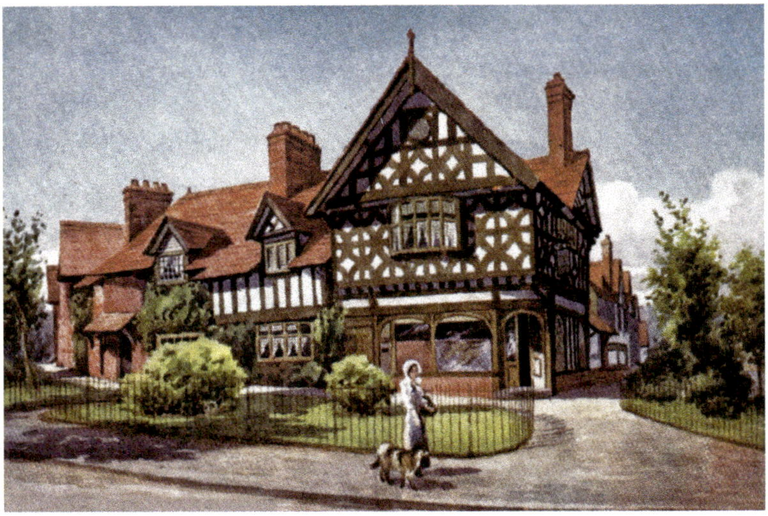

The post office, Port Sunlight.

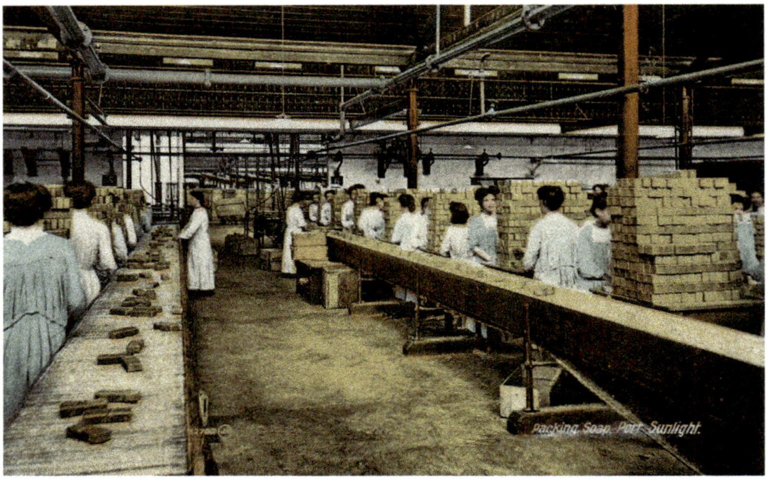

Workers packing soap in the works at Port Sunlight. Mrs W. H. Lever performed the ceremony of cutting the first sod at Port Sunlight on 3 March 1888 following the decision to move production of 'Sunlight' soap from Warrington. Lever Brothers was founded by William Hesketh Lever and by 1884 a decision was made to specialise in the manufacture and marketing of soap. He leased a factory in Warrington in 1886 and went into partnership with his brother, James Darcy Lever. Port Sunlight was chosen as a location for the works as it allowed room for future expansion and was close to a pool of labour. It was also ideally placed with its road, rail and water links. The first factory was opened in 1889 followed by the construction of the first cottages two years later, and the original village was completed in 1897. At the International Housing Conference at Port Sunlight in 1907 Lever stated that, 'The building of ten to twelve houses to the acre is the maximum that ought to be allowed. Houses should be built a minimum of 15 feet from the roadway and every house should have space available in the rear for a vegetable garden. Open spaces for recreation should be laid out at frequent and convenient centres. A home requires a garden in front of it, just as much as a cup requires a saucer.' Lever was created a baronet in 1911 and a baron in 1917, taking the maiden name of his late wife Elizabeth Hulme to form the title Leverhulme. Elizabeth died in 1913 as Lady Lever, but never Lady Leverhulme. In 1922 he was raised in the peerage to the rank of viscount.

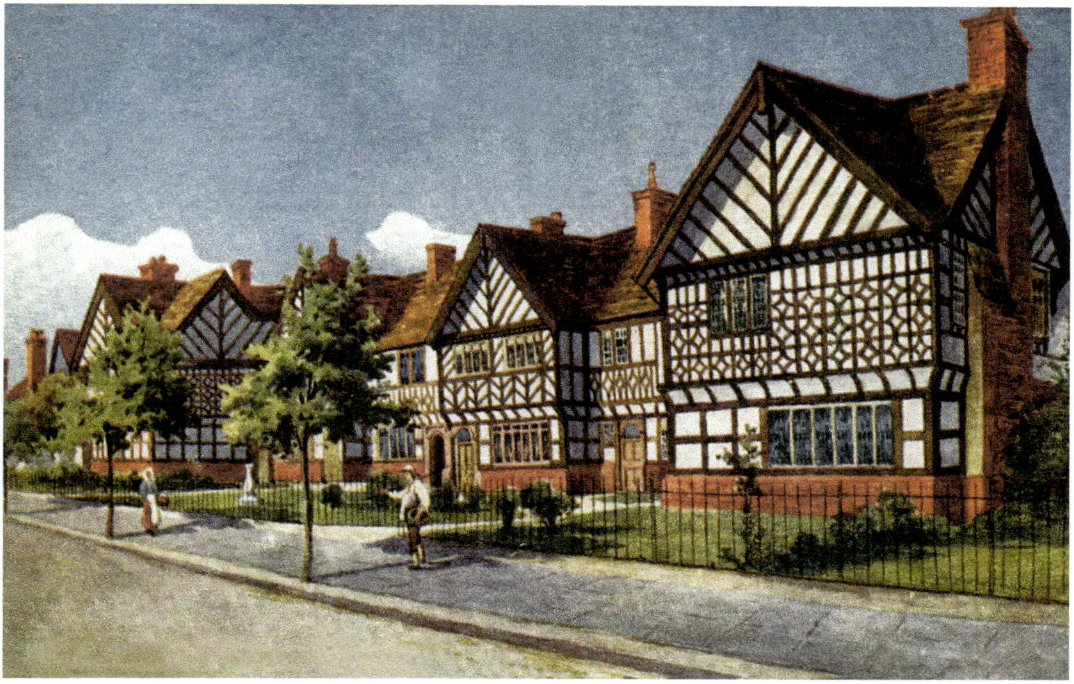

Above: Cottage Houses, Greendale Road, Port Sunlight.

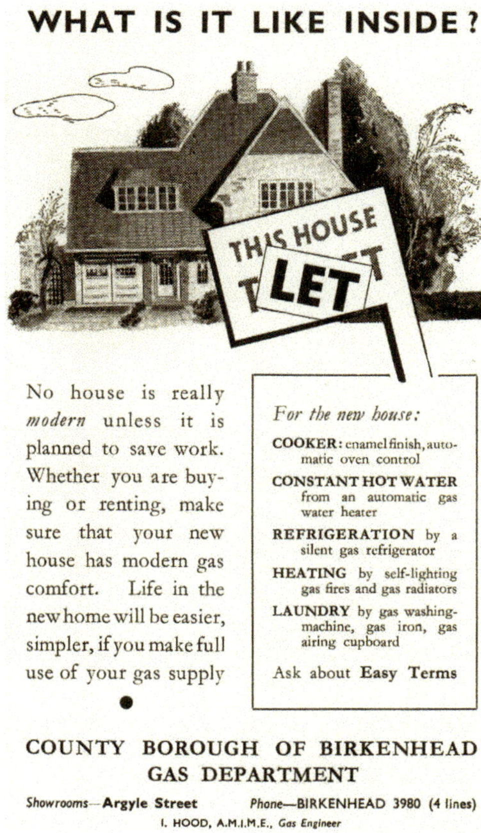

Above: County Borough of Birkenhead Gas Department, 1938.

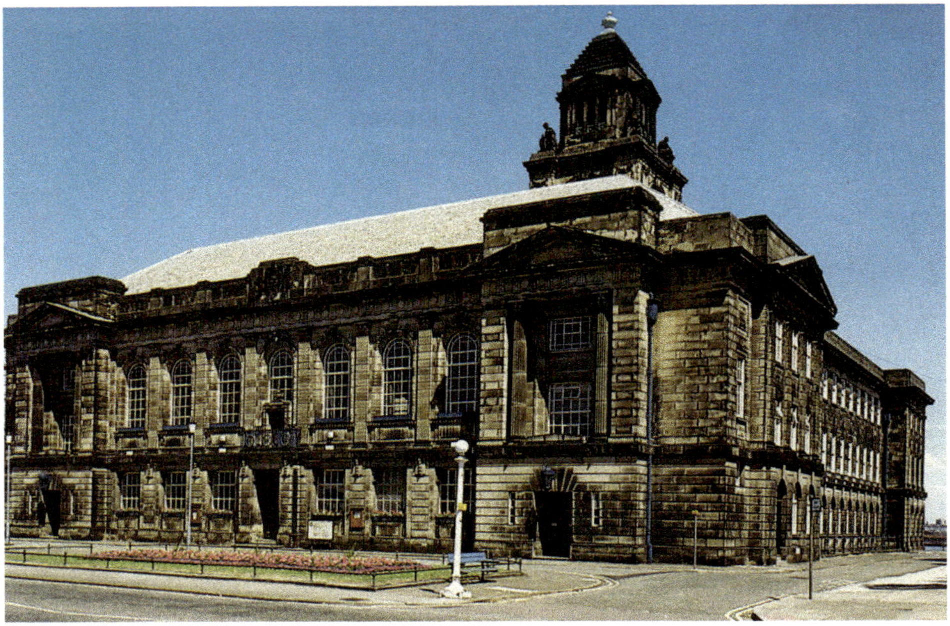

Wallasey Town Hall. Although the foundation stone for the new Town Hall was laid by George V on 25 March 1914, it was not opened until 3 November 1920 as it had been used as a military hospital during the First World War. Wallasey became a Parliamentary Borough in 1918 and the mayor's oak-panelled parlour overlooks the river, with the marbled grand staircase leading to the round room where weddings are carried out.

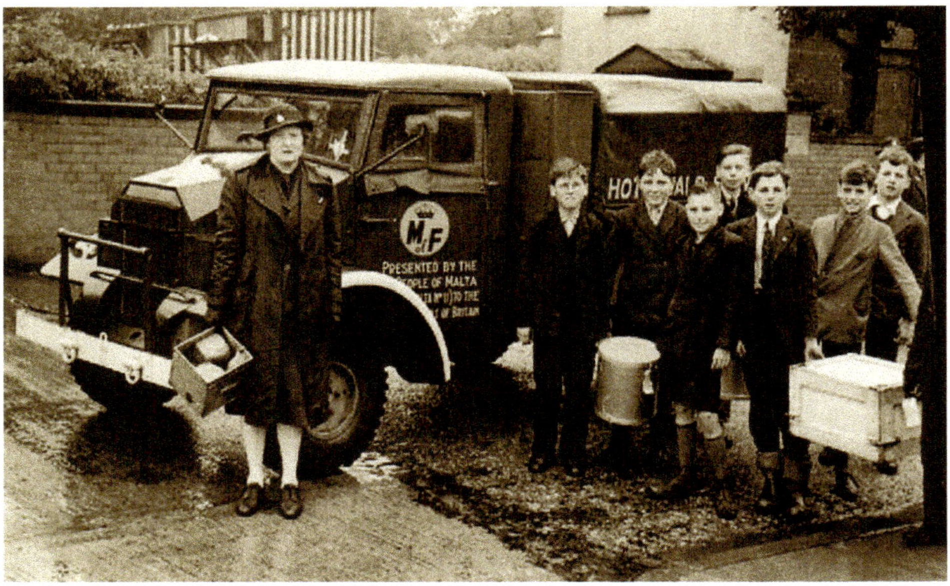

A meals on wheels service was provided by the Ministry of Food. The van states that it was 'Presented by the people of Malta.' Meals on wheels originated in the United Kingdom during the Blitz, when many people lost their homes and the ability to cook their own food. The Women's Volunteer Service provided the food and the system developed after the war when local authorities provided daily meals to the elderly and disabled people.

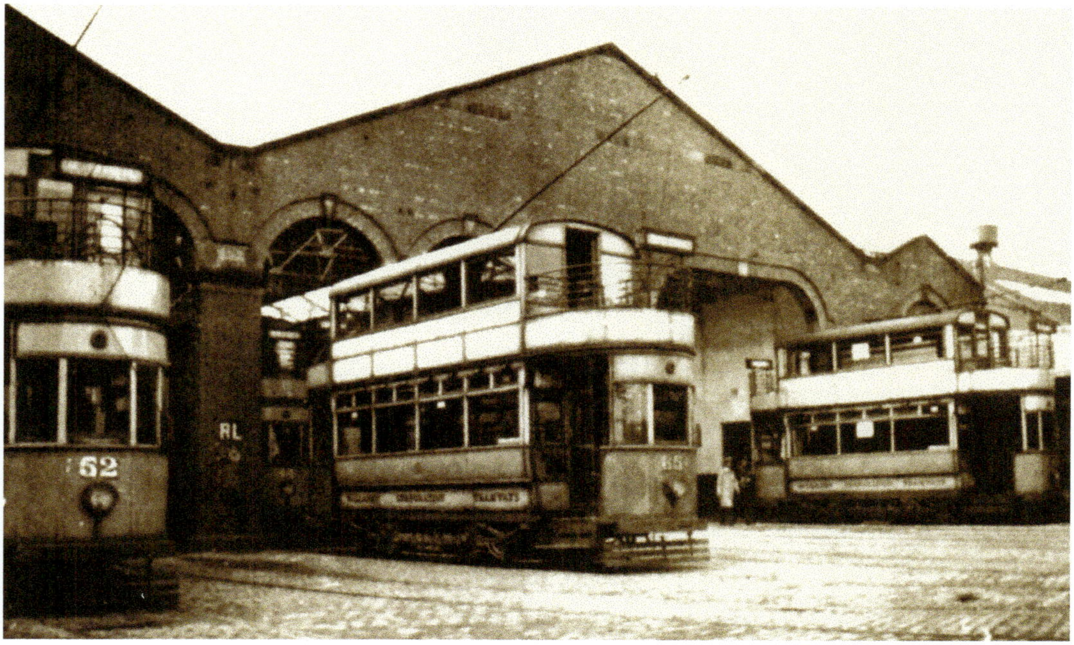

Trams at Seaview Road depot.

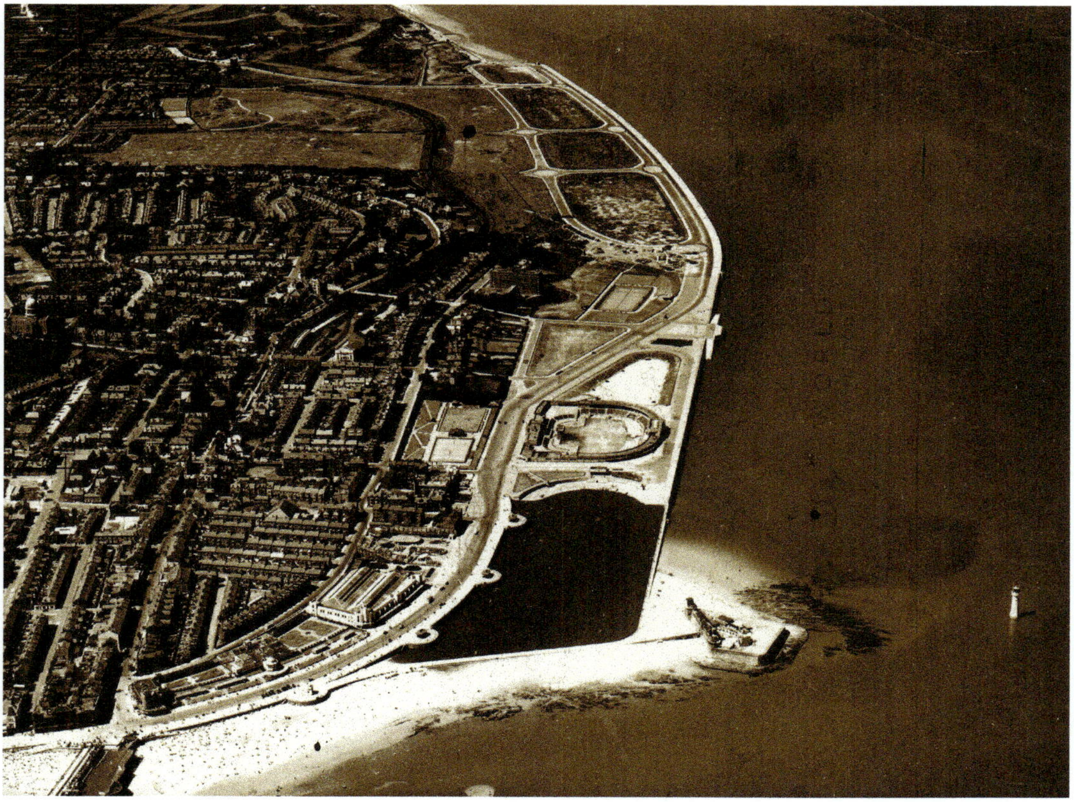

New Brighton showing Fort Perch Rock, the lake and the swimming baths.

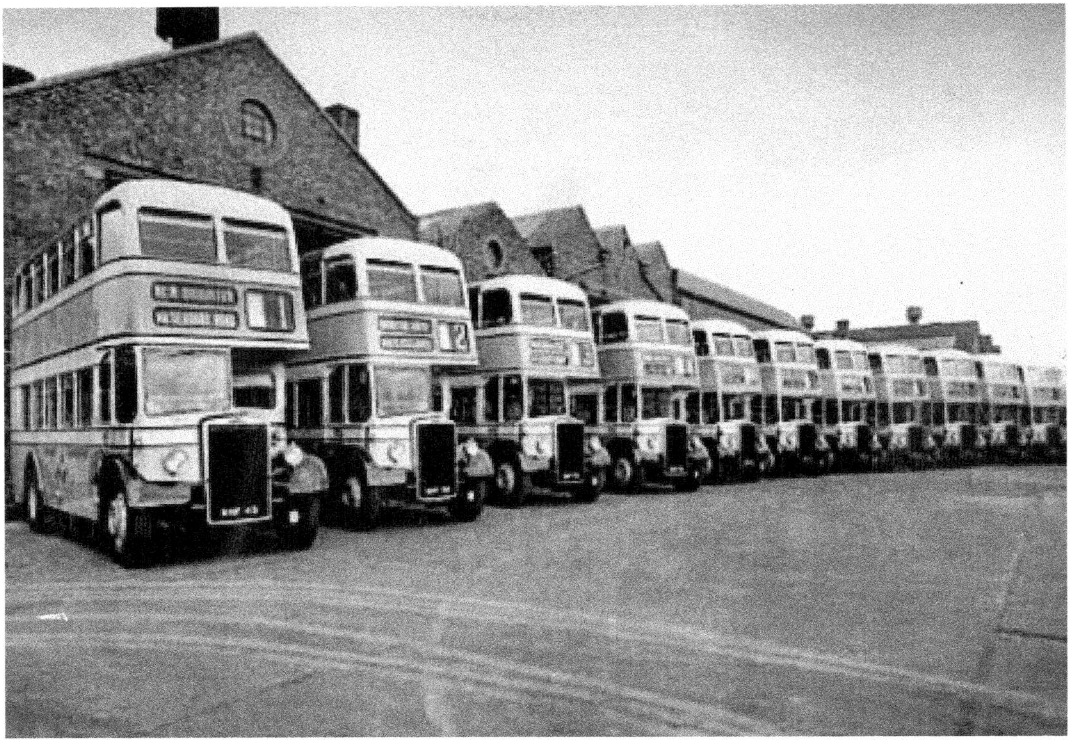

Above and below: Wallasey Corporation buses lined up at the Seaview Road depot.

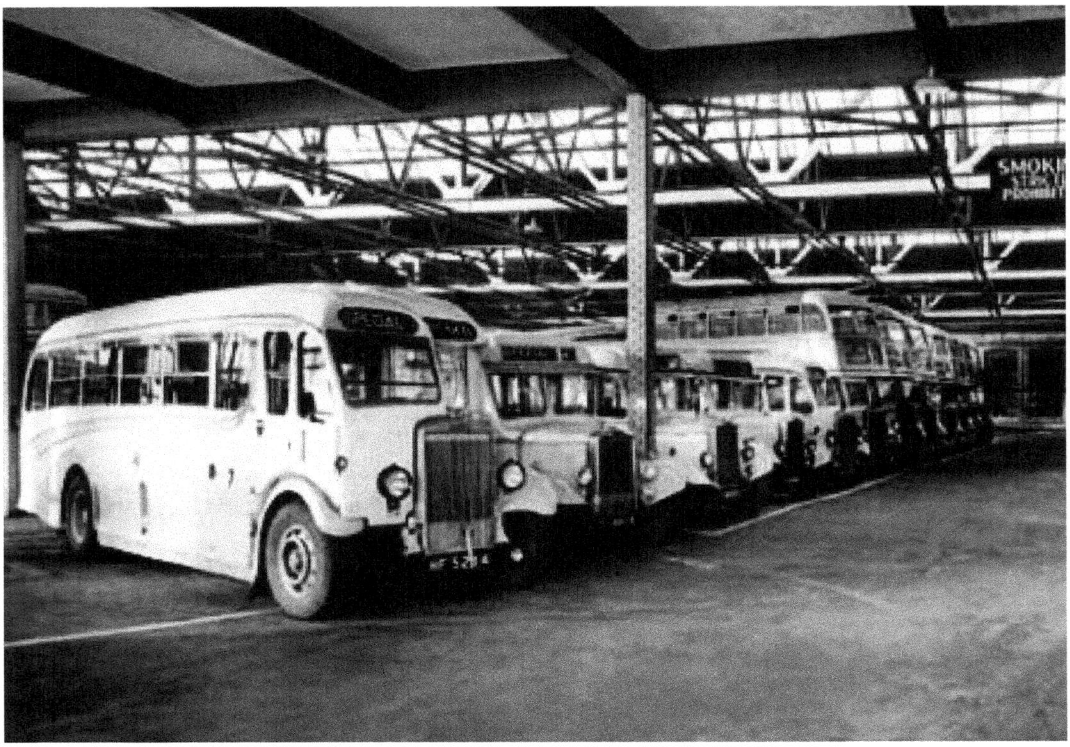

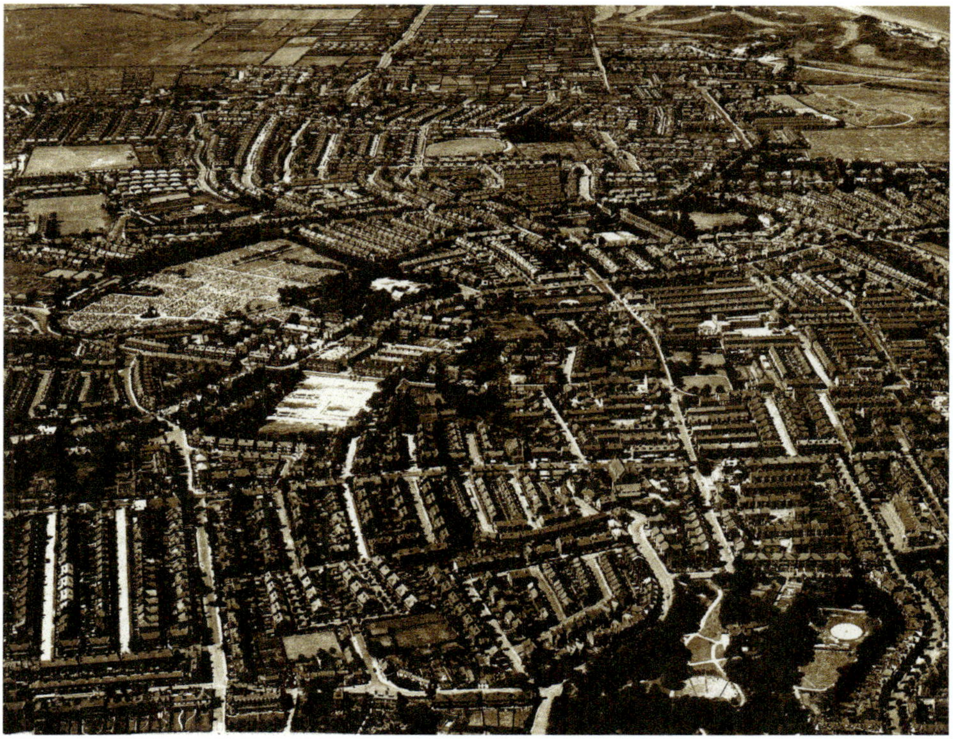

New Brighton from the air around the late 1940s.

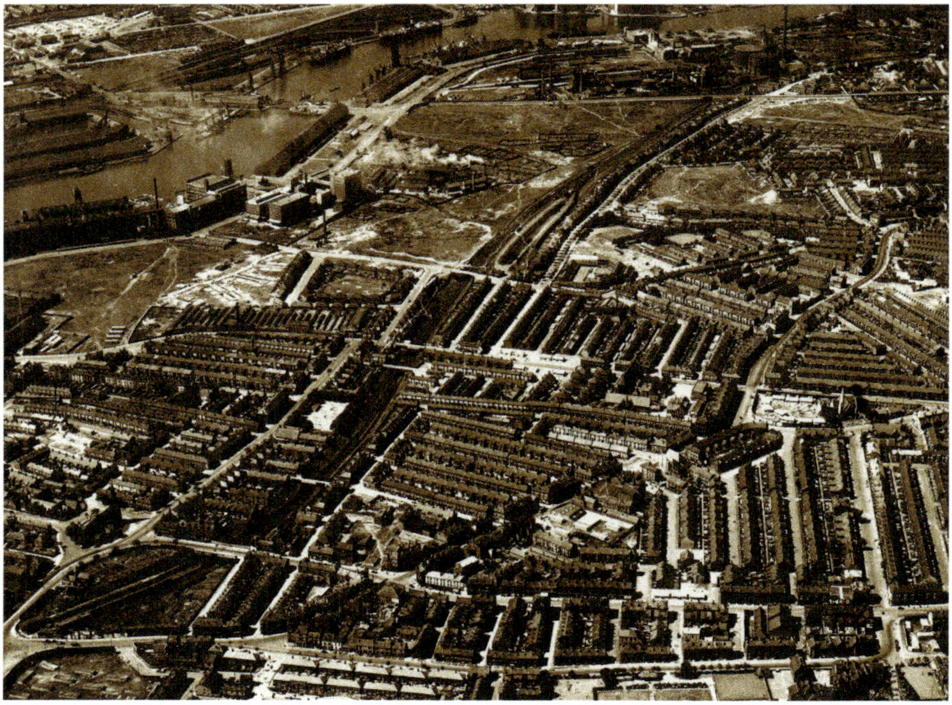

The docks and Seacombe Railway line.

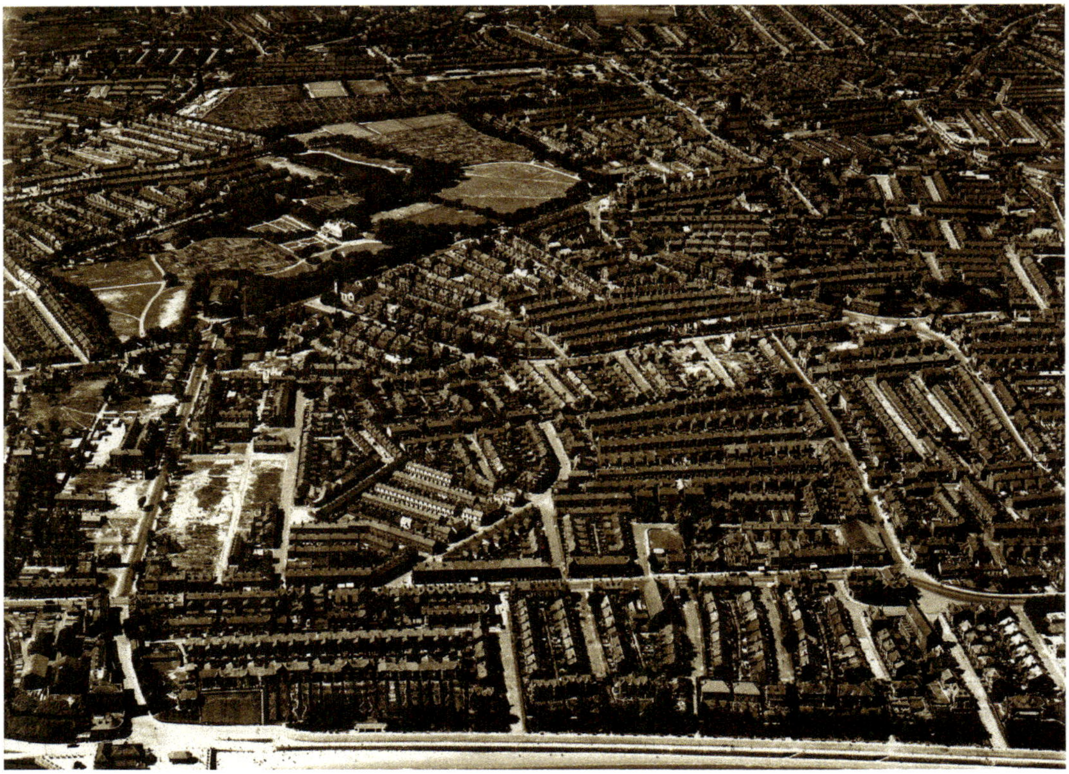

Wallasey Town Hall and Egremont.

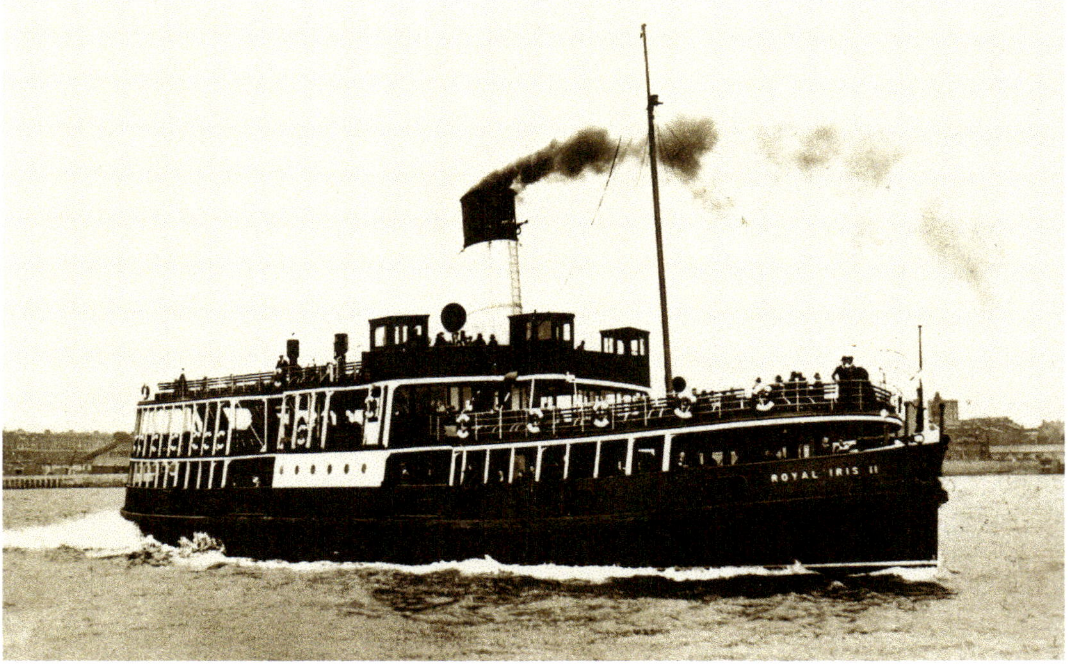

Wallasey Ferries' *Royal Iris II* was built in 1932 and was 607 gross registered tonnage.

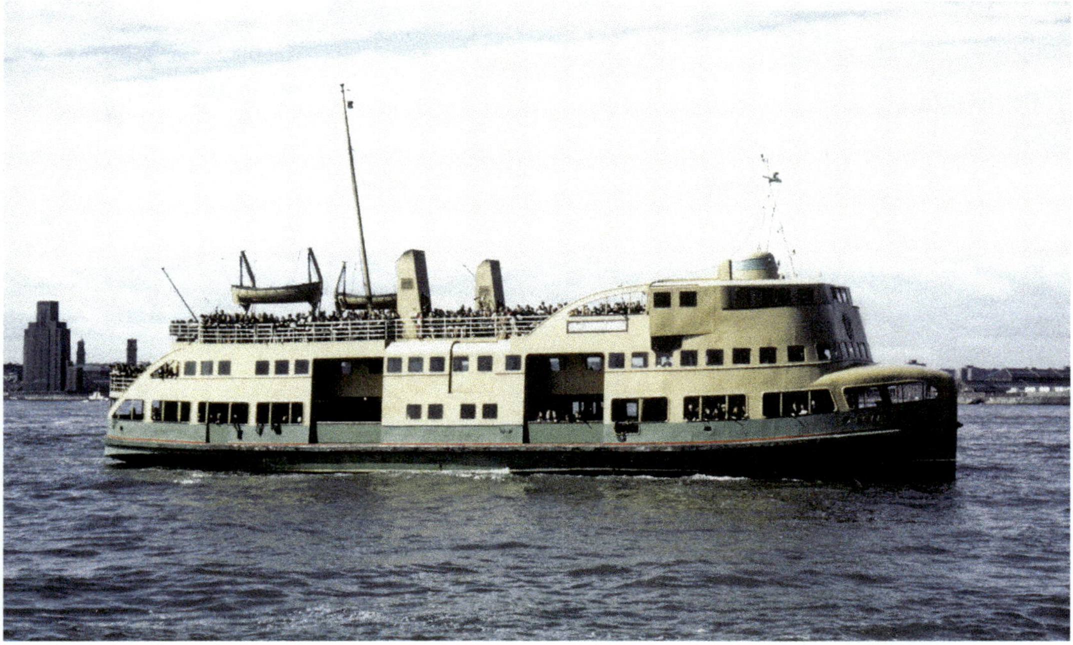

Above: A new *Royal Iris* was introduced in 1951. Wallasey Ferries claimed that they gave the lead to the transport world by the introduction of shore-based radar control, and were again in the fore with the revolutionary design of their new diesel electric ferry vessel, *Royal Iris*. She was planned to give the greatest possible comfort to passengers, whether engaged in ferry service or on the famous sea and river cruises.

Right: Wallasey Corporation Ferries Dance Cruises advertisements.

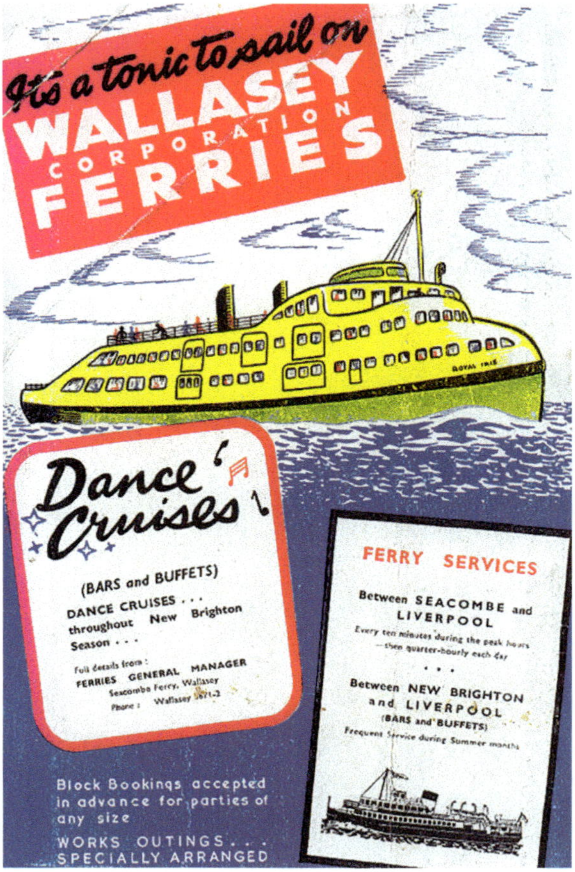

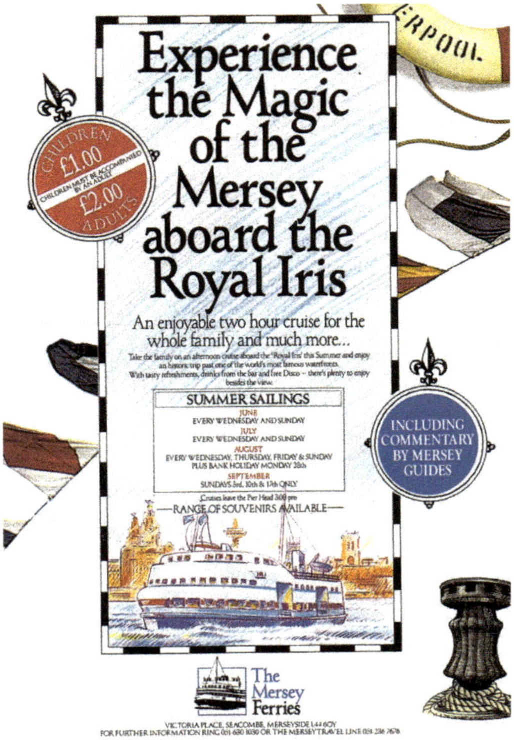

Mersey Ferries' *Royal Iris* two-hour cruise leaflet.

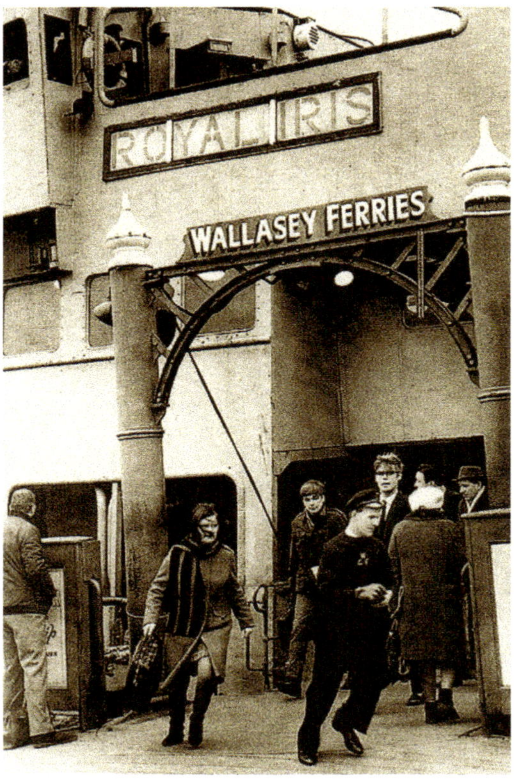

Royal Iris on the commuter service at Seacombe.

BIRKENHEAD CORPORATION FERRIES.

INSTRUCTIONS AS TO NAVIGATION IN FOG.

Under the Regulations for Preventing Collisions, this Vessel must in a Fog go at a moderate speed, having careful regard to existing circumstances and conditions.

When under way in dense Fog, the Vessel should proceed at a speed sufficient only to maintain steerage way, and, if necessary, for the attainment of such speed the engines should be alternately stopped and put ahead, due regard being had to the state of the tide and other conditions.

The utmost vigilance must be observed in all respects including the picking up of the bells and whistles of other vessels.

When under way in dense Fog the lookout (forward) must be doubled.

W. E. LANGSHAW, Manager.

Woodside, December 8th, 1916.

Above: Instructions as to navigation in fog dated 8 December 1916.

Right: Roberts & Harland advertisement, 1962.

Roberts & Harland

J. R. HARLAND F.S.V.A. W. R. HARLAND A.R.I.C.S. A.R.V.A.

ESTATE AGENTS SURVEYORS & VALUERS

ARUNDEL AVENUE-£35,950
A pleasant and bright modern detached property situated quiet cul-de-sac off the Oval. Central heating 25'10' garage, good gardens, fully fitted cloaks, lounge, dining room, kitchen, spacious landing, three good bedrooms, combined bathroom.

STEEL AVENUE—£29,500
Extremely well maintained four bedroomed semi. Central heating, garage and neat gardens, Attractive hall, lounge, dining room, morning/kitchen, bathroom, separate w.c.

SOMERSET ROAD—£25,250
Larger than average detached property situated quiet residential area. Conven. Wallasey Village station, shops, buses and M53 link to tunnel. Hall with cloaks, lounge, dining room, extended kitchen 20'6 long, three good bedrooms. Manageable gardens.

LISCARD ROAD—£21,500
Six bedroomed terraced, adjacent to above property. Many good features. Combined properties suitable for commercial project.

LISCARD ROAD—£22,500
Six bedroom terrace, excellent order. Fully fitted kitchen, large lounge and dining room, breakfast kitchen 25'3' long. Extremely well decorated. Attractive gardens, hard standing for two cars.

BURTON AVENUE—£21.500
Attractive 1930's semi detached in Wallasey Village. Quiet cul-de-sac, convenient Mersey Rail, schools and shops. Well planned accommodation includes hall, lounge, dining room, kitchen, three bedrooms, bathroom, good sized gardens with detached garage.

WILLOUGHBY ROAD—£19,750
Extensively modernised semi-, re-plumbed, modern windows additional features lighting and gas fires, modern kitchen and bathroom, three bedrooms. Nice gardens.

HALTON ROAD—£17,950
Completely refurnished and decorated three bedroomed semi.

CAVENDISH ROAD—£17,000
Compact five bedroomed house, convenient Marine Park promenade, Mersey Railway station and local shops, spacious entrance, lounge, dining room, breakfast room, kitchen, five bedrooms, combined bathroom.

RADNOR DRIVE—£15,950
Attractive double fronted semi. Spacious accommodation. Elevated position, convenient promenade. Hall, lounge, living room, kitchen, separate bathroom and toilet, five bedrooms, box room, basement workshop.

TRAFALGAR ROAD-£15,300
Just off Serpentine Road having southerly aspect and fulll grant work three years ago, convenient local shops and technical college. Lounge, dining room, kitchen, three good bedrooms, secluded rear garden.

MORLEY ROAD—£13,000
Attractive semi detached. Pleasant kitchen and modern bathroom ideal first time buyer, hall, lounge, dining room, kitchen (fitted) three bedrooms, modern bathroom, G/rent £4 p.a.

ILCHESTER ROAD—£11,750
Compact three bedroomed house convenient local shops and trasport. Modernised through lounge and modern kitchen. Ideal first time buyer, lounge/dinette, kitchen, three bedrooms-combined bathroom.

TO LET

Furnished Houses and flats
WALLASEY-Liscard
£130 per month
First floor fully furnished s.c. flat. Sleep 4, on No. 31 & 32 bus route direct to Liverpool. Completely redecorated and refurbished. Available 12 months.

LIVERPOOL 12
Eaton Rd. North £185 per month
Fully furnished modern semi all facilities, central heating, fridge, freezer, washing machine convenient city centre. Sleep 3-5 persons, garage and gardens. Availabe 12 months. Vieing by appointment.

PROPERTY SALES & MANAGEMENT
BUILDING SOCIETY & PRIVATE VALUATIONS
COMPULSORY PURCHASE & COMPENSATION
VALUATIONS FOR PROBATE & CAPITAL TAXES
IMPROVEMENT GRANT APPLICATIONS
RATING

65 LISCARD VILLAGE
WALLASEY
051-638 4104

AGENTS TO Burnley Building Society

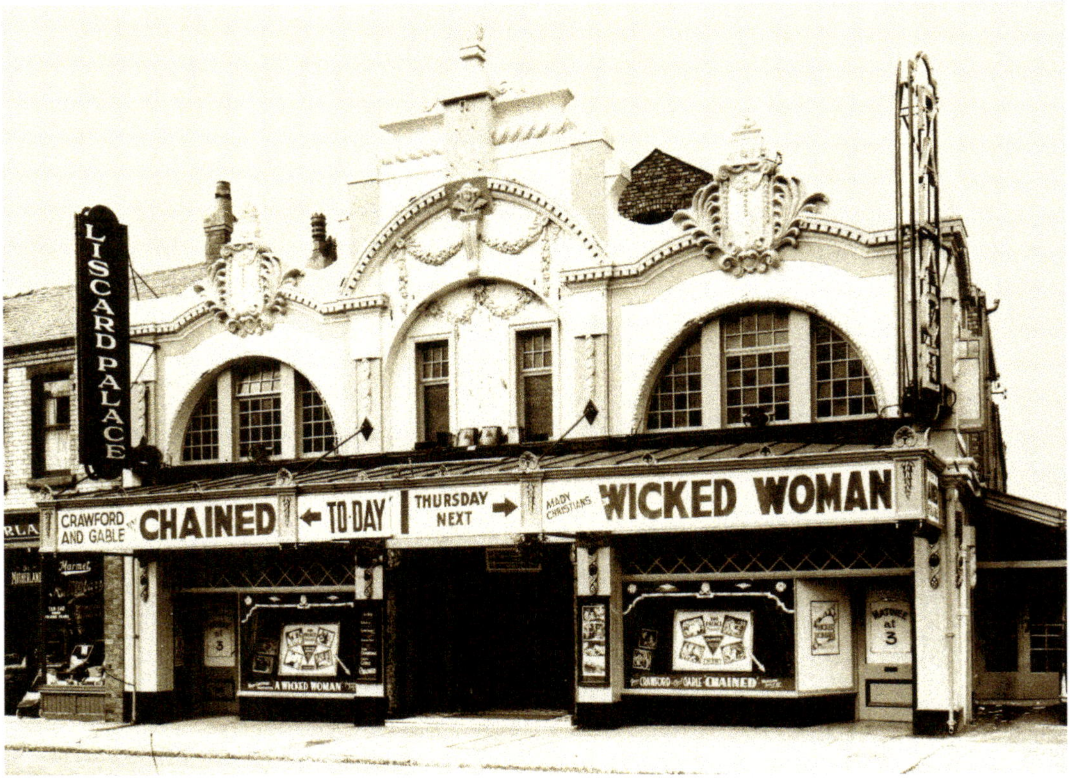

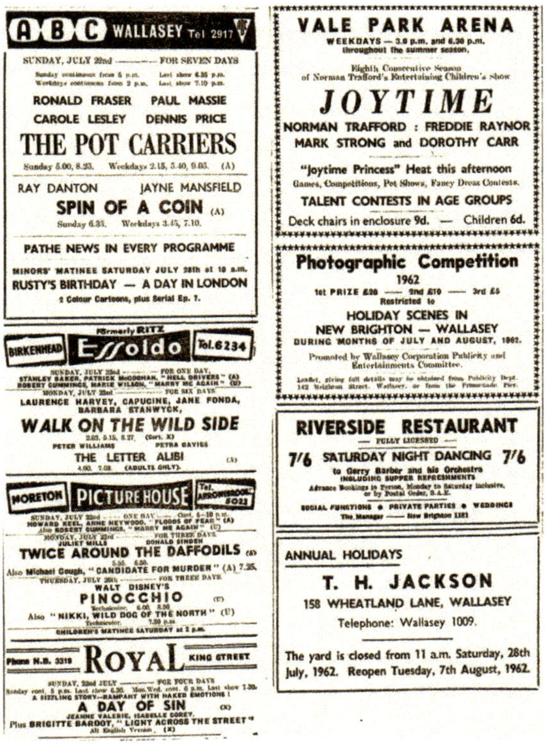

Above: The Liscard Palace cinema opened on 25 November 1911 in Seaview Road. The entrance had shops on either side and was covered by a large glass canopy, plaster covered façade, which included three arched window features, and was illuminated at night by hundreds of lights. The building was extended in 1920 and the seating capacity increased to 1,000. The two shops at the entrance were incorporated into the cinema two years later, and this provided additional waiting room accommodation. The first colour film to be made was shown in 1923 and the building was redecorated five years later. A new rustic façade replaced the original in the early 1950s, when a CinemaScope screen was fitted. The last film was shown on 3 June 1959, and it later became a supermarket and a shoe market.

Left: 1962 cinema advertisements.

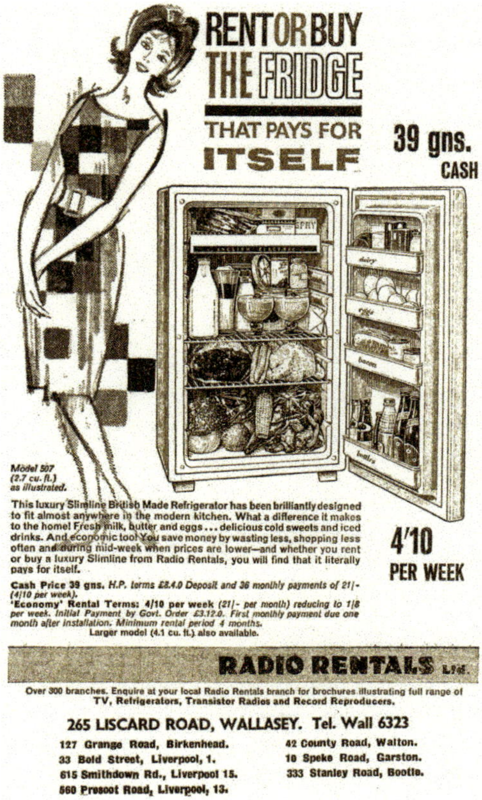

Right: 1962 Radio Rentals advertisement.

Below: Liscard shopping centre with the Boot Inn in the distance. There has been a public house on the site of the Boot since Elizabethan times and the present building was erected in 1926, when the road was widened. The origin of the name dates back to the reign of Elizabeth I. A traveller arrived with a large boot in his hand, and as the landlord was serving him, he heard the sound of coins and deducted that they had been stolen. The landlord overcame the man just as three men arrived to confirm that the gold coins had been stolen. The thief was hanged, the landlord rewarded and the boot was left as a sign for the inn. Another theory is that the name derives from the boot shop next door to the inn.

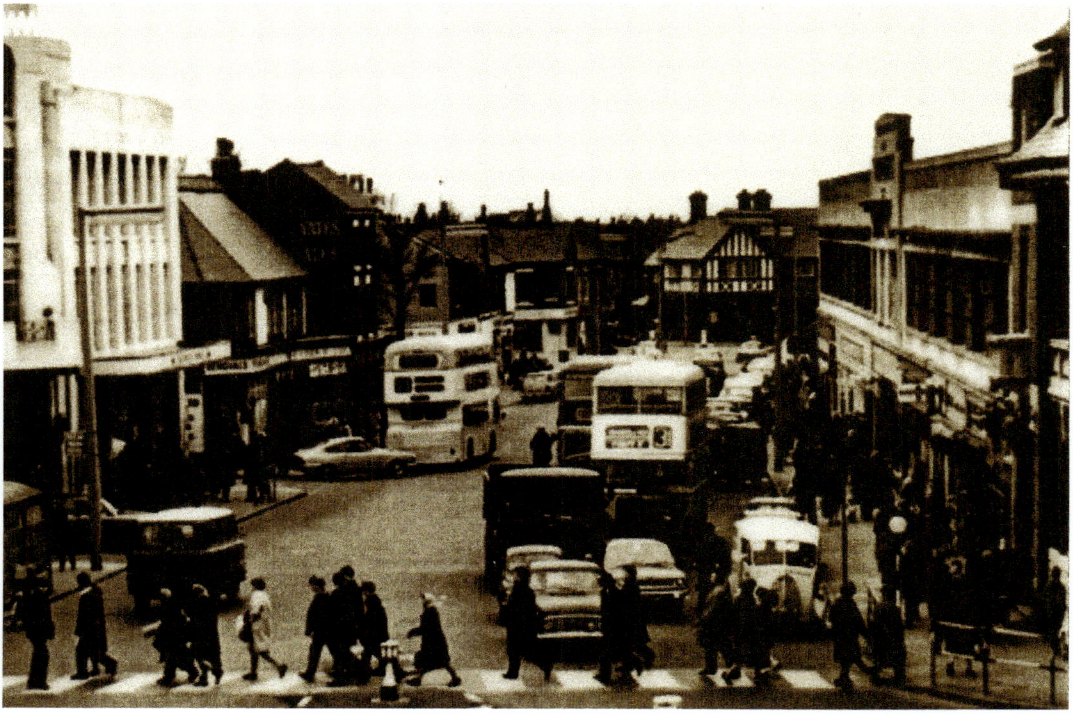

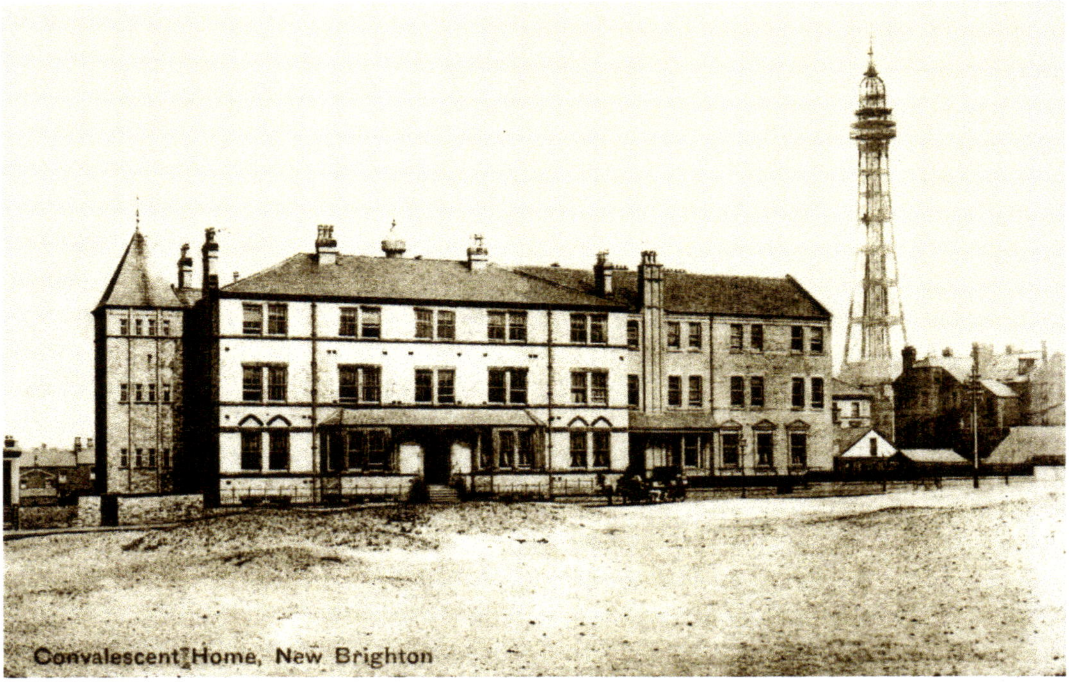

The Convalescent Home was located at the bottom of Rowson Street. It was closed at the end of the First World War and was reopened in 1924 as the Maris Stella Covent, which was New Brighton's first Roman Catholic high school. The school was closed in 1970 and the building was demolished two years later.

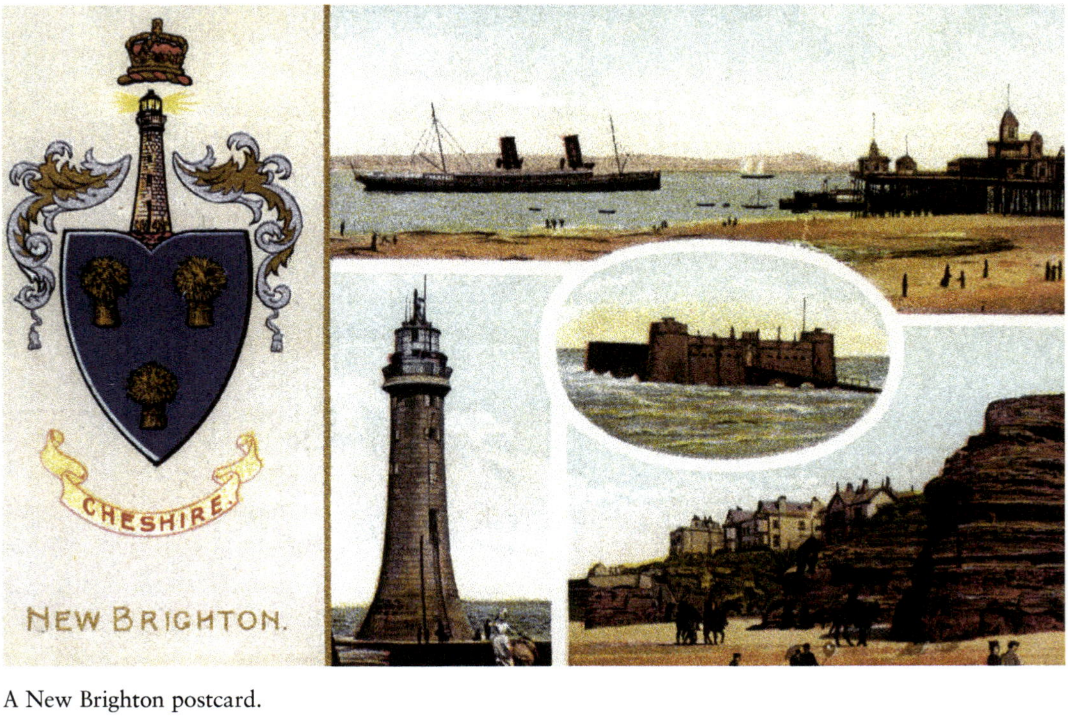

A New Brighton postcard.

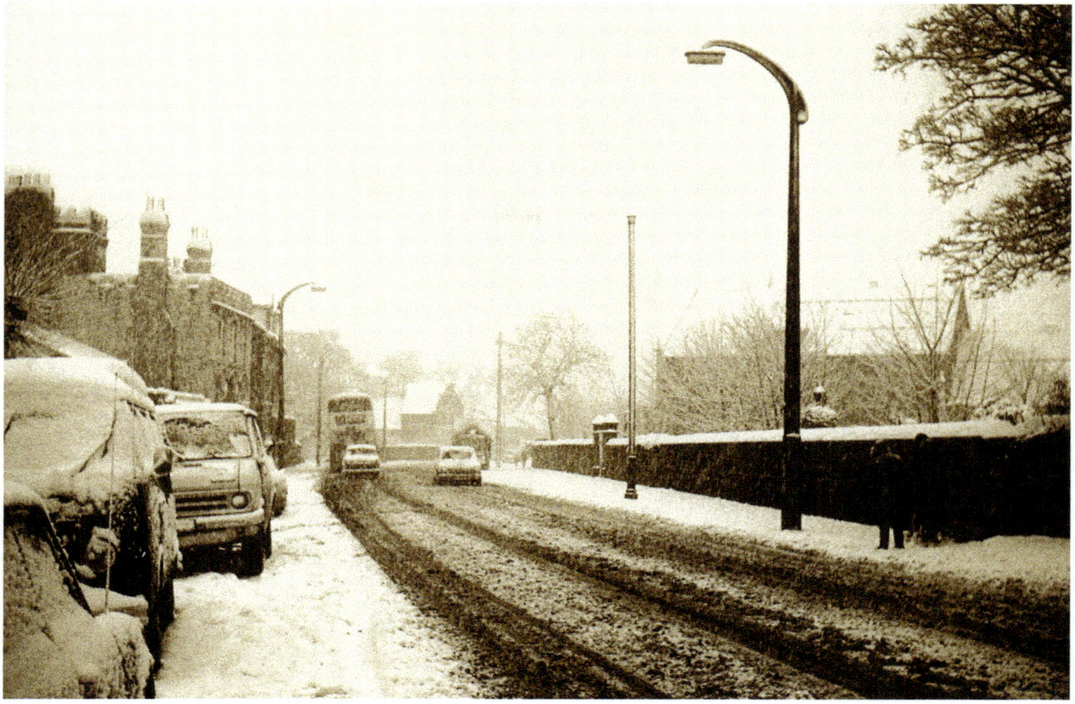

A winter's scene in Rake Lane, New Brighton, looking towards Liscard village.

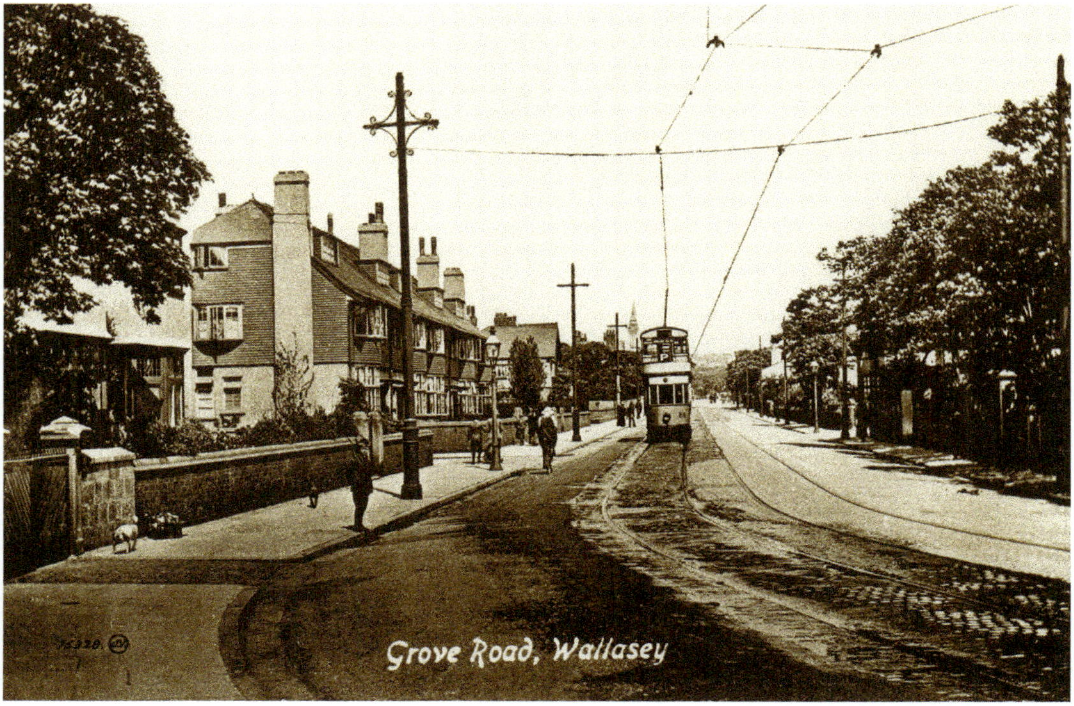

A tram heads up Grove Road. The tram route through Wallasey village opened on 7 February 1911 and New Brighton Tower can be seen to the left of the tram in the distance.

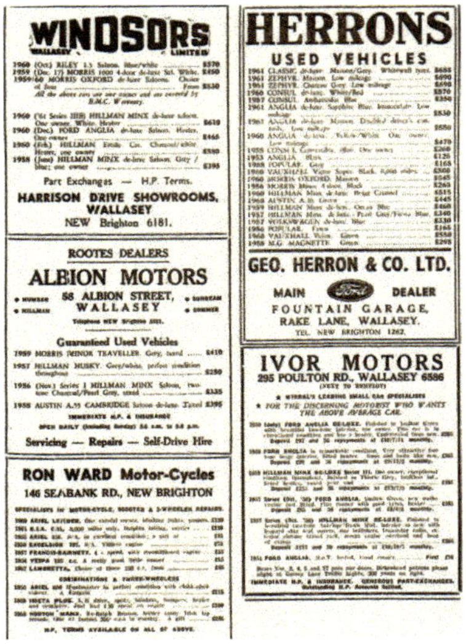

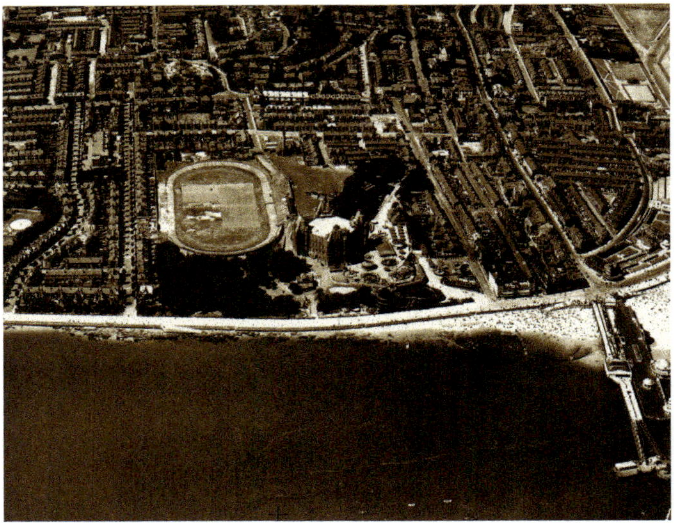

Above left: 1962 Wallasey car dealer's advertisements.

Above right: Tower Grounds and New Brighton Pier. Work commenced on building the tower on 22 June 1896, and it was completed in 1900 at a cost of £120,000. The tower was 567 feet 6 inches high and 621 feet above sea level. The architects for the project were Maxwell & Turk of Manchester and it was built by Handysides & Co. of Derby. The New Brighton Tower and Recreation Co. was established with a share capital of £300,000, and an area of 20 acres at the Rock Point Estate was purchased. The idea was based on the Eiffel Tower in Paris and it was to include an Assembly Hall, Winter Gardens, refreshment rooms and a cycle track. The tower was to be more elegant than Blackpool Tower and £1 shares were offered to investors. There were six workmen killed during the construction of the building and others seriously injured. It was the highest building in the country on completion, and suffered its first suicide shortly after it was opened when a man threw himself off the balcony. It cost *6d* to travel to the top of the tower by one of the four lifts, and it was possible to see the Isle of Man, Great Orme's Head at Llandudno, the Lake District and the Welsh Mountains. Half a million people visited the tower in the first year it was opened. As there was little maintenance work carried out on the tower during the First World War, the steel structure was neglected and was very expensive to repair or replace. Consequently, it was decided to dismantle the structure, with work commencing on 7 May 1919 and being completed in June 1921. The main building, comprising the ballroom and theatre, remained and during the Second World War the basement was used as an air-raid shelter. On 5 April 1969 the building was destroyed by fire, leaving the shell, which was later demolished. The site was grassed over, providing a recreation area for the community and the old athletic ground was purchased by a property developer and housing was built on the land.

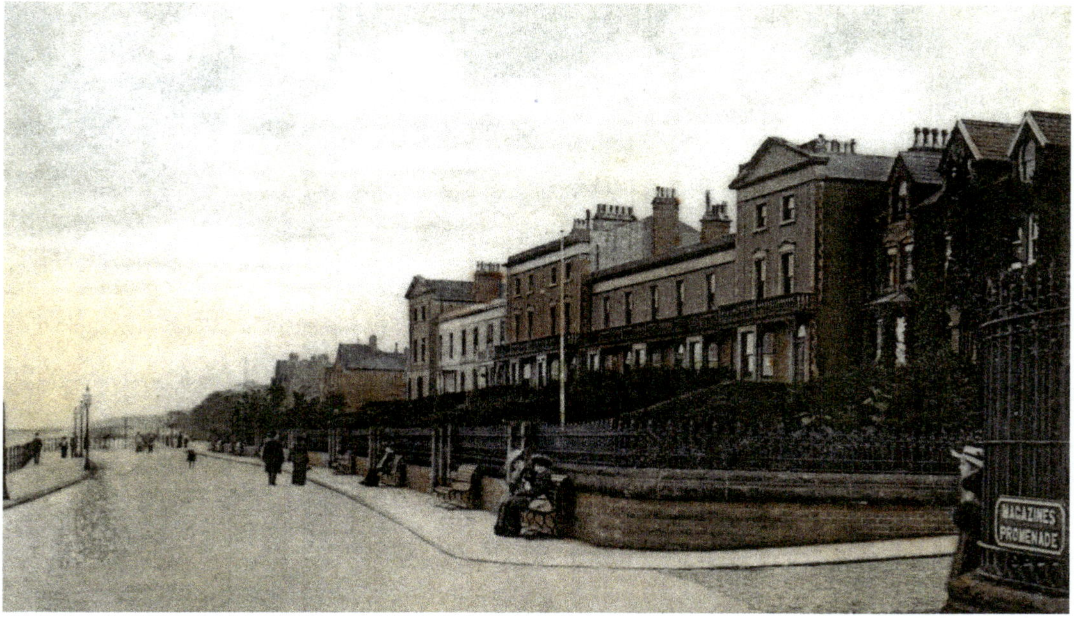

Above: The Magazines, New Brighton. All ships entering the port of Liverpool had to place its gunpowder into storage, and the location near Liscard was chosen in the 1750s. The stores were moved in the 1850s to hulks anchored in the Mersey at Bromborough and houses were built on the land.

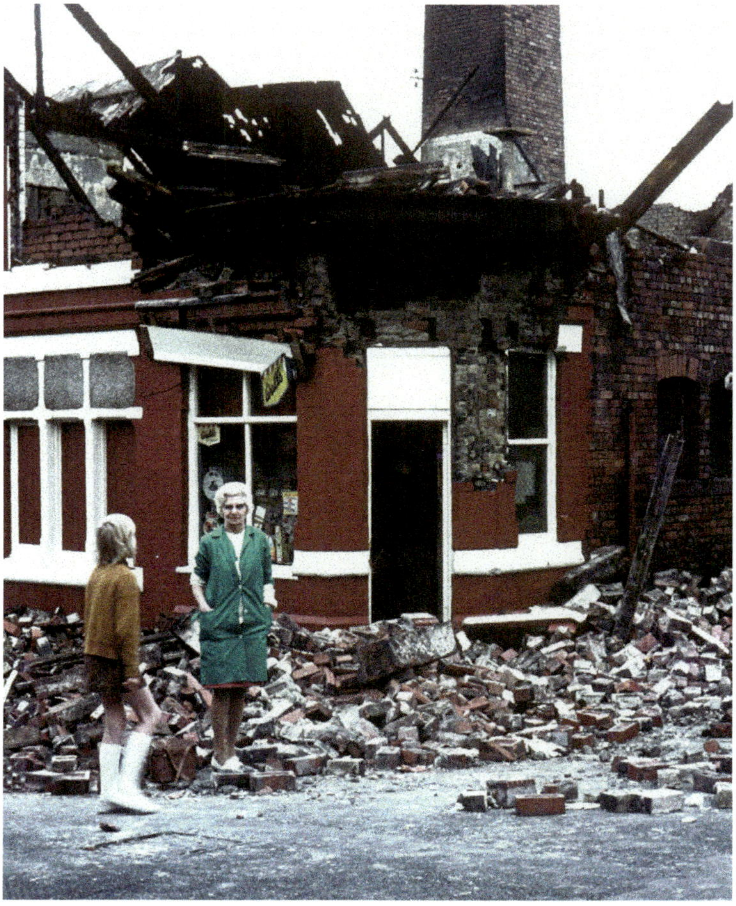

Right: The laundry at Granville Street, New Brighton. The building was demolished and thirty flats in sheltered accommodation were built on the site. The care provided at Granville Court includes twenty-four-hour staffing seven days a week. There is a lift, lounge, dining room, laundry, guest facilities, garden, community centre and a hairdressing salon.

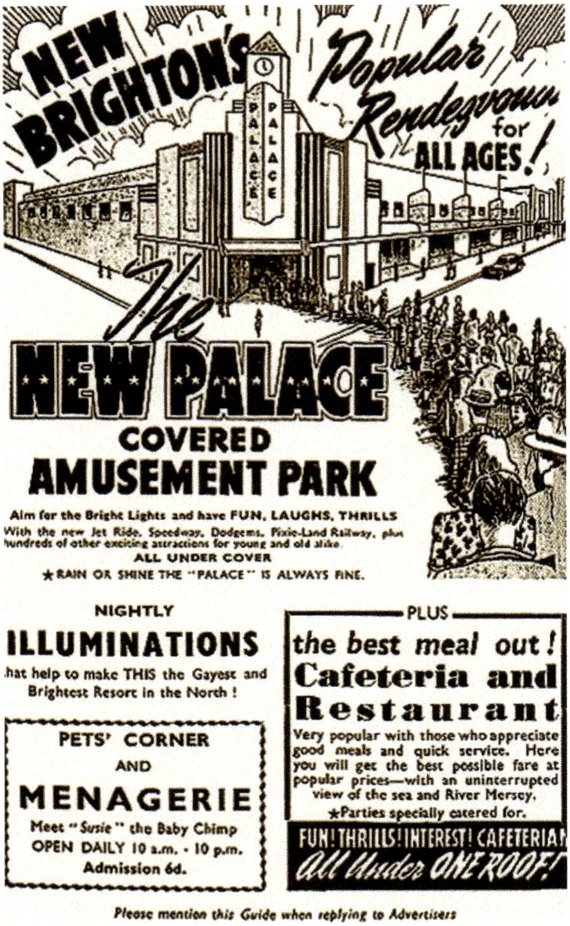

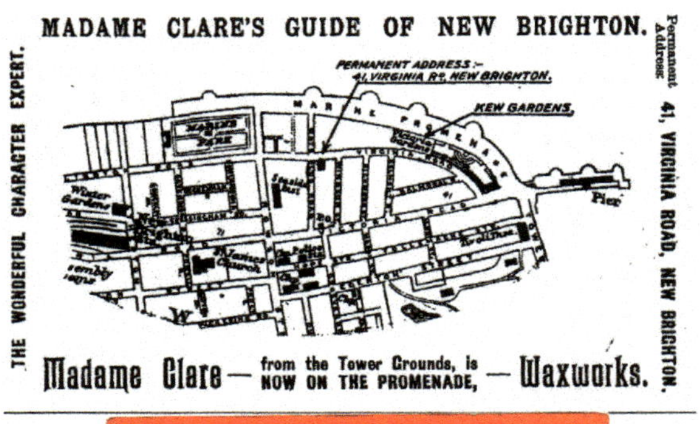

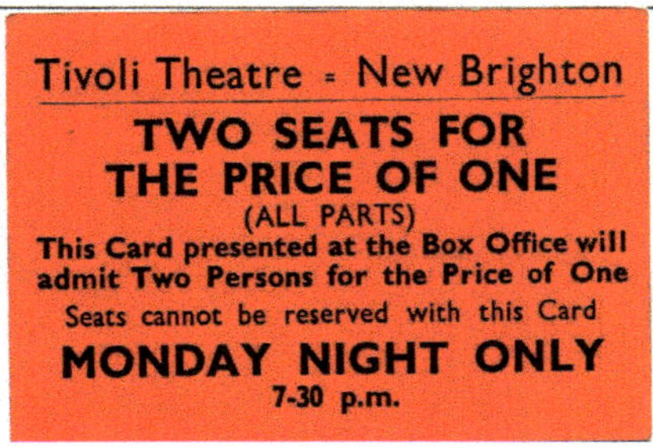

Advertisement for the New Palace covered Amusement Park at New Brighton. The Palace's indoor amusement arcade contained dodgems and other activities including bingo and food stalls. The facility also includes an outside area with numerous other rides and attractions.

The Tivoli Theatre at New Brighton opened in 1914, starring Lily Langtree. It was sold to Pat Collins in 1923 and then to William Swire by auction in 1925. The following year it was acquired by its original owners, The Tivoli Leases Ltd, and it was then purchased by the Gaumont British Company in 1928. It operated for a short time as a cinema, and in 1937 it became the New Tivoli. The building was closed in 1938 and reopened by Leam Productions Ltd in 1945, who presented twice-nightly variety shows in the summer months and a repertory production in the winter until 1955. It then operated as an amusement arcade until a fire in 1976. The building was later demolished and apartments were built on the site.

New Brighton advertisements.

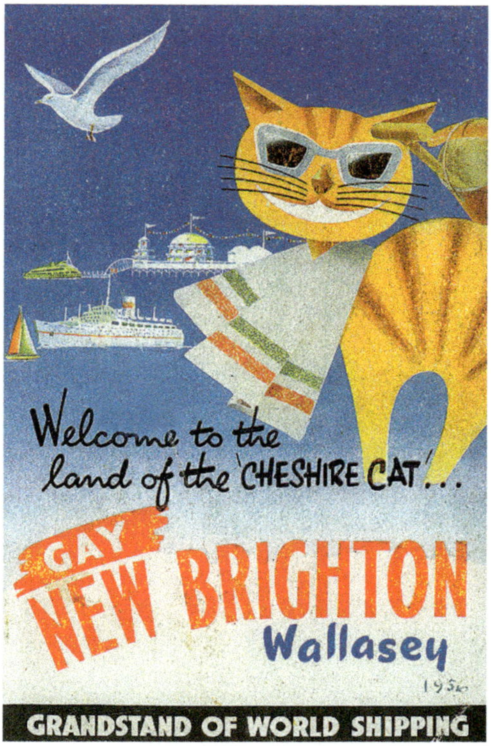

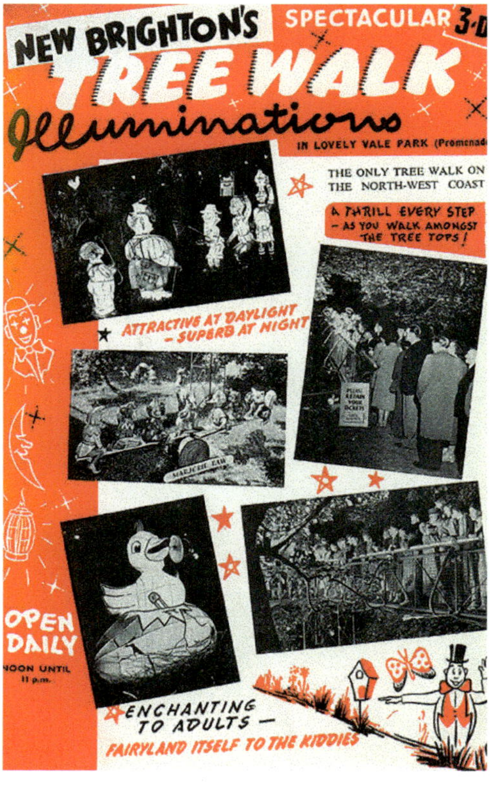

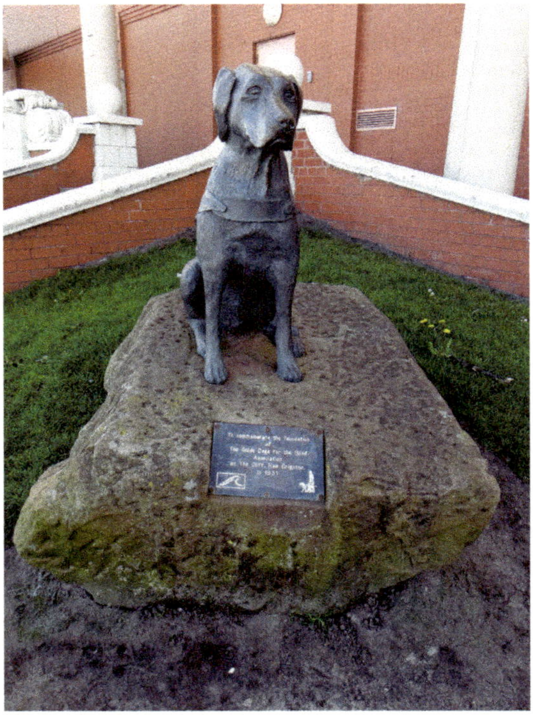

A plaque and model commemorating the foundation of The Guide Dogs for the Blind Association at The Cliff, New Brighton in 1931. The first four guide dogs – Judy, Flash, Folly and Meta – were trained at Wallasey in 1931 and The Guide Dogs for the Blind Association was formed. Muriel Crooke and Rosamund Bond were breeders of German shepherds and responsible for training the first guide dogs. Captain Nikolai Liakhoff became the first permanent trainer, and in 1941 and the premises at The Cliff was taken over for war purposes and the association moved to new headquarters at Leamington Spa.

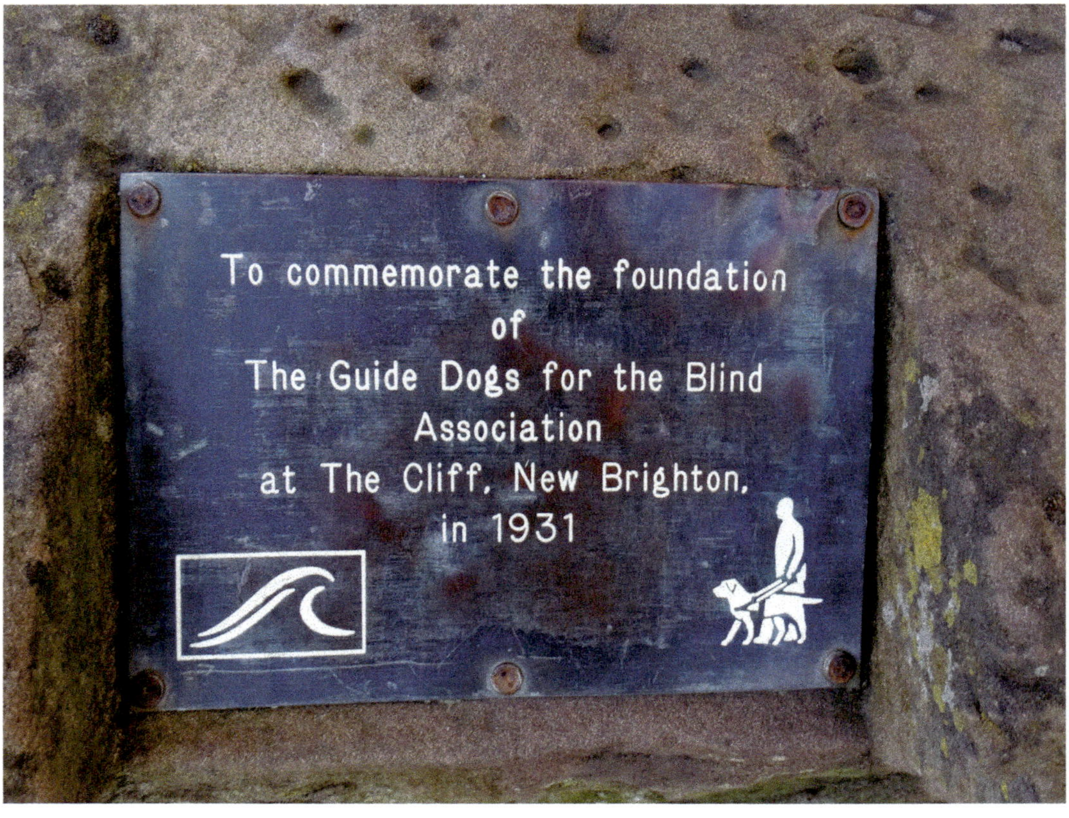

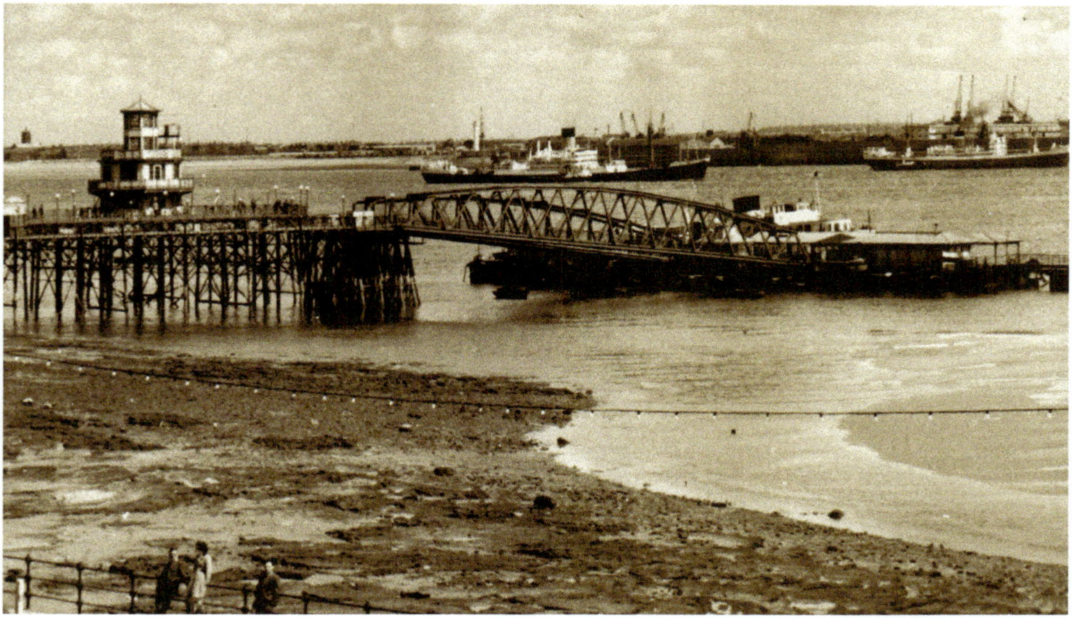

Above: The Wallasey ferry *Leasowe* at the landing stage at New Brighton. Vessels of the Blue Funnel and Ellerman lines prepare to berth at Liverpool Docks. In the 1950s and 1960s it was quite common to see several large vessels anchored mid-river awaiting tugs to take them into the dock system to load or discharge their cargos.

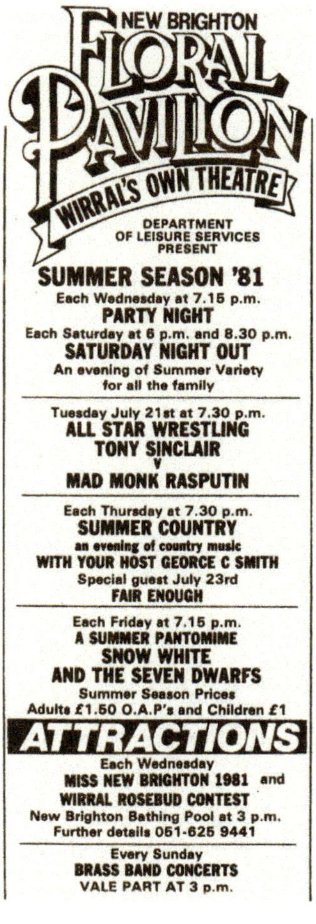

Right: 1981 programme of events at the Floral Pavilion Theatre, New Brighton.

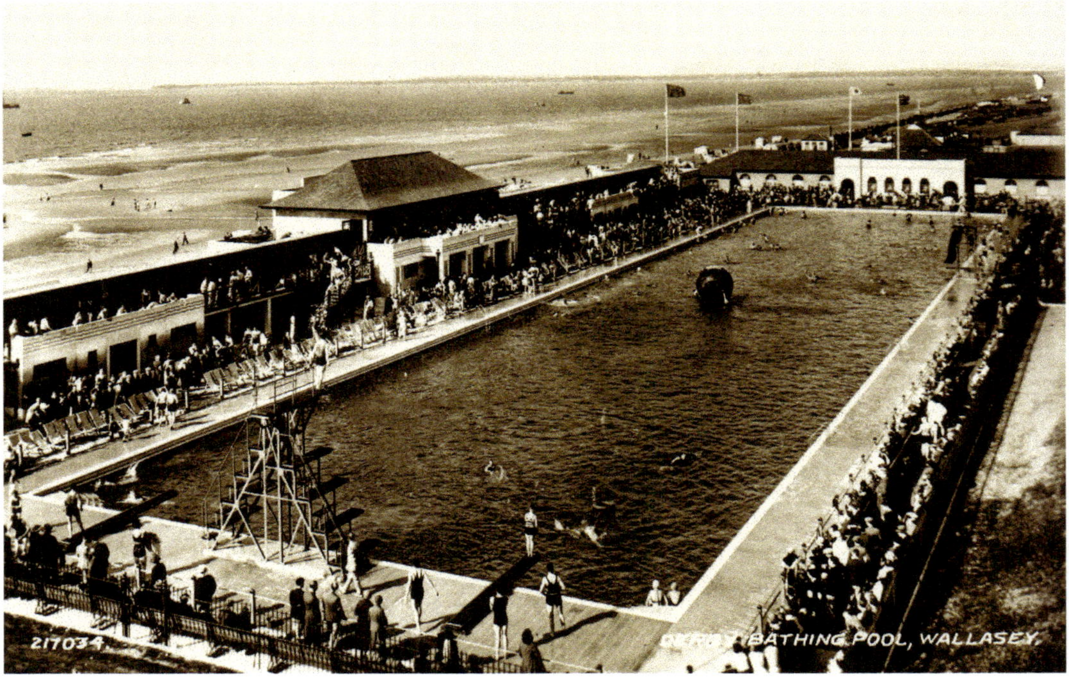

The Derby Pool at Harrison Drive was opened by Lord Derby on 8 June 1932. The baths could accommodate 1,000 bathers and 2,000 spectators. It was demolished in the 1970s and a public house named the Derby Pool was built on the site.

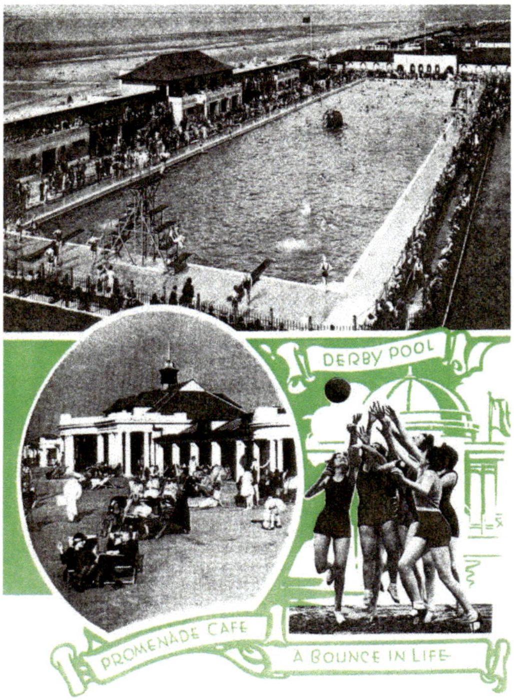

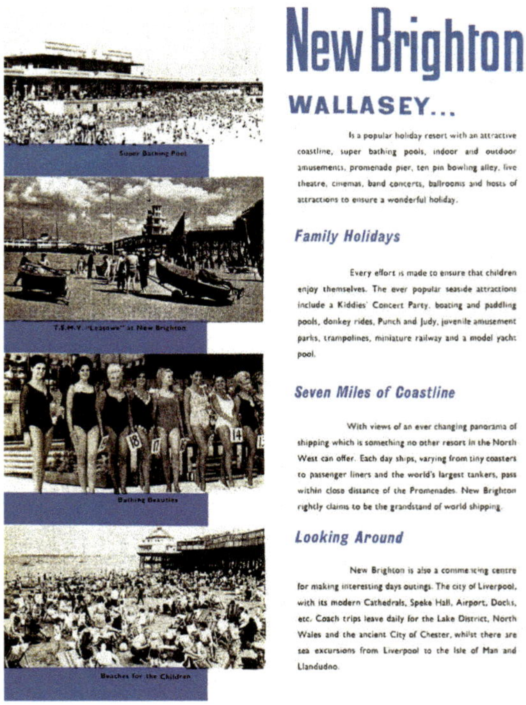

Advertisements for the Derby Pool and the facilities for family holidays at New Brighton.

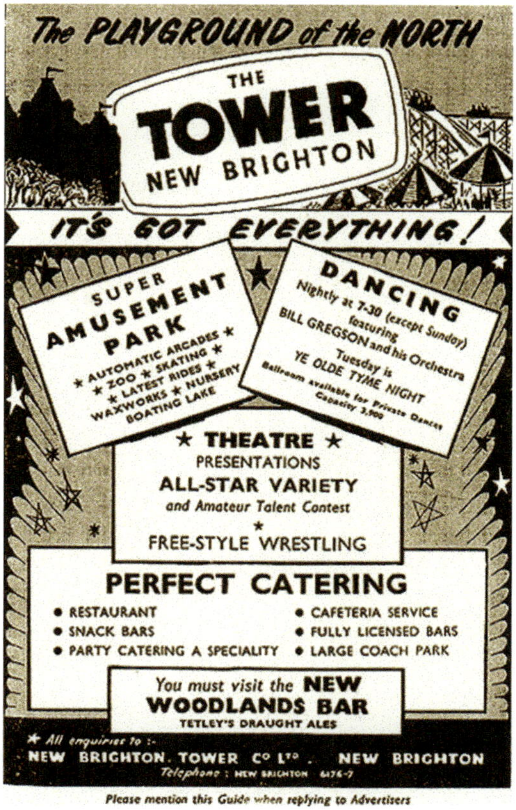

Right: Advert showing the facilities at New Brighton Tower.

Below: A beauty contest at New Brighton Bathing Pool. The pool hosted many such competitions during the summer months, which were judged by local and national celebrities, and some were televised live by the BBC.

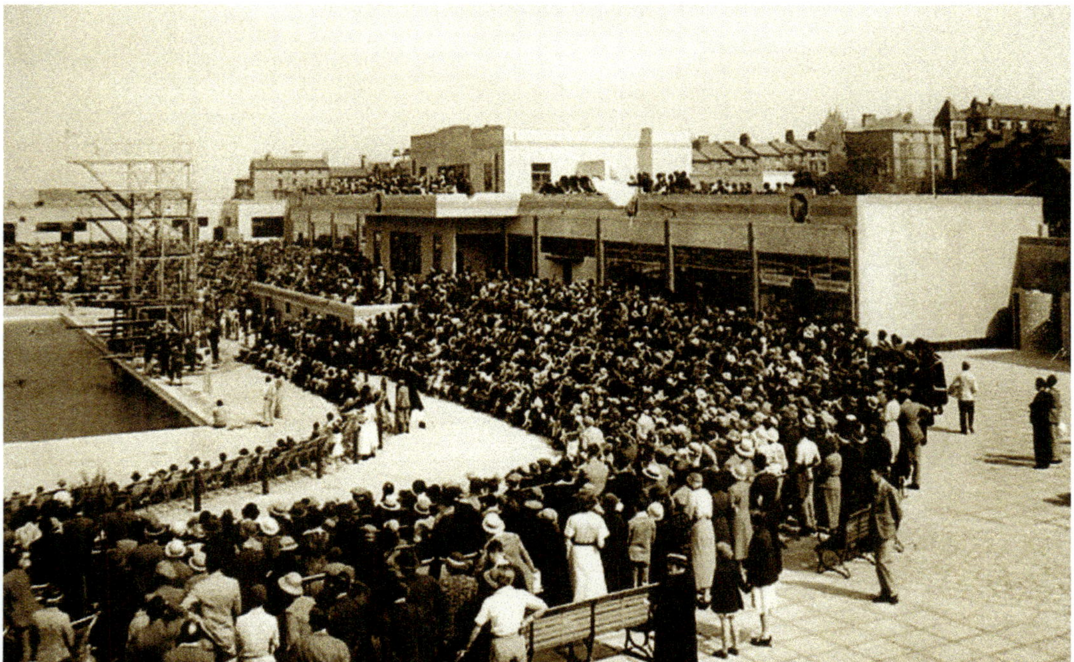

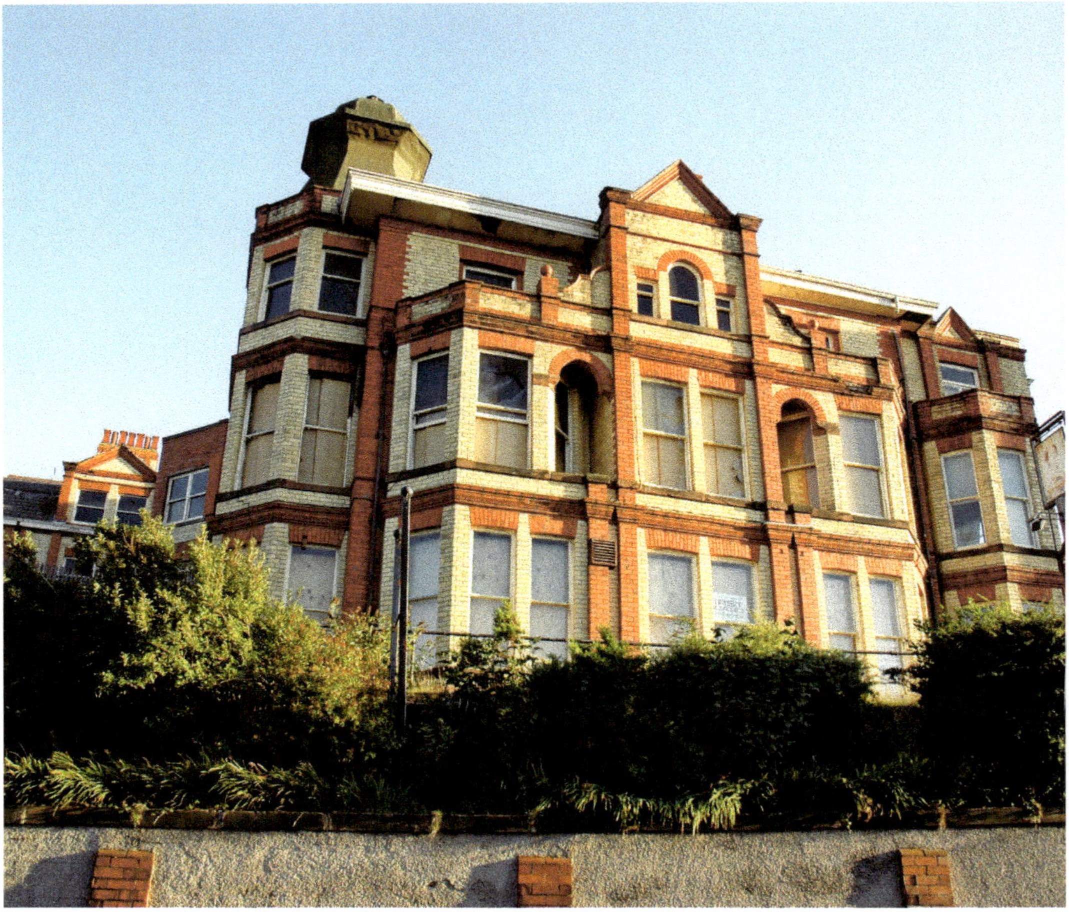

The Hotel Victoria at New Brighton was built of yellow and red brick in 1896. The hotel was designed with twenty-two rooms and had hot and cold water in each room. The Assembly Rooms were built in 1855 and were later combined with the Hotel Victoria. The hotel was advertised as the 'Premier Residential Hotel in the Wirral Peninsular. Delightfully situated with private rooms for weddings, banquets etc., with a large ballroom and suite available, and spacious car park.' The hotel closed in 2007. It was quickly demolished and a block of luxury apartments was built on the site.

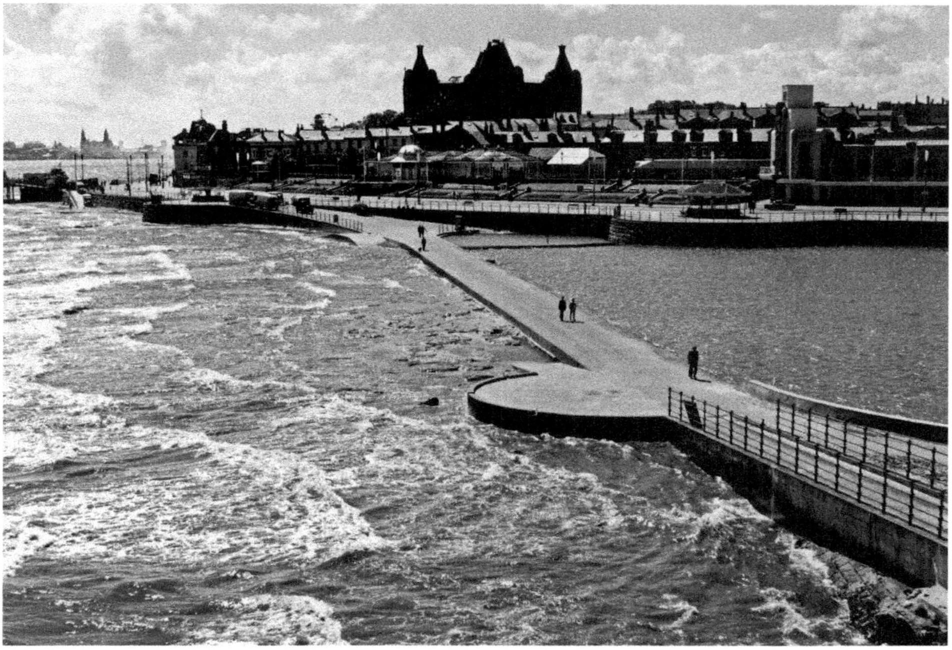

Above and below: The New Brighton Tower and Marine Lake. The Marine Lake was completed in 1933 at a cost of £95,000. It covers 10 acres and visitors could hire boats to sail on the lake. In recent years the area around the lake has been developed, and new restaurants, cafés and other facilities have been provided for the visitor to the resort.

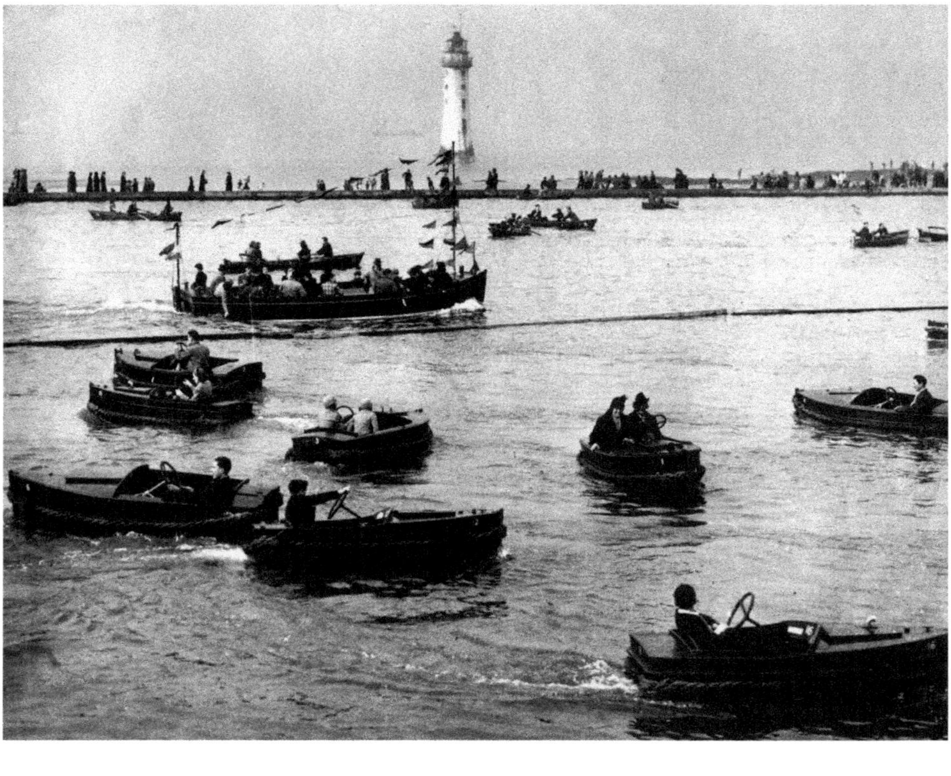

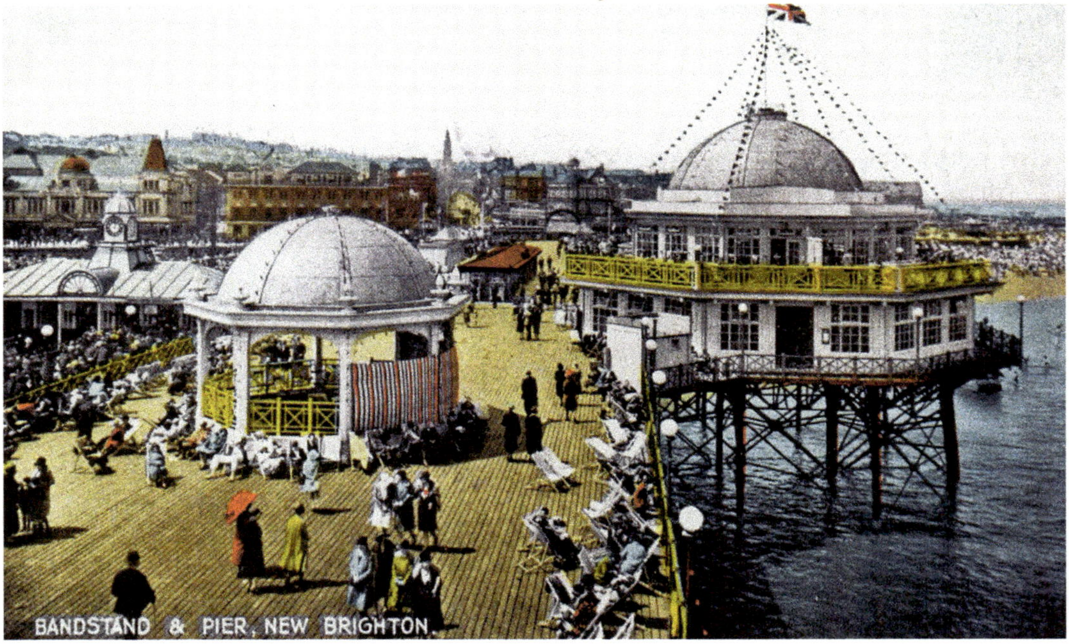

The grandstand and pier at New Brighton.

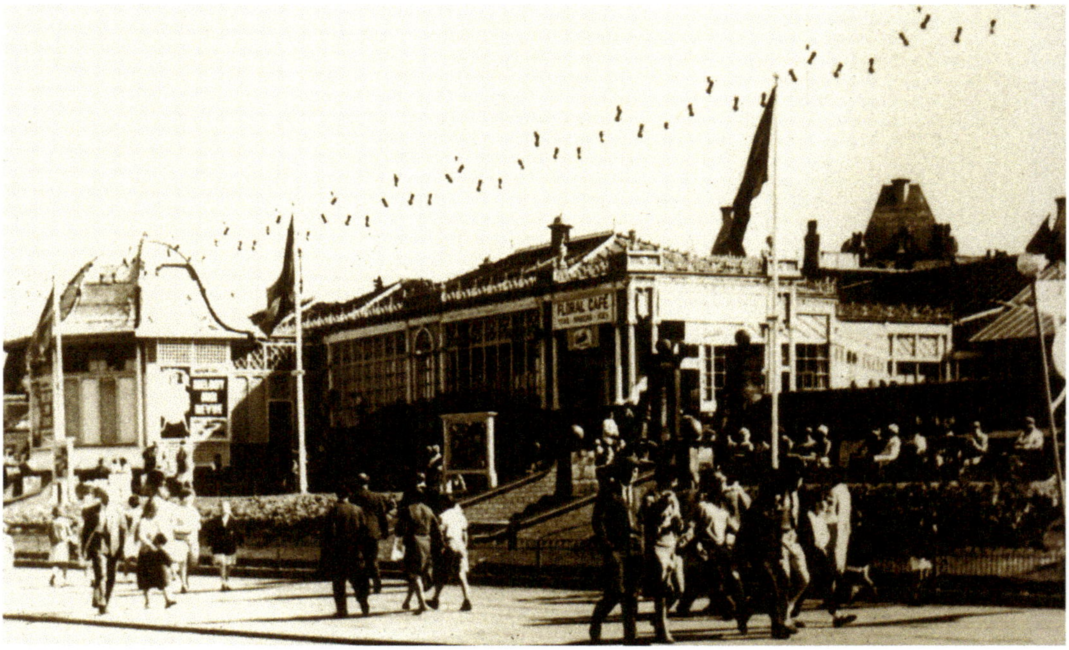

The Floral Pavilion Theatre at New Brighton opened in 1913 as an open-air summer theatre within the Victoria Gardens. It was covered by an iron and glass roof in 1925 and in the mid-1960s it was rebuilt with a metal roof. As part of a £60 million redevelopment of New Brighton it was demolished in 2007 and a new theatre was built, which opened the following year. The new building has an enlarged auditorium with seating for over 800 people, and the complex also provides for conference facilities and contains a large multipurpose lounge area.

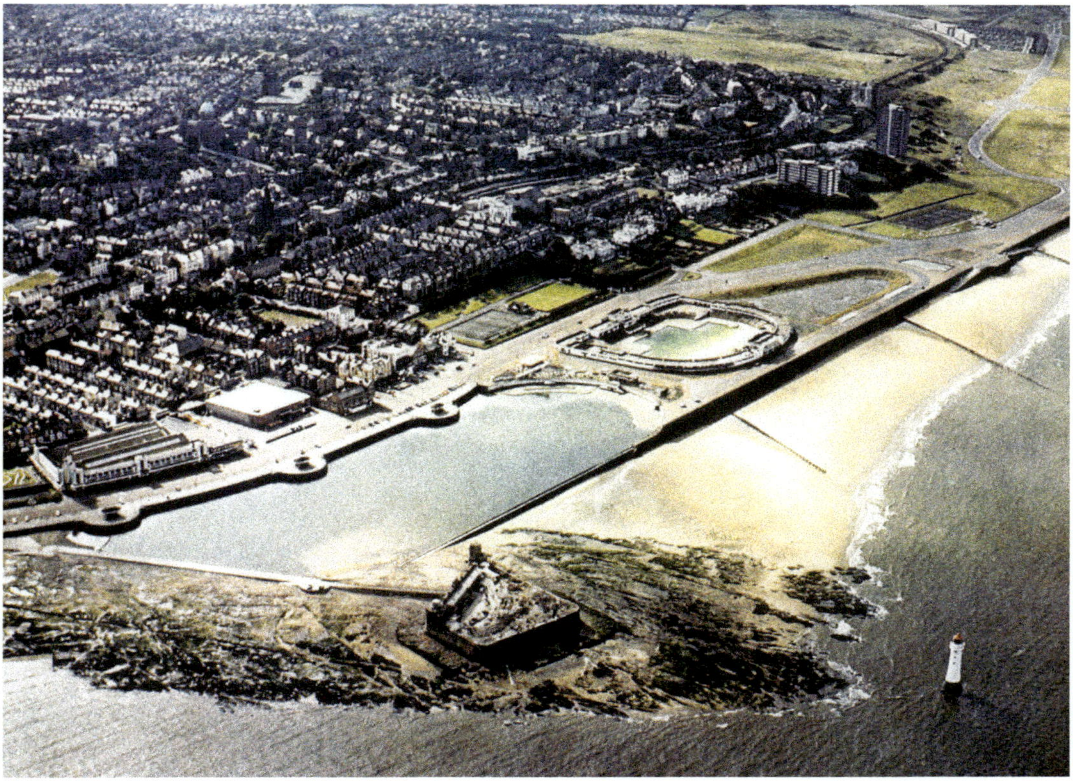

Fort Perch Rock, the Marine Lake and New Brighton Swimming Baths. Rocky reefs at the north-east angle of Wirral, in part exposed at low water, were a danger to vessels entering the estuary, and the position of the rocks at New Brighton was indicated by a wooden 'perch'. It was recorded as early as 1683 in an order of Liverpool Corporation, providing that every foreign vessel coming into the harbour of Liverpool should pay *6d* in respect of the perch. The perch was replaced by the present 'Rock' lighthouse standing on the rocks at New Brighton, which began operating a light on 1 March 1830. The fort was constructed between 1826 and 1829 on the Black Rock. The sandstone was quarried at Runcorn, and floated down by barges. It was designed to hold 100 men, but was normally staffed by a handful. In the 1850s the Rock Channel began to silt up and traffic entered the Mersey via the Crosby Channel. Also, the building of iron-clad armoured ships meant that there was a need for more powerful guns. The defences at the port were replaced in 1893 by a pair of Maxim machine guns, and three Mark VI 6-inch guns were fitted in 1899. They were replaced in 1910 with Mark VII 6-inch guns, which had a range of 20,200 yards. An observation post, searchlights and temporary huts were installed in 1919, and the bridge was replaced by a causeway in 1930. During the Second World War the fort was disguised as a tea garden. The guns were last fired in 1951, during the Festival of Britain and were then move to Woolwich Arsenal. It was sold for £4,000 in 1958, and again in 1969. In 1976 it was acquired by Norman Kingham, who owned it until 1997. It is normally open to the public throughout the year.

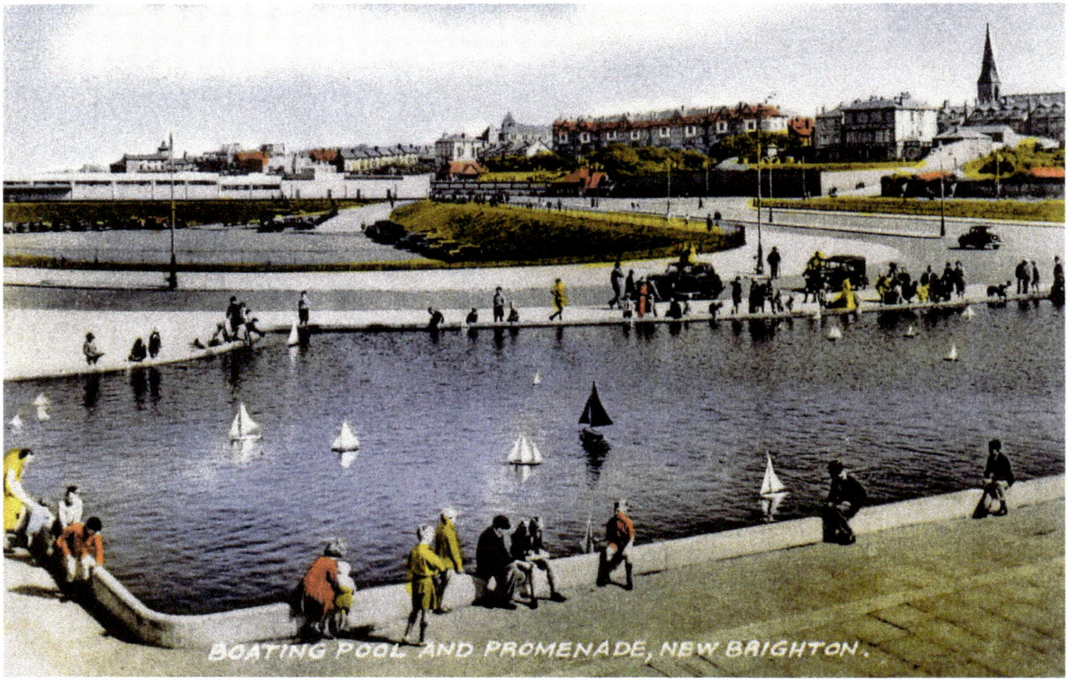

Model boating lake and promenade, New Brighton. On Sundays and Wednesdays it is used by model ship enthusiasts who bring a variety of sailing and powered ship models to take part in competitions on the lake. The Wallasey Model Boat Society was founded in 2011 to provide a place for model boating enthusiasts to meet and learn new skills.

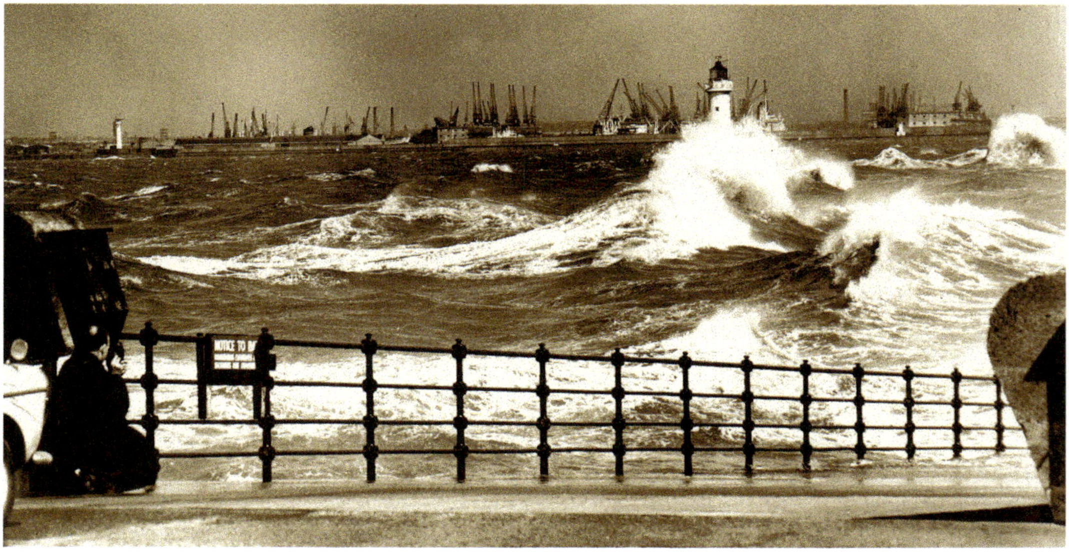

Rough seas at New Brighton.

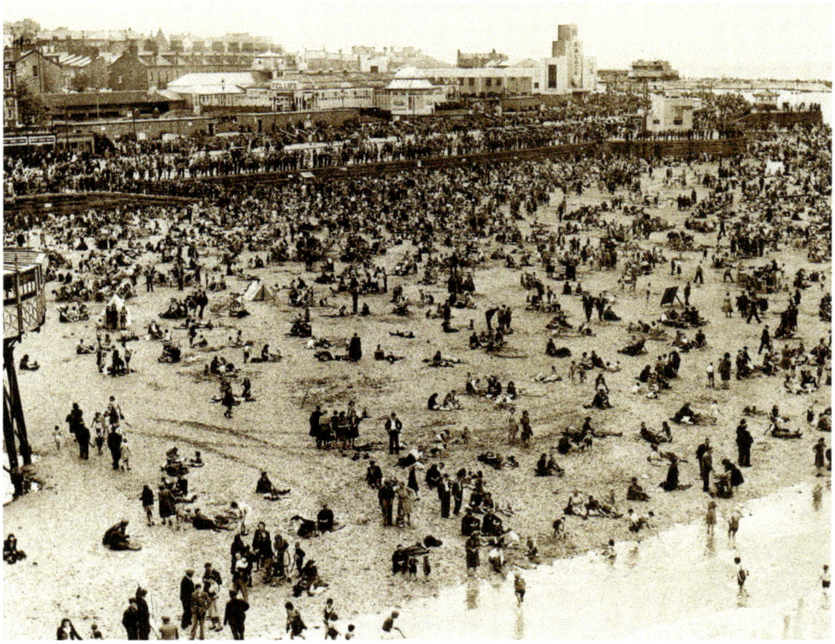

A summer's day at New Brighton in 1948. The photograph was taken from the pier and the Floral Pavilion and New Palace covered amusement arcade can be seen on the promenade. The Marine Lake and its facilities are in the distance.

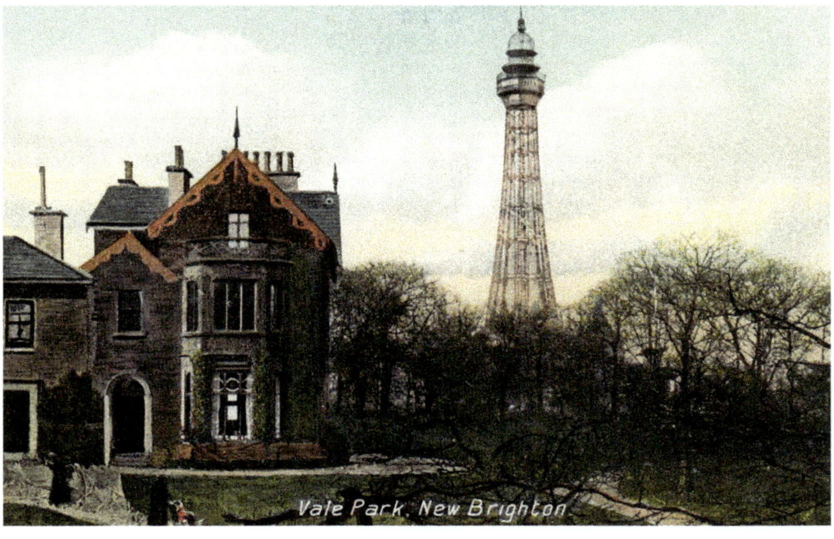

Above: Vale Park and the tower at New Brighton. The Woodlands and Liscard Vale House were purchased by Wallasey Corporation to create Vale Park. Liscard Vale House was retained and now provides a meeting venue and a café for visitors to the park. Vale Park also contains a large bandstand where concert performances by bands and groups take place in the open air, usually during the summer months. A talent show called Joy Time took place in the park for several years. This was organised by Uncle Norman and Aunty Dorothy and was very popular with the local children. A floral clock, which was 16 feet in diameter, was constructed in 1948 and maintained by the council greenkeepers.

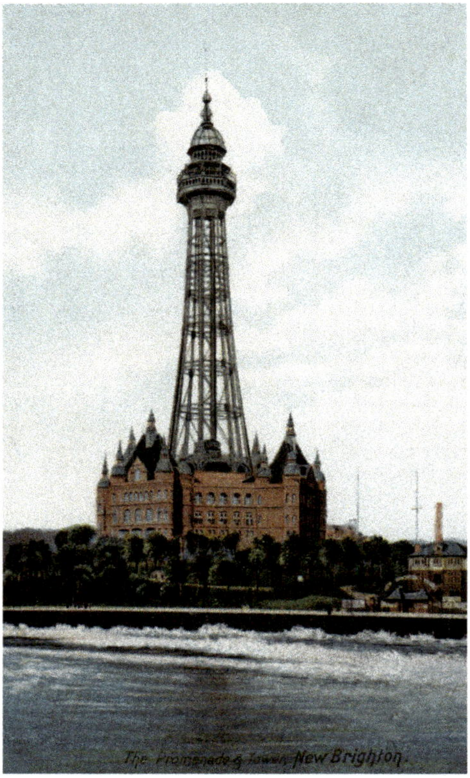

New Brighton Tower. A plaque on the promenade near where the tower stood commemorates that the Beatles performed at the New Brighton Tower twenty-seven times during their early career. Rory Storm and the Hurricanes, Gerry and the Pacemakers, the Remo Four, Kingsize Taylor and the Dominoes, Little Richard and the Rolling Stones also played at the Tower Ballroom.

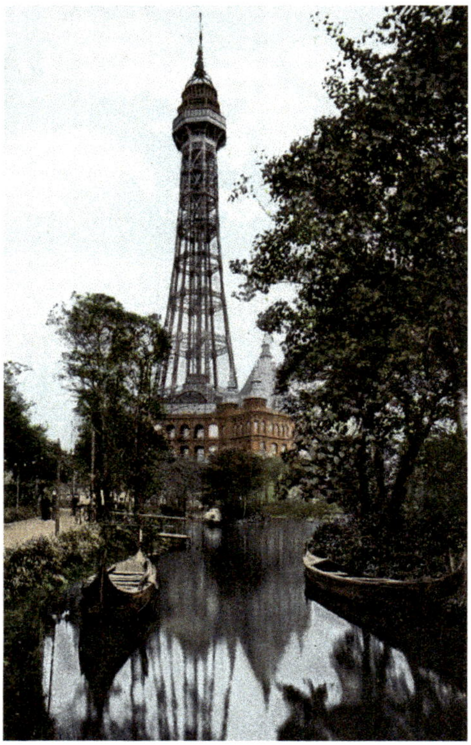

New Brighton Tower and boating lake in 1905.

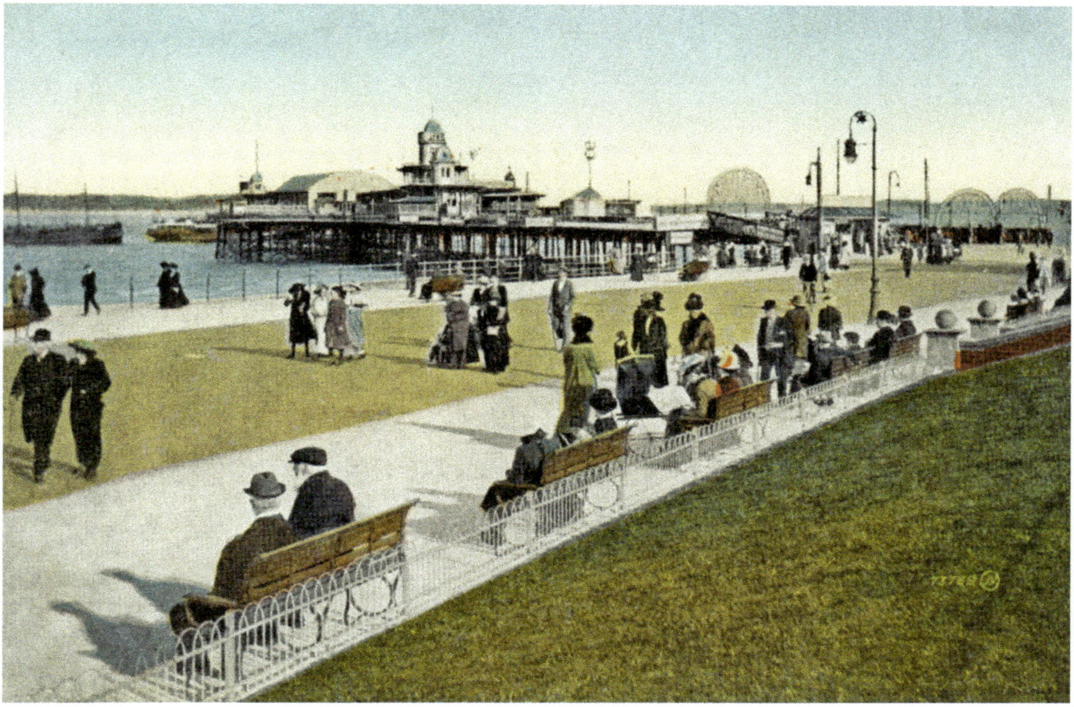

New Brighton Pier from the Marine Promenade.

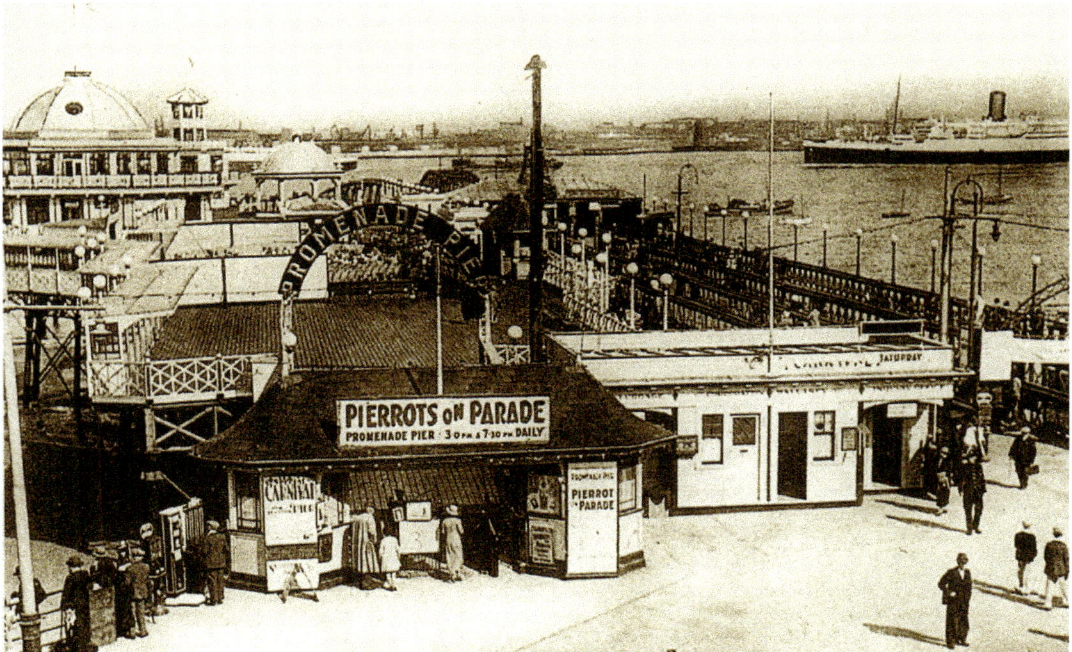

New Brighton Pier from the bottom of Victoria Road. The pier was opened in September 1867, replacing one dating back to 1830. The ferry pier for services to Liverpool is on the right and the Promenade Pier contained amusements, Pierrot shows and a bandstand.

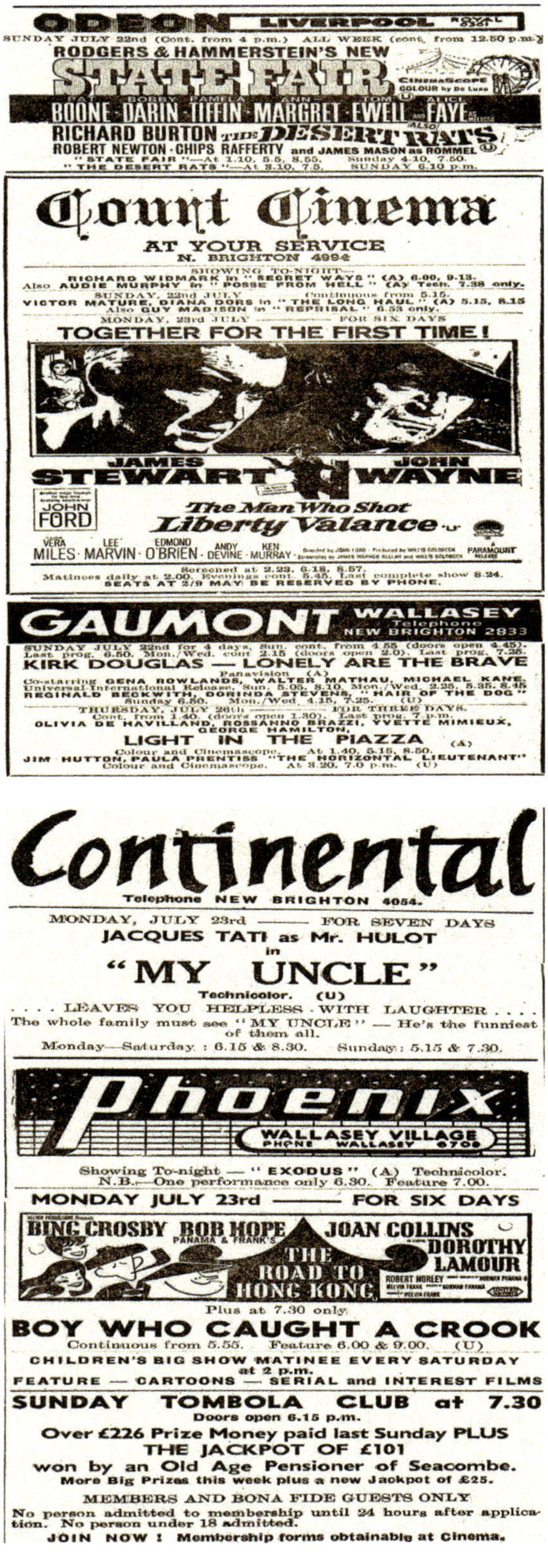

1962 Wallasey cinema advertisements.

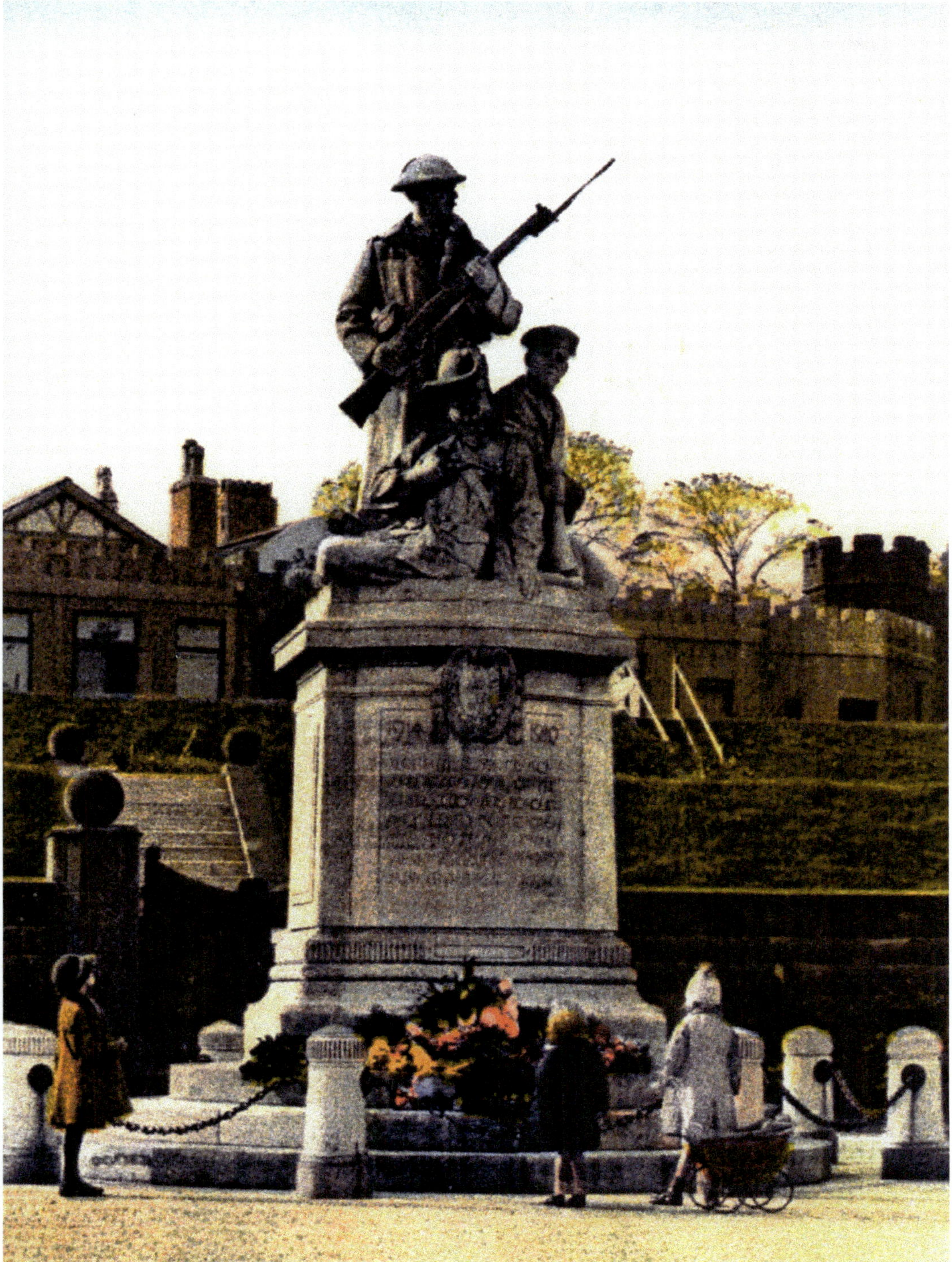

The Cenotaph, New Brighton, is situated near to the entrance to Vale Park at Magazine Promenade. It was unveiled in 1921 by Lord Derby to commemorate the fallen of the First World War and later those who died during the Second World War.

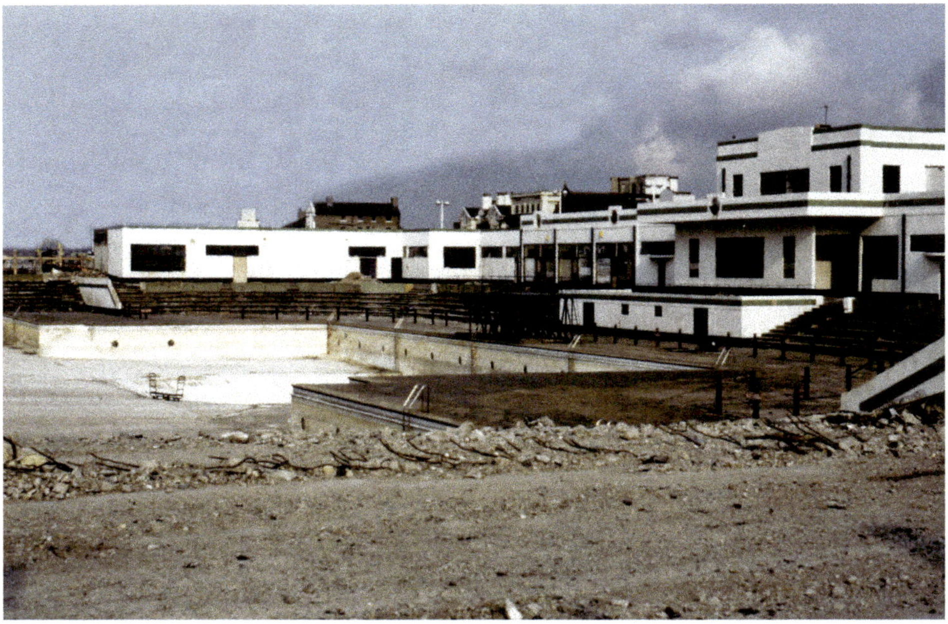

New Brighton Bathing Pool was opened on 13 June 1934 by Lord Leverhulme and was advertised as the largest outdoor swimming pool in Europe. It was designed to accommodate over 2,000 swimmers and 10,000 visitors. The bathing pool was damaged during a severe storm in 1990 and was demolished. A large supermarket, shops, casino, restaurants, hotel and a public house were later built on the site.

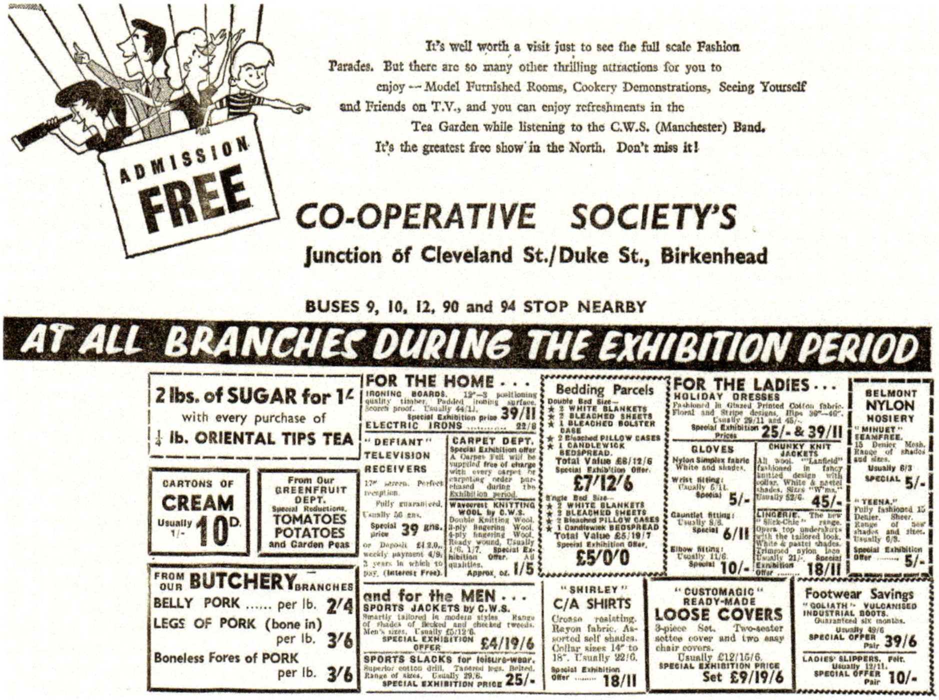

1962 prices at the Cooperative Society's stores in Wirral.

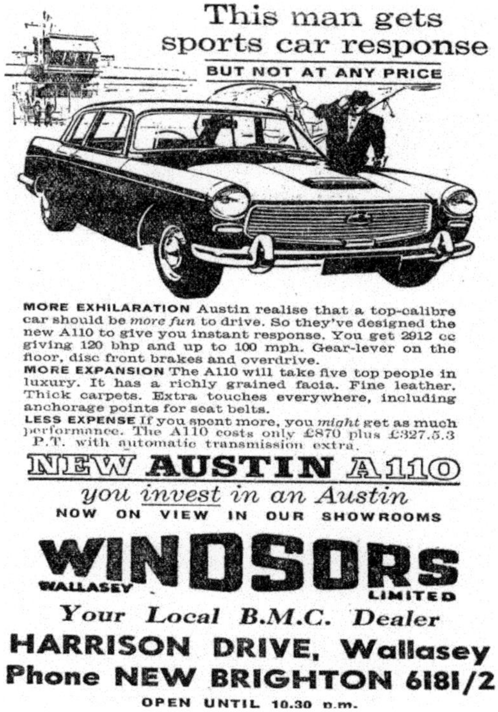

Windsors and F. W. Apperley & Sons 1962 advertisements.

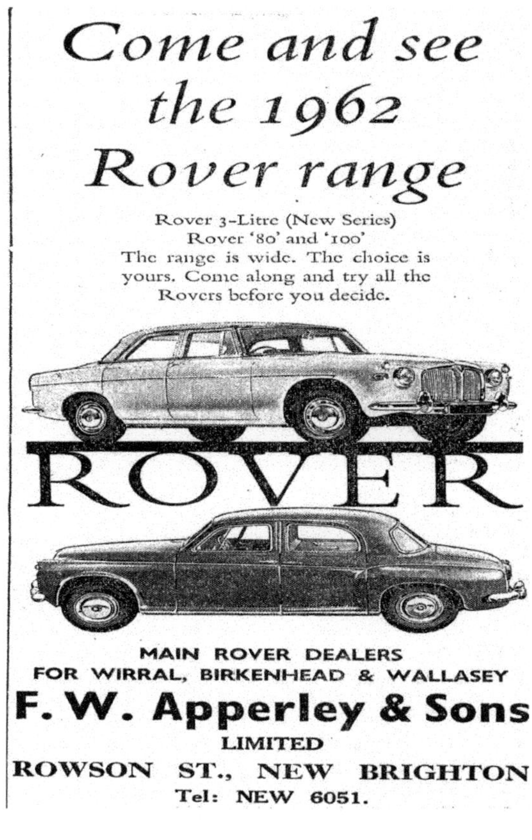

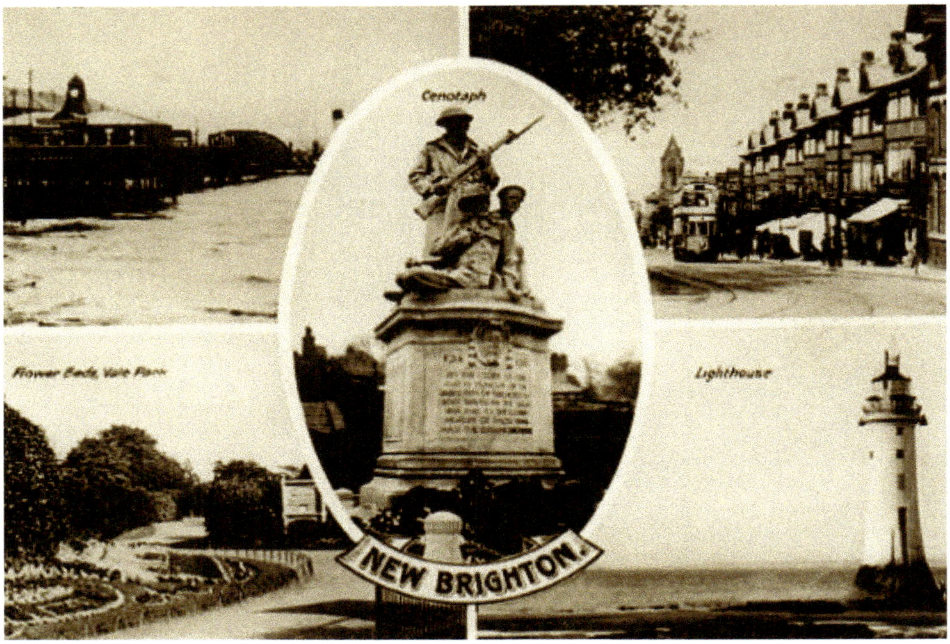

A New Brighton postcard.

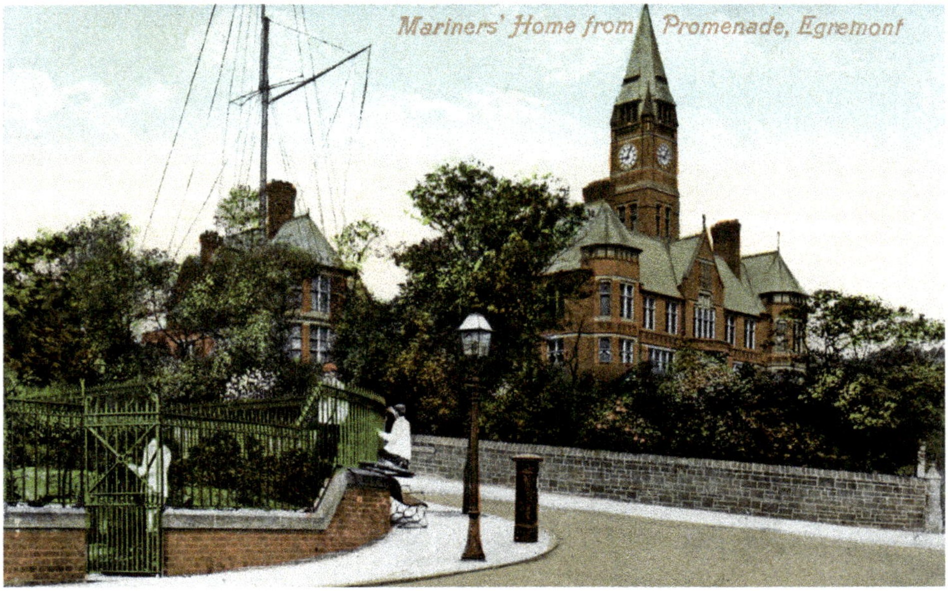

The Liverpool Home for Aged Mariners at Egremont was built by William Cliff, a Liverpool merchant, in memory of his daughter Rosa Webster. The grounds surrounding the building were the gift of the trustees of the late Roger Lyon Jones. The main building was surrounded by a tower 135 feet high, which contained a clock and bell. The arms of the donor, and the Mercantile Marine Service Association were on the gable, with the Liver bird above. The homes were opened by HRH the Duke of Edinburgh on 16 December 1882. They were closed in 1977, and have since been demolished. A new home has been built, and there are a number of bungalows, apartments and houses on the site for retired mariners and their widows.

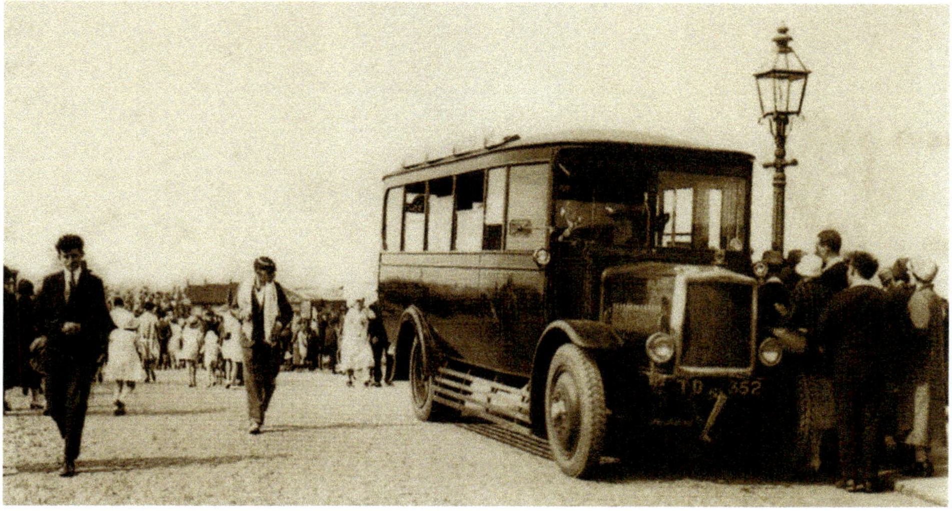

In 1901 Harrison Drive was named after the Harrison family, who had donated the adjoining Harrison Park five years earlier. The church and vicarage were erected by Frederick James Harrison and Sir Heath Harrison in memory of their father and mother James and Jane Harrison, who lived at the Laund, Wallasey, from 1857 to 1879. The church was originally known as the Harrison Memorial Church, but was later named after St Nicholas, the patron saint of voyagers. The foundation stone was laid by Miss A. J. Harrison on 26 April 1910 and it was consecrated by the Lord Bishop of Chester on 29 November 1911. St Nicholas is one of the few churches to have the chancel built west facing on account of the exposed position of the north-westerly gales. Harrison Hall contains three halls, the main hall, the middle hall and the north hall. A recent legacy has enabled the congregation to invest in modern equipment, toilet facilities and ramps to all three halls. New stage lighting and a sound system have also been installed to encourage youth and adult theatre groups to use the hall.

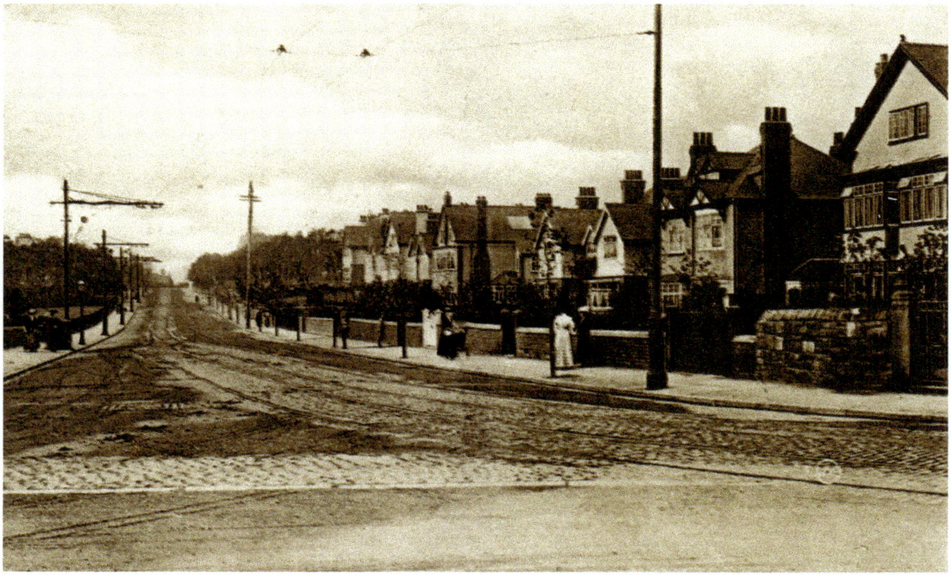

Warren Drive in New Brighton was named after Warren Villa, which got its name from the number of rabbits in the area. This image is from around 1900, and shows its junction with Grove Road.

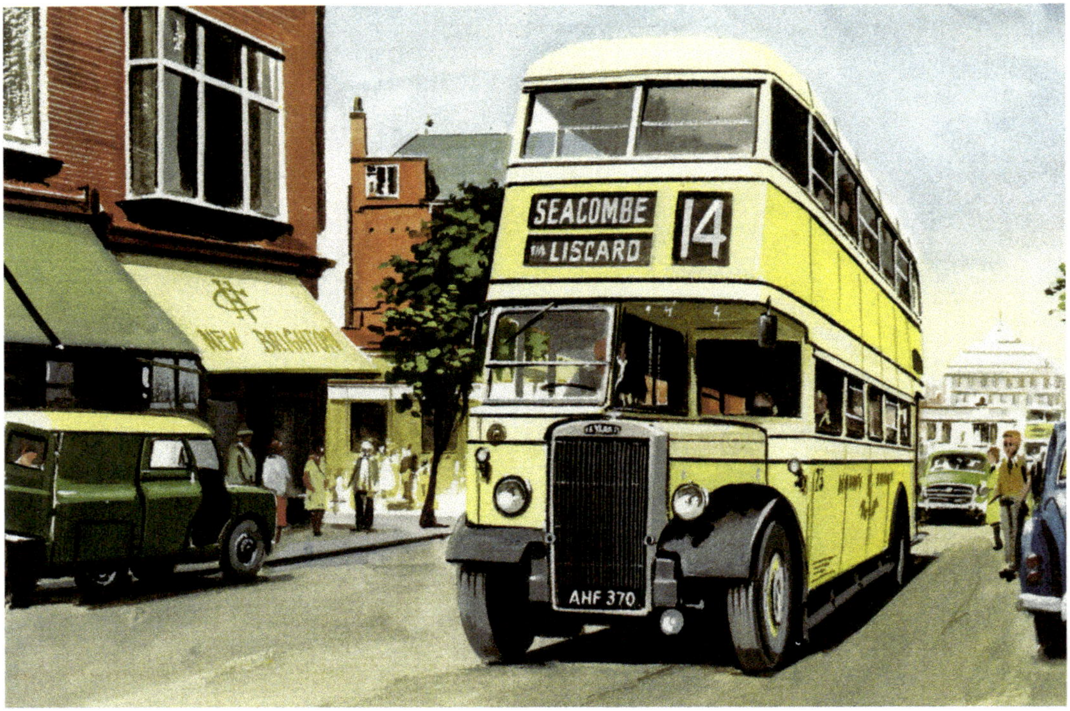

The Wallasey Corporation No. 14 Seacombe via Liscard bus in Victoria Road, New Brighton (www.cooperline.com).

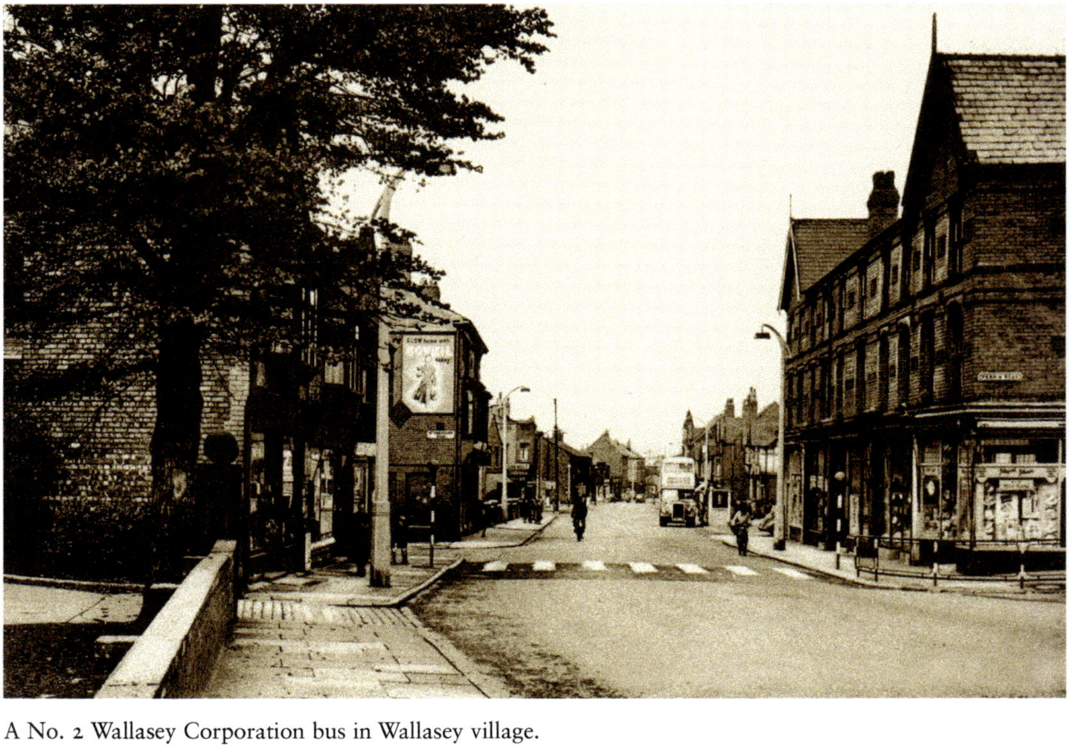

A No. 2 Wallasey Corporation bus in Wallasey village.

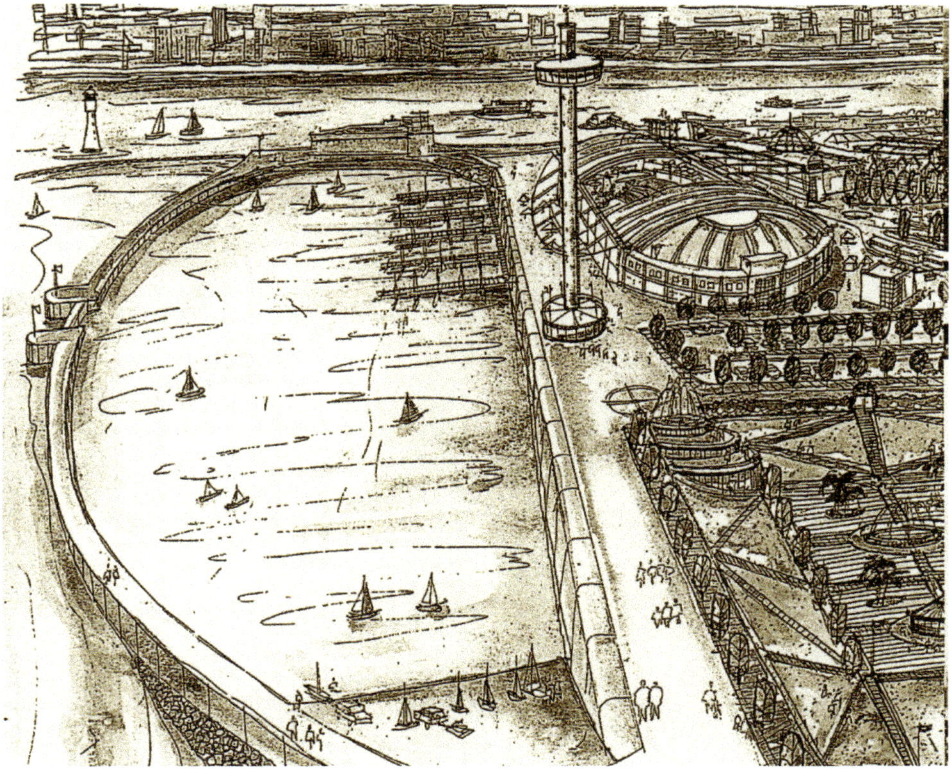

The proposed Dome at New Brighton.

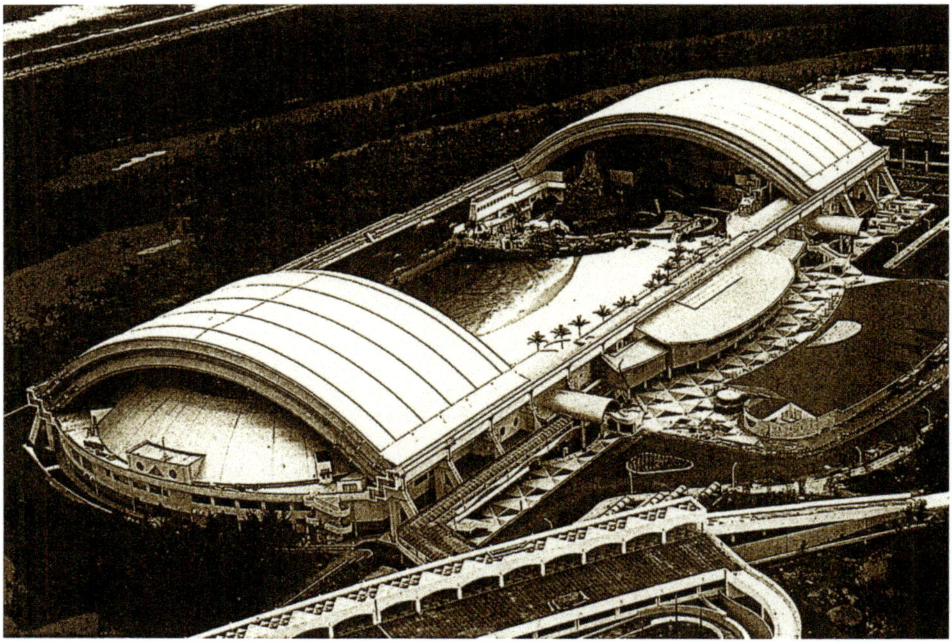

It was envisaged that the new Dome at New Brighton would have a removable roof, which could be opened during good weather in the summer months.

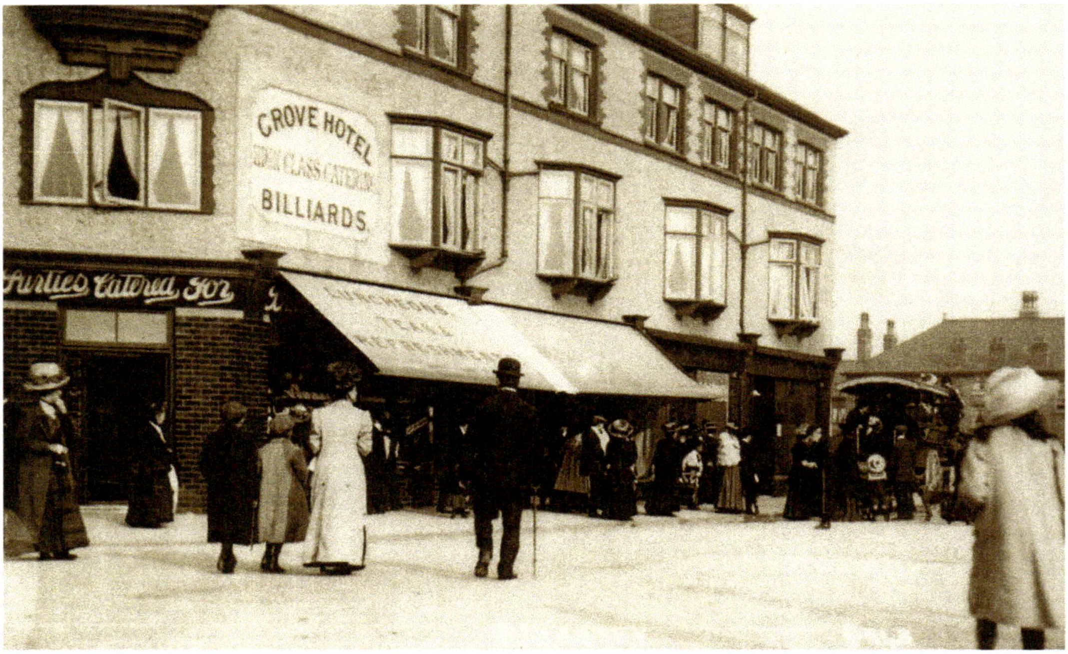

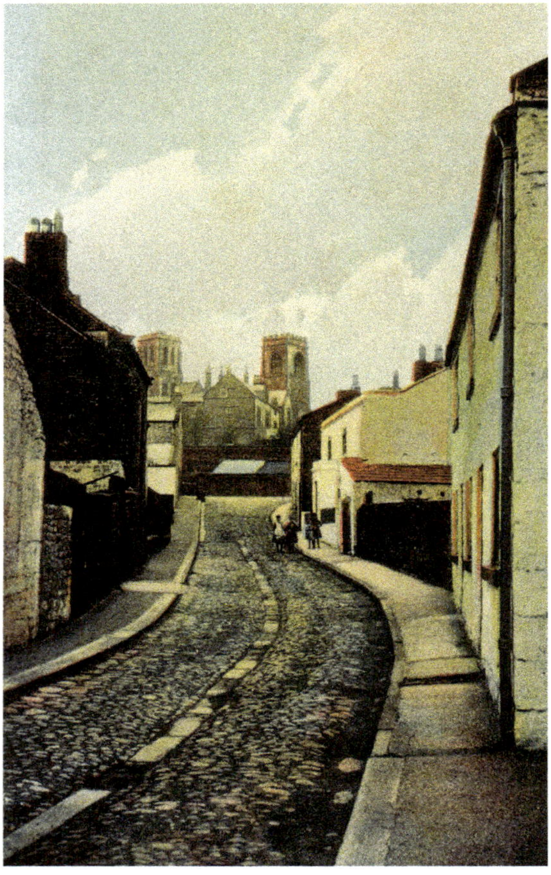

Above: The Grove Hotel in Grove Road. The hotel was built in 1908 and later became Reece's café. The Melody Inn Club was established on the first floor of the building but it was damaged by fire in 1968 and the structure was demolished.

Left: Wallasey village looking up the hill towards St Hilary's Church. From earlier days the area around Wallasey village was known for its light soils, consisting of sandy material with a little clay, which are suitable for intensive cultivation where continuous attention is available. The subsoil in parts of Wirral is seen to consist of disintegrated sandstone, or sand which in some cases appears to have been more or less assorted or distributed by water. It was found that the success of the early production of vegetables for local markets at Wallasey village was because of the favourable conditions for such cultivation at the western and southern slope of a sheltered ridge. It is interesting to note that many of the old village settlements in Wirral stand on the western or south western side of a sheltering ridge such as Burton, Heswall, West Kirby, Prenton, Storeton and Wallasey.

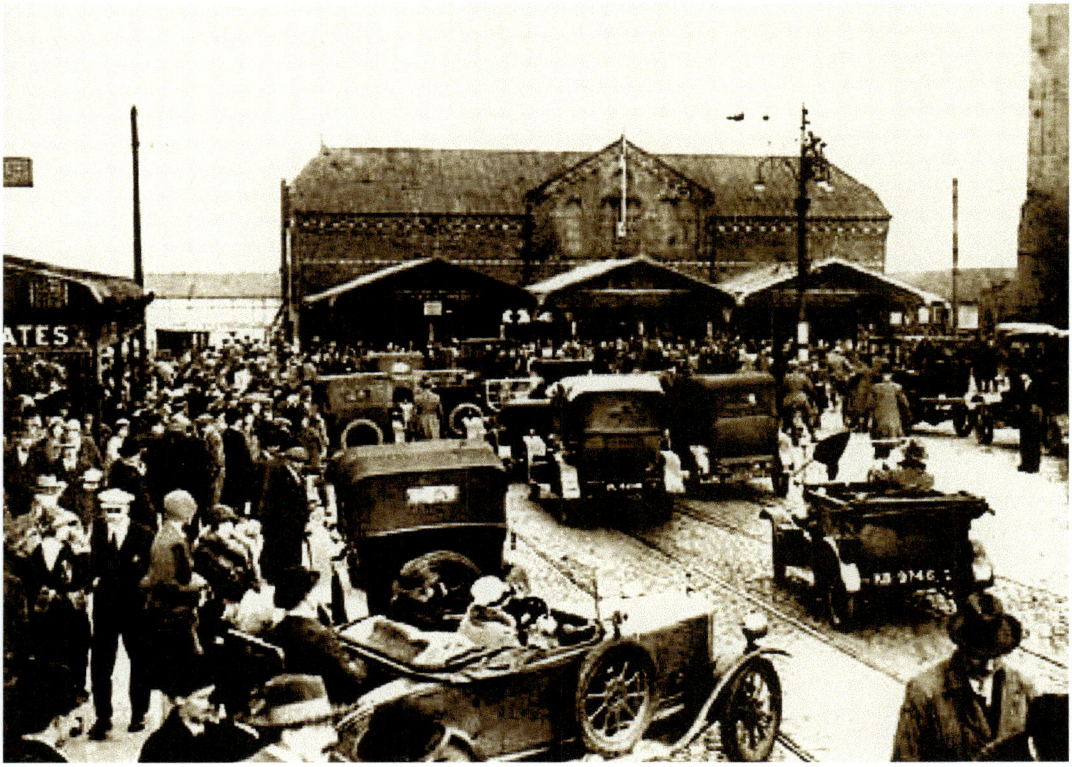

Seacombe Ferry Terminal. Sailing boats were used to take people across the River Mersey to Liverpool up until 1823 when they were replaced by steam-driven vessels. By 1840 a floating landing stage was installed at Seacombe, and the ferry was connected to the Seacombe Hotel. In 1865 the ferry fleet consisted of the paddle boats *Tiger*, *Elizabeth*, *Wallasey*, *Thomas Wilson*, *Fairy*, *James Atherton* and *Queen of Beauty*. By 1876 the ferry annual passenger traffic had reached nearly 2 million and it was decided that a new larger terminal was required at Seacombe. *Daisy* and *Sunflower* were delivered in 1879, *Primrose* in 1880, *Wallasey* in 1881, *Violet* in 1883, *Crocus* and *Snowdrop* in 1884 and in 1885 *Woodchurch* was purchased from Birkenhead Corporation and renamed *Shamrock*. *Thistle*, *John Herron*, *Pansy*, *Rose*, *Lily*, *Seacombe*, *Iris*, *Daffodil*, *Bluebell* and *Snowdrop* all followed into service. The new pier at Seacombe had been opened in 1880 and a floating roadway was added in 1925 so that vehicles could be transported across the river. In 1933 there were sixteen bus routes in Wallasey and buses waited at Seacombe for passengers to embark from the ferry.

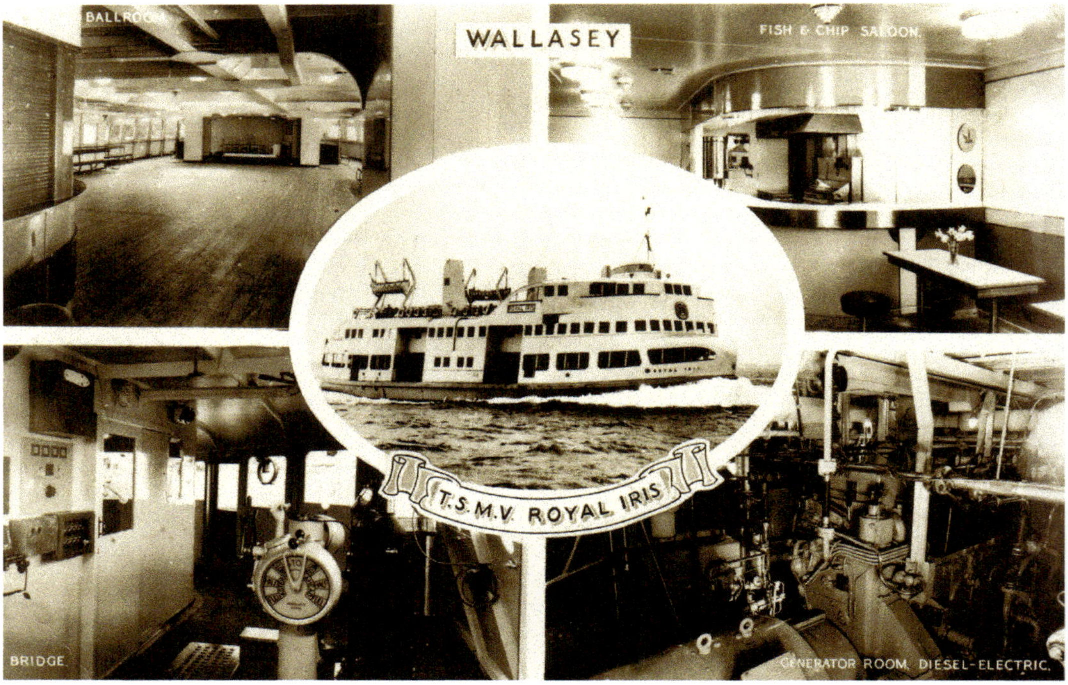

Above and below: Postcards showing Wallasey Corporation ferries.

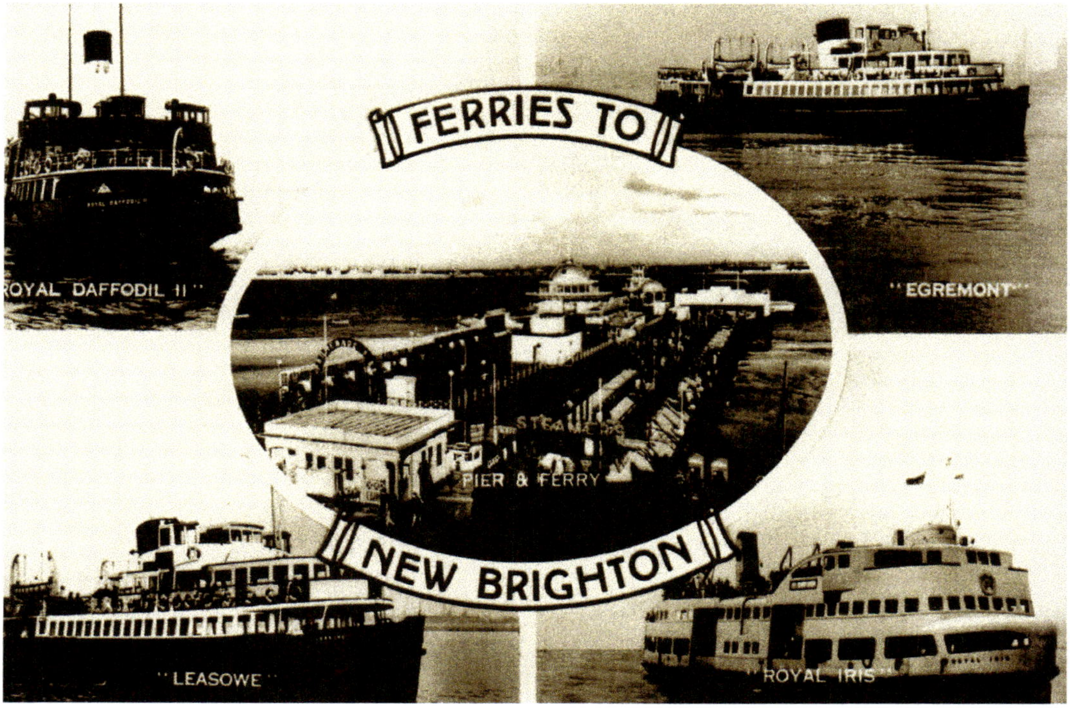

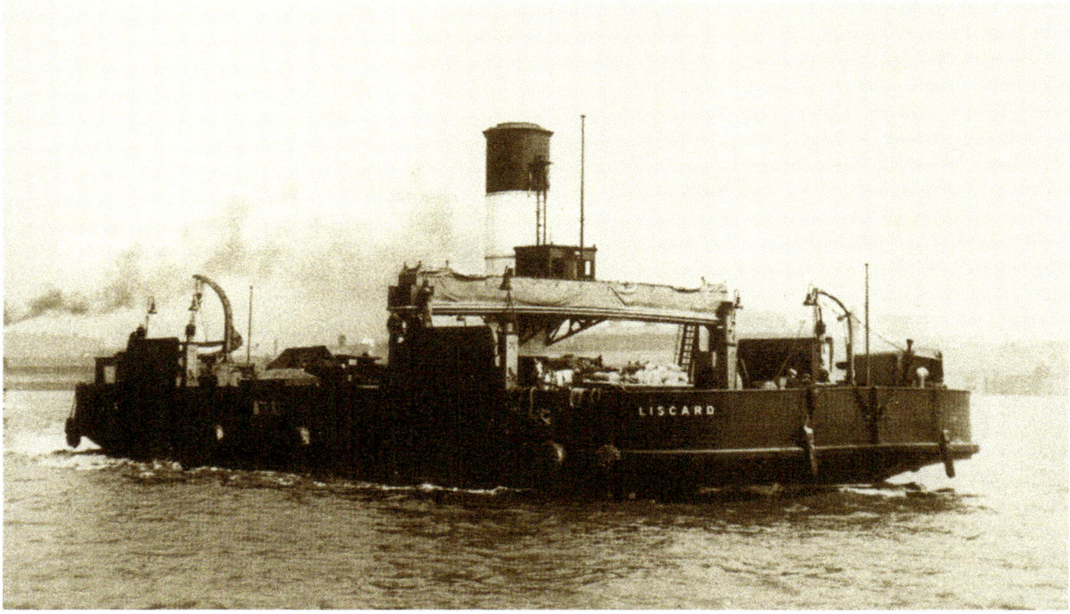

The luggage boat *Liscard* was built in 1921 by J. L. Thornycroft & Co. and was a sister of the *Leasowe*, which was delivered that year by the same builder. *Liscard* was converted into a floating crane in 1941 for service on the Mersey. She was sold to Danish operators in 1946 and converted to a salvage vessel, becoming *Lisca*. *Leasowe* survived in service until 1948, when she was sold and broken up.

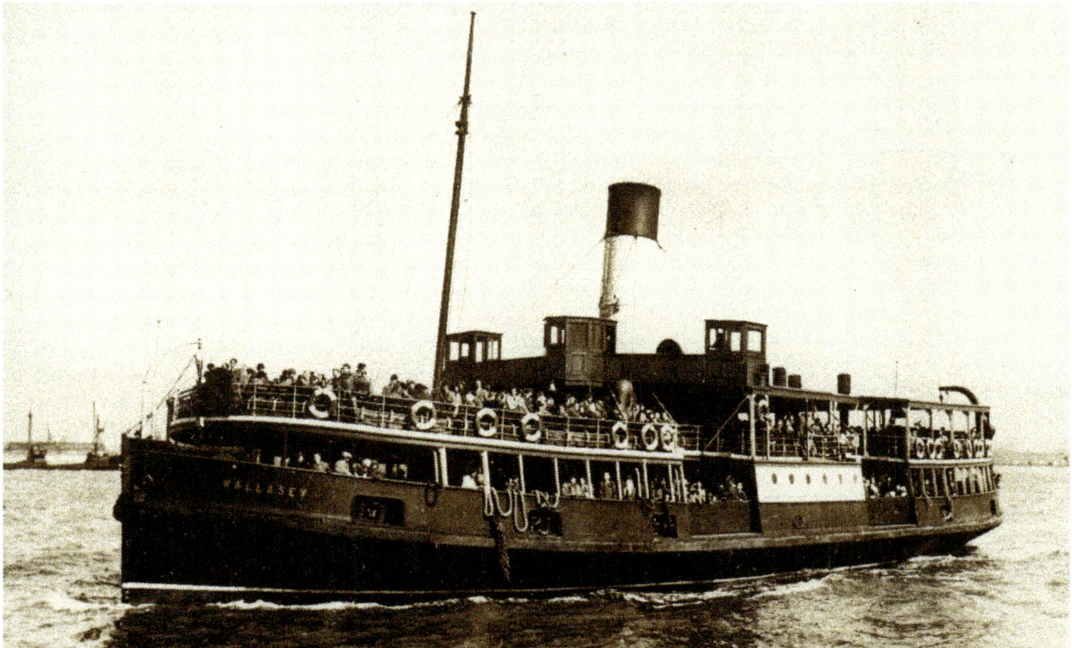

Wallasey Corporation ferry *Wallasey* was introduced on 19 July 1927 and was the third vessel of the same name built for the authority. She cost £42,298 and was certified to carry 2,233 passengers. She was reconditioned by Harland & Wolff in 1958 and sold to Belgium ship-breakers in 1964.

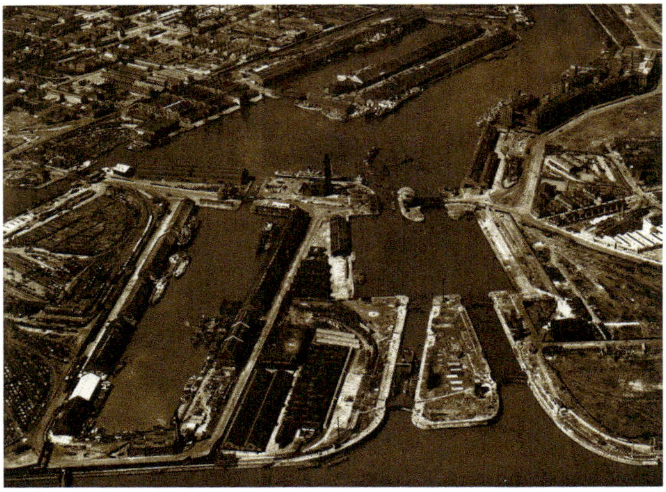

Alfred Dock entrance, the Four Bridges and Seacombe.

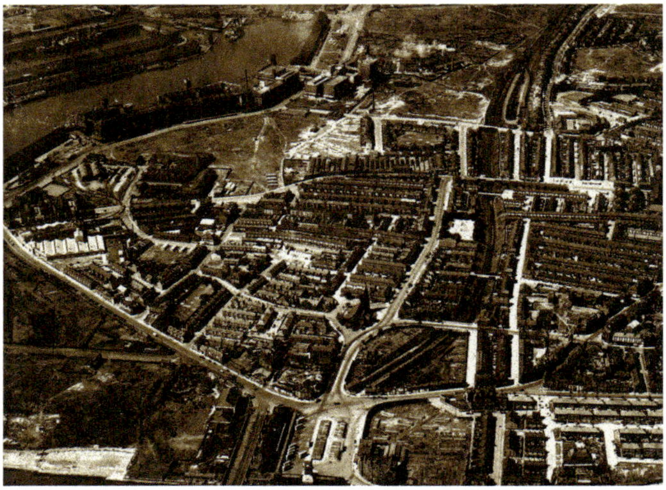

Seacombe and the dock estate.

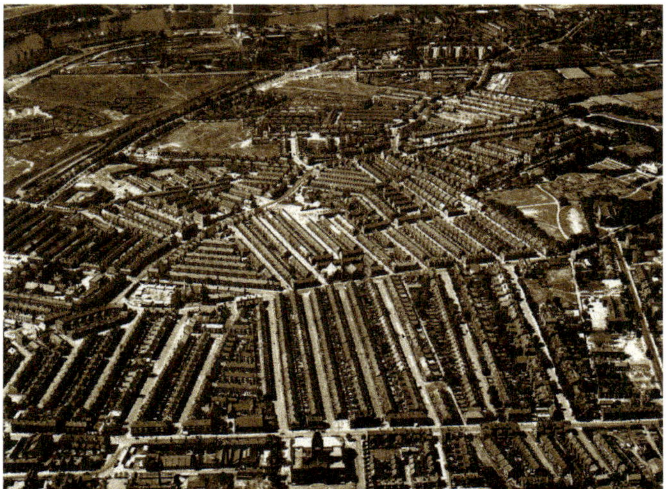

Wallasey Town Hall and Egremont.

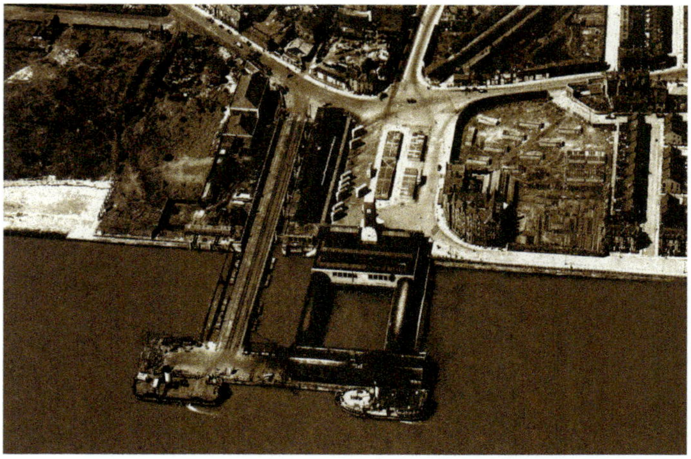

Seacombe Ferry in the late 1940s.

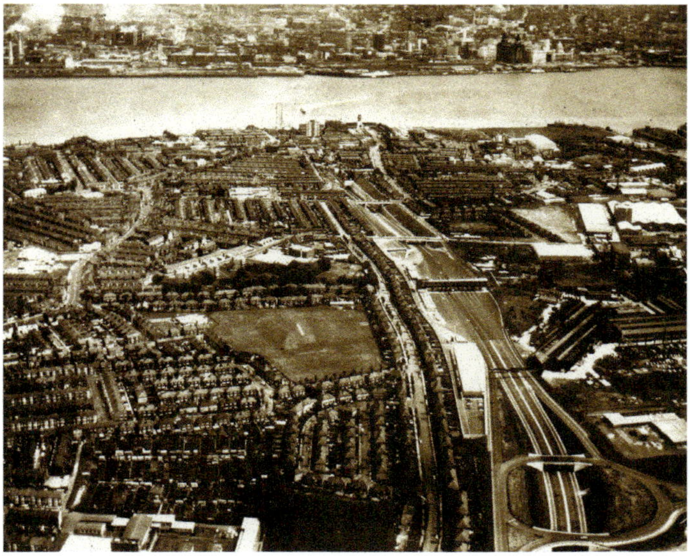

The Wallasey Tunnel and approach roads. Plans were drawn up in 1964 for a second road tunnel under the Mersey and for approach roads from the M53 along the old Seacombe railway line. Construction began in 1966 and the first tube of the tunnel was opened by Her Majesty the Queen on 24 June 1971. The motorway link roads were opened the following February.

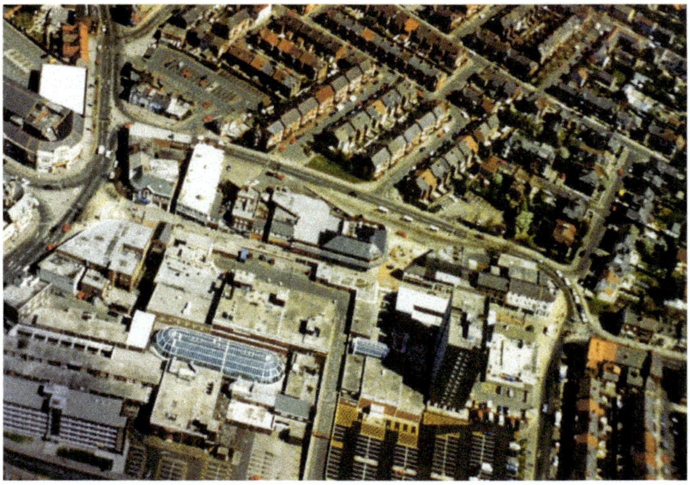

Liscard town centre and the Cherry Tree Shopping Centre.

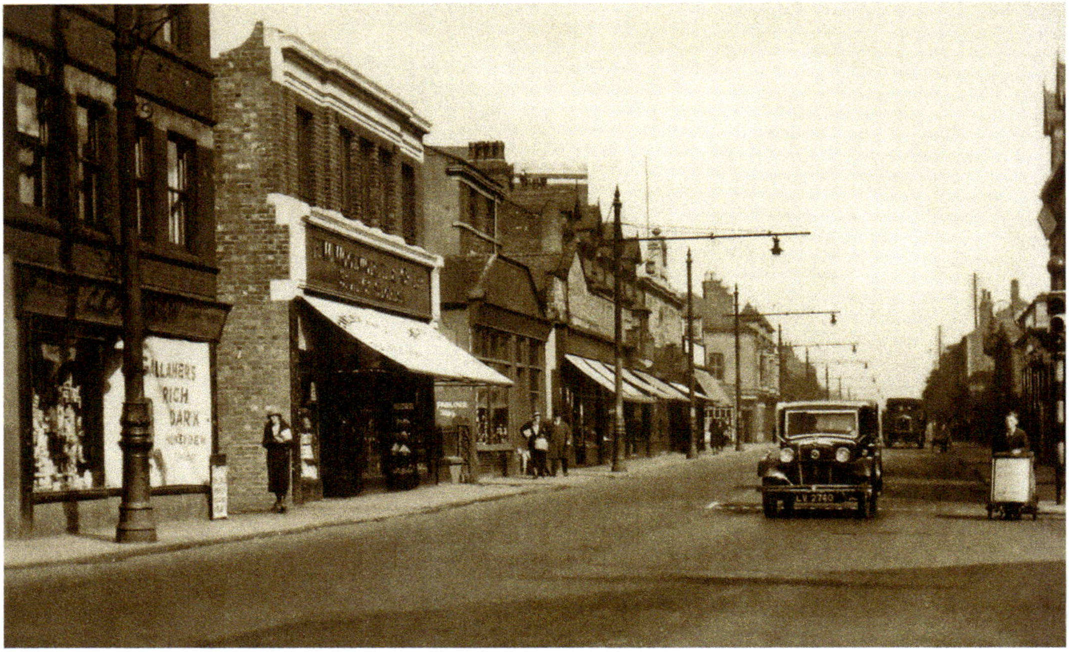

New Ferry shopping centre at the New Chester Road. New Ferry was originally called 'The Pastures', and was common grazing land, of which a small piece only now remains unenclosed. The open common land that at one time occupied large areas of the Wirral have mostly been enclosed, mainly during the nineteenth century.

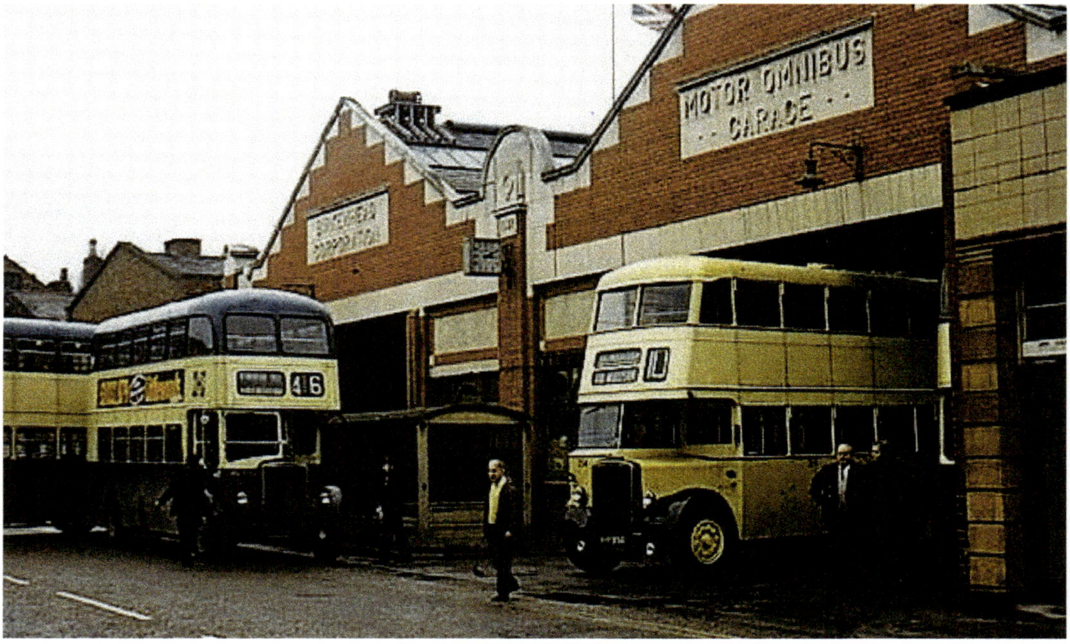

When the New Ferry trams were withdrawn on 27 December 1931 the bus depot at New Ferry was built, replacing an earlier depot built for the horse-drawn trams. The depot was closed on 3 March 1973 and a post office built on the site.

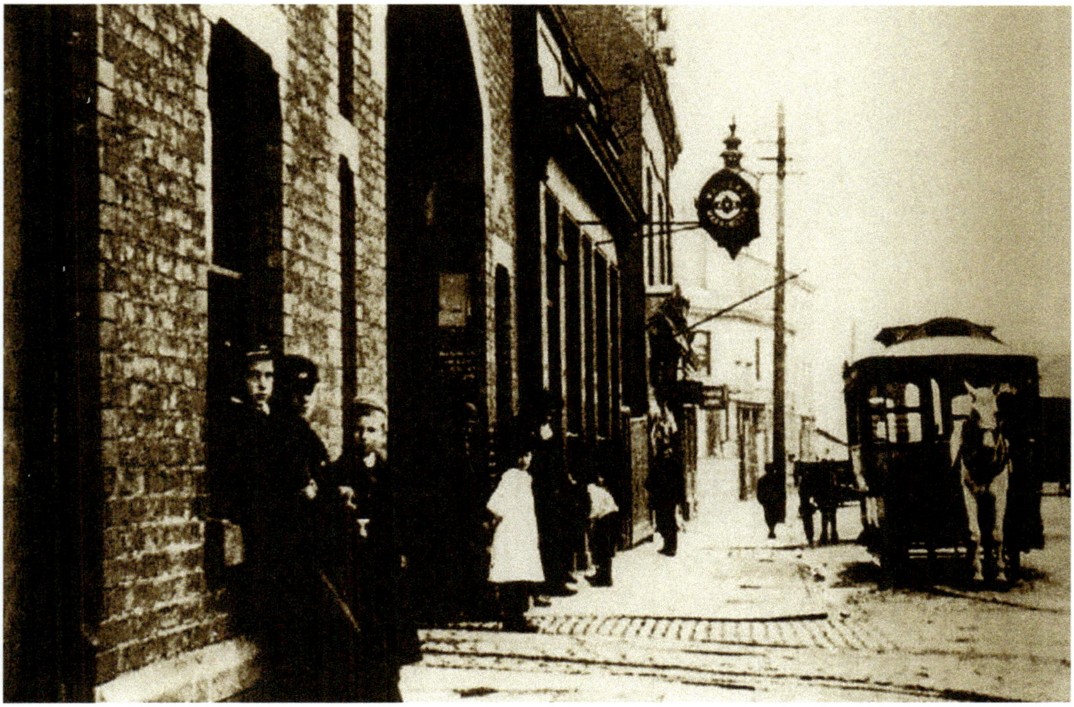

A horse-drawn tram at New Ferry.

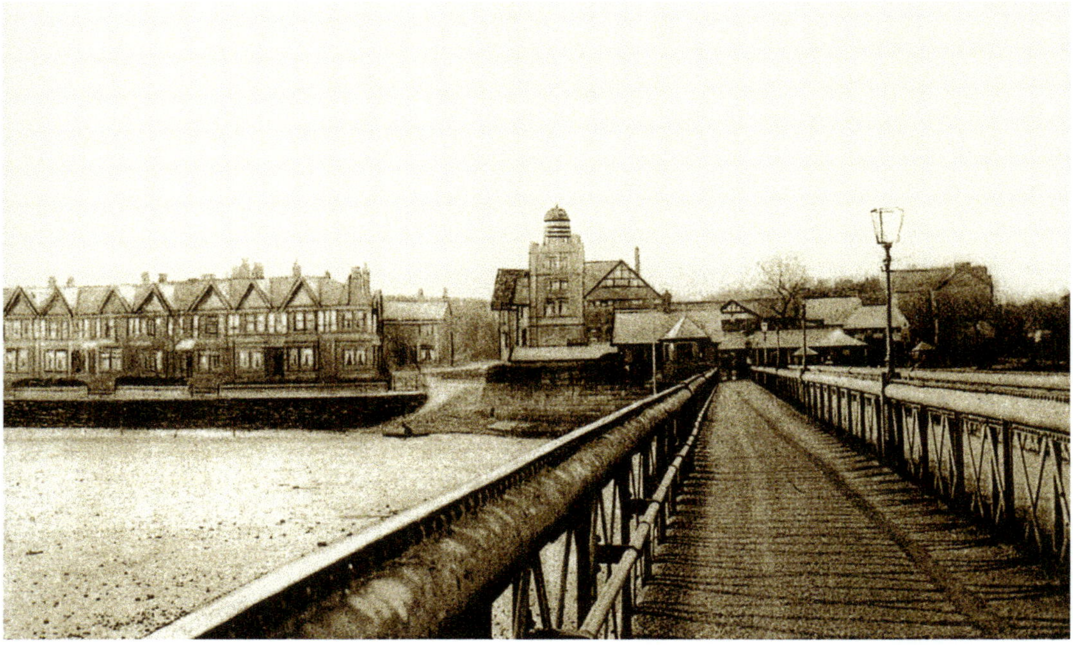

The pier at New Ferry was opened in 1865 and was 856 feet long. The ferry was originally operated by the Mersey River Steam Boat Co. Ltd. The 'new ferry' was advertised to operate between Princes Landing Stage and the New Ferry Pier, calling (except in low water spring tides) at the company's South End Landing Stage (situated at the foot of Park Street).

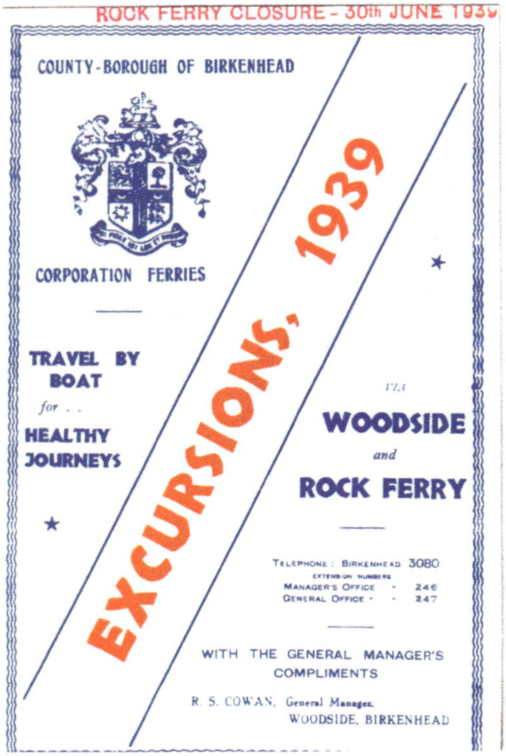

THROUGH RETURN FARES

FERRIES . . .

and MOTOR BUSES . . .

From Liverpool Landing Stage (via Woodside Day Boats

(Book at the Turnstiles, Woodside Ferry)

	ADULTS	CHILDREN UNDER 14
Arrowe Park Gates	10d.	5d.
*Arrowe House Farm	10d.	5d.
Barnston (via "Crosville" only)	1/2	6d.
Bidston Village	8d.	4d.
Bromborough Cross	10d.	5d.
Bromborough Pool Lane End	8d.	5d.
*Eastham Village	1/-	6d.
*Heswall	1/4	7d.
Landican Lane	8d.	5d.
Leasowe, Reeds Lane	8d.	4d.
Lower Bebington Village	8d.	5d.
Moreton, via Arrowe	1/-	6d.
Moreton, via Bidston	10d.	5d.
Oaklea Road, near Irby	1/-	6d.
Pensby (via "Crosville" only)	1/2	6d.
Spital Cross Roads	8d.	5d.
*Thingwall Corner	1/-	6d.
Thurstaston (via Irby)	1/2	6d.
Upton Manor (via Arrowe)	10d.	5d.
Upton Cricket Ground	10d.	5d.
Upton Station	8d.	5d.

* Also available via "CROSVILLE" Buses.

Available for return by Passenger Day Boats, on day of issue or following day. Tickets issued on Saturdays are available for return on the following Sunday or Monday.

SEE PAGE 3 NO LUGGAGE ALLOWED

County Borough of Birkenhead official notification of the closure of the ferry service from Rock Ferry on 30 June 1939.

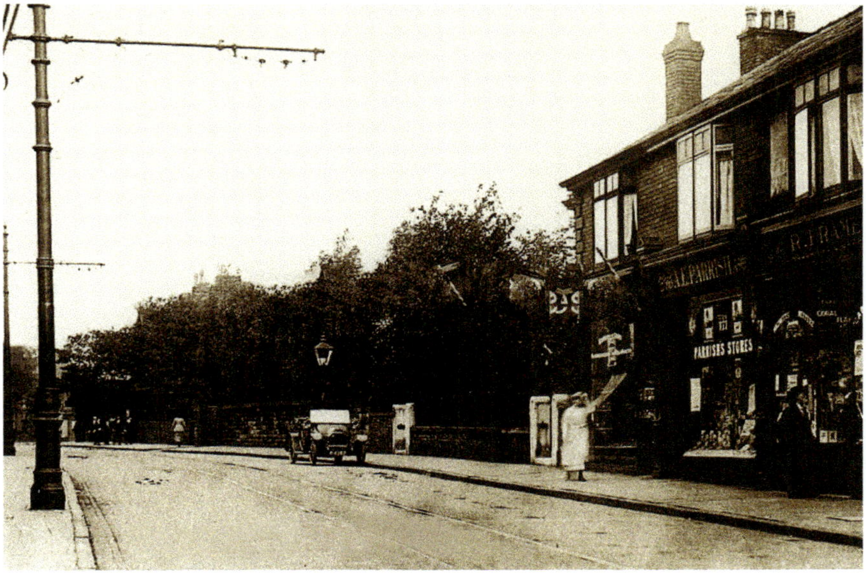

Church Road, Tranmere. The main road form Chester was met at Lower Tranmere by a tidal inlet of Birket Pool over which, in the early part of the nineteenth century, was carried an embankment to connect with the Birkenhead ferries. In 1839–40, a straight and level road, the New Chester Road, was constructed by Thomas Brassey from Tranmere to Bromborough, with a substantial stone bridge over the lower part of Bromborough Pool. The crossing at Birket Pool was originally by a ford at low water and the dangers of this were shown in the findings of a coroner's jury in 1659, when a rider drowned when 'going towards Chester at a certain place called Birket Poole'. Many of the coaches from Chester dropped their passengers at Tranmere, who then made their way to the Birkenhead ferry by way of a wooden trestle bridge across the pool. It is thought that in earlier times the crossing of the tidal pool was avoided by the old road continuing along the line of Bebington Road over the high ground of Tranmere and down Whetstone Lane to connect with Grange Lane.

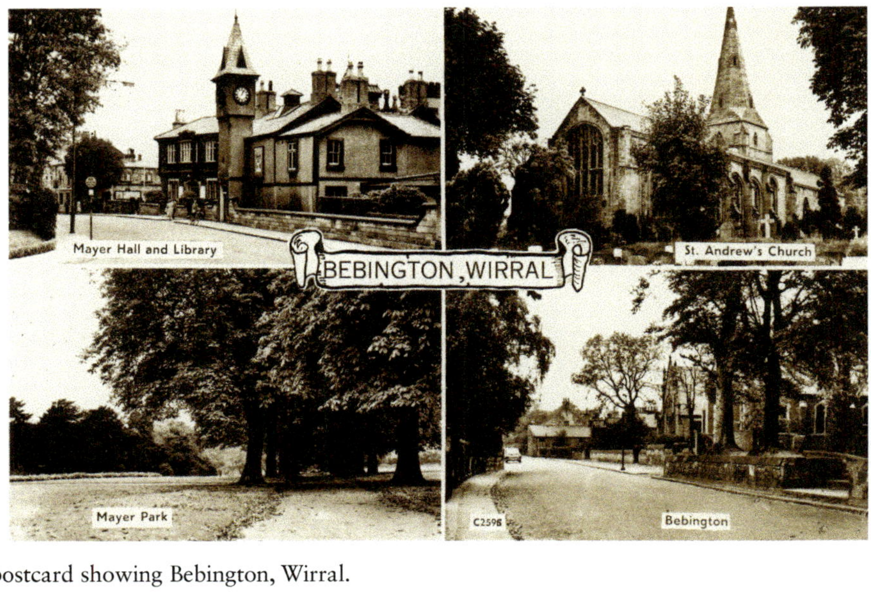

A postcard showing Bebington, Wirral.

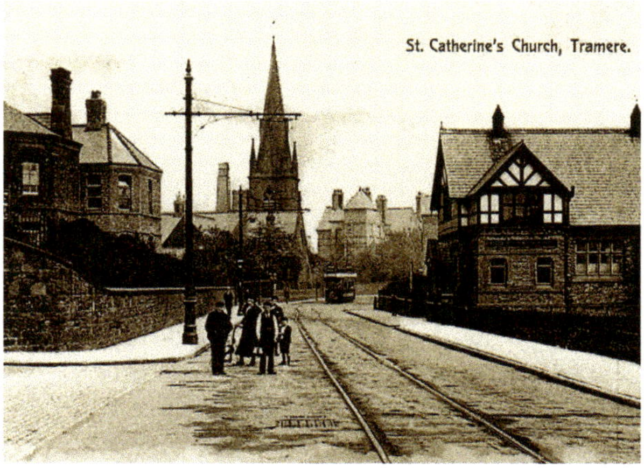

St Catherine's Church in Tranmere was built in 1831, enlarged in 1875–76 and the tower and spire were added in 1879. The land for the church was donated by the Hough family. Tranmere was a small village of 1,168 people and 213 houses, surrounded by farmland and Tranmere woods, with a windmill along the road from the site of the church. The stained-glass window is in memory of Eliza Mortimer, whose husband was vicar from 1868 to 1886. The Charles Whiteley pipe organ was installed and dedicated in memory of Dr E. E. Marshall, who was vicar from 1908 to 1931. It is one of only three of its kind. One of the others is believed to be at Eaton Hall, the home of the Duke of Westminster.

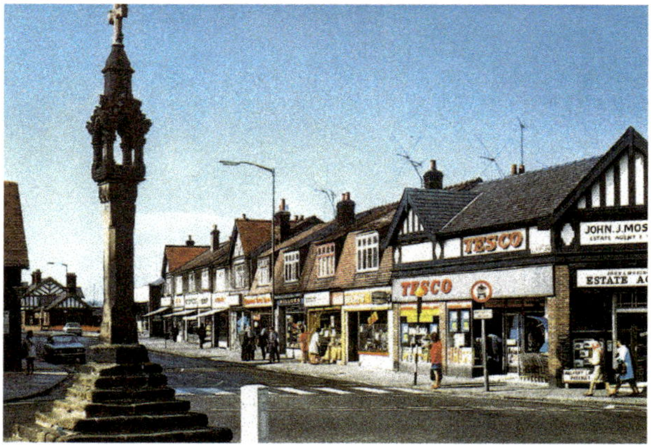

Bromborough Cross dates back to the thirteenth century, and a new shaft and canopied head was added in 1874. In AD 937 the Battle of Brunanburh took place at Bromborough, and this helped maintain England as an Anglo-Saxon kingdom. A charter for a market to be held each Monday was granted by Edward I in 1278 to the monks of St Werburgh's Abbey. The market was established near the cross as it was thought that this would promote more honesty with all involved in dealing with the goods and items sold. The cross was the traditional centre of the village and an assembly point for all farm labourers available for hire. The steps of the cross are from the original thirteenth-century monument, and the cross itself was presented to the town by the Bromborough Society. The Domesday Book recorded a watermill, which was likely to have been the oldest mill on the Wirral. It was located on the River Dibbin at Spital Dam, and was worked until 1940. It was demolished in 1949. A windmill, built in 1787 on the higher ground, was destroyed around 1878. Because of the increase in road traffic in the 1930s Bromborough Hall, built in 1617, was demolished in 1932 to create a bypass and a number of farm buildings and cottages around Bromborourough Cross were demolished and replaced by shops.

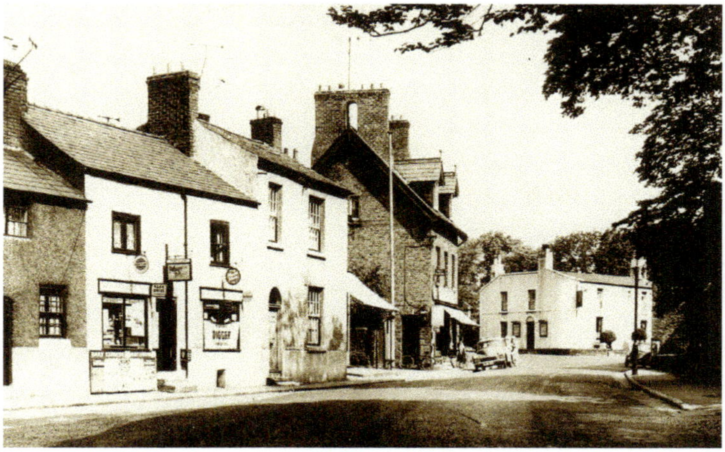

It is claimed that Eastham is one of the oldest villages on the Wirral and has been inhabited since Anglo-Saxon times. The name derives from ham (home), situated east of Willaston, which was the main settlement. St Mary's Church is at the centre of the village and the grounds contain an ancient yew tree. A ferry service operated from a pier to Liverpool and paddle steamers were introduced to replace the earlier sailing vessels. However, the demand for the service declined with the opening of a railway service between Chester and Birkenhead in 1846. The Manchester Ship Canal was opened by Queen Victoria in 1894 and a Jubilee Arch was built in 1897 to commemorate the Queen's diamond jubilee. The Eastham Ferry Hotel was built by Thomas Stanley and the Pleasure Gardens were later added to attract visitors to the town. In the summer months people were entertained by acts like Blondin, who was a tight rope walker, and in 1894 he wheeled a local boy across a high wire in a wheelbarrow. The ferry steamers continued until 1929 and the pleasure gardens fell into disrepair during the 1930s. The iron pier and Jubilee Arch were dismantled in 1970 and the area was designated a country park. Torr Park situated in the centre of the village, was founded by the Stanley family and is home to the village cricket club.

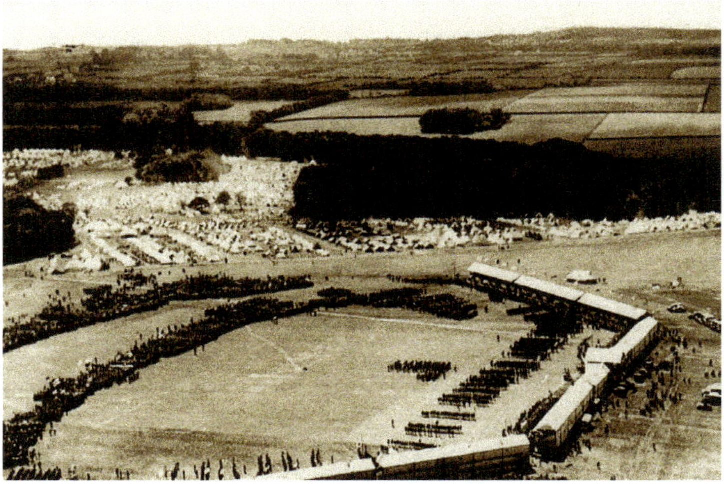

The opening ceremony of the Pageant of Nations in front of the nine-section grandstand at the Arrowe Park International Scout Jamboree, which took place from 31 July to 13 August 1929. The Jamboree was attended by Lord Baden-Powell, the chief scout, and was chosen because it was the twenty-first anniversary of the inaugural meeting of the movement at Birkenhead YMCA on 24 January 1908.

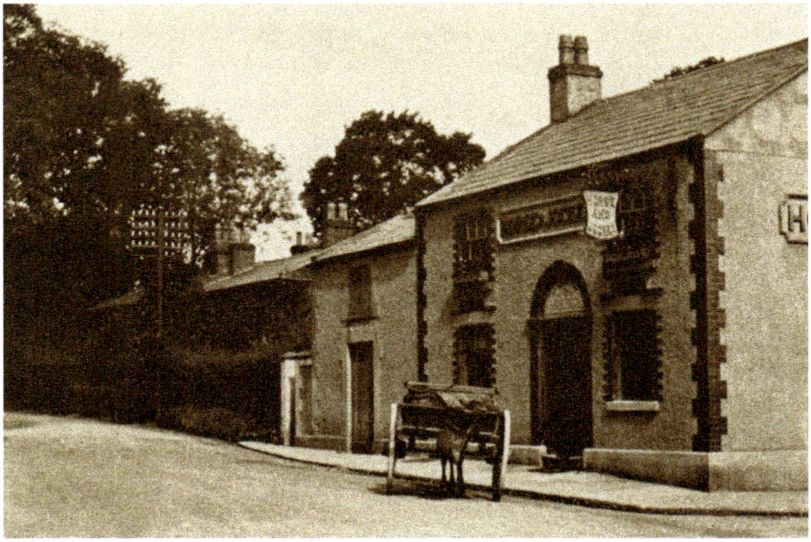

The Horse and Jockey at Woodchurch was opened around 1850. When the Arrowe Park Hotel opened in 1936 the licence was transferred to it from the Horse and Jockey and the public house was then demolished. The Arrowe Brook runs north along a valley to the west of the Thingwall and Arrowe Park ridge to Saughall Massey, near where it is joined by the Greasby Brook, rising near Thurstaston village and running in a northerly direction through the valley between Thurstaton Hill and Irby Hill. The combined streams run north and then north-east across the lowland to join the Birket near Leasowe Lighthouse. Woodchurch village was little more than a hamlet, and in 1801 it had a population of only fifty-two, and by 1911 this had increased to 138 persons. It was not mentioned in the Domesday Book, as it is believed to have been included in the adjoining township of Landican. Wudechurch is named in the charter of 1093 as being given to the Abbey of St Werburgh by Earl Hugh. Records do not show if the name is derived from a wooden church building, or a church in the woods.

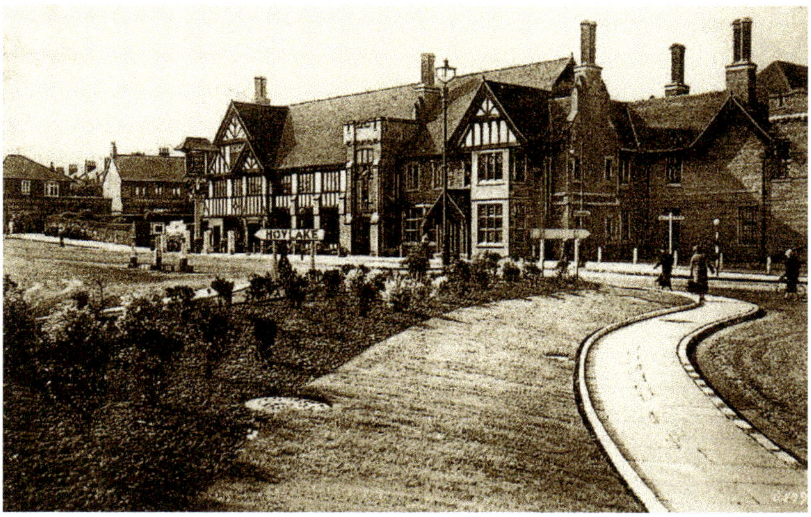

The Coach & Horses at Moreton replaced the previous hotel, which was demolished. The road was widened and shops were also built on the site. A supermarket occupies the land next to the Coach & Horses, which was previously the site of the old bowling club.

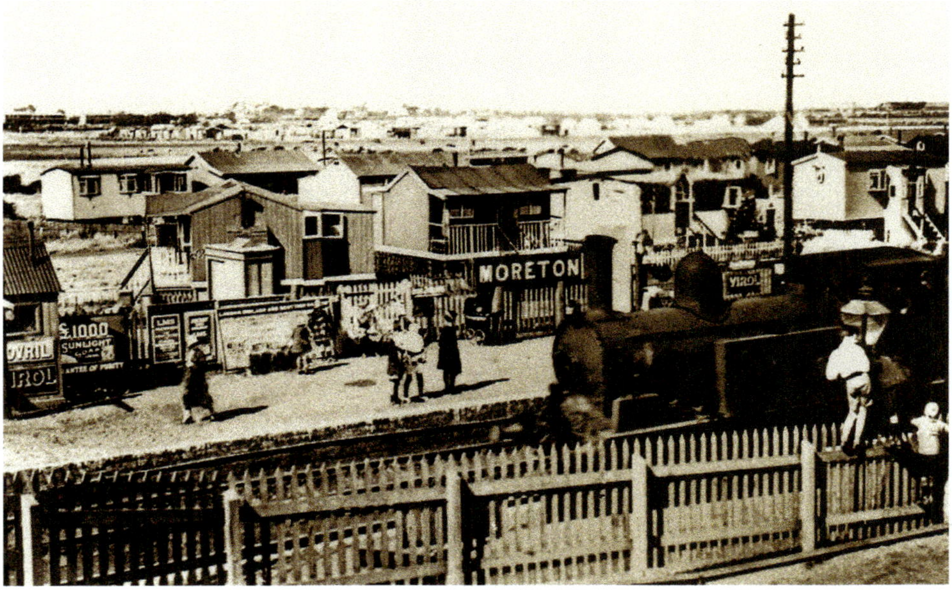

Wooden bungalows were built next to Moreton railway station. They were used by people from various areas of Merseyside and allowed families to enjoy weekends and short holidays by the sea. At the end of the First World War there was a housing shortage and people began to live in these properties on a permanent basis. As the building was on low-lying land many were constructed on stilts or had wheels, which allowed them to be moved. In 1928 Wallasey Corporation took over responsibility for the area and most of the properties were condemned. Cadbury's opened a factory on the site in 1953 and this was served by its own siding until 1971.

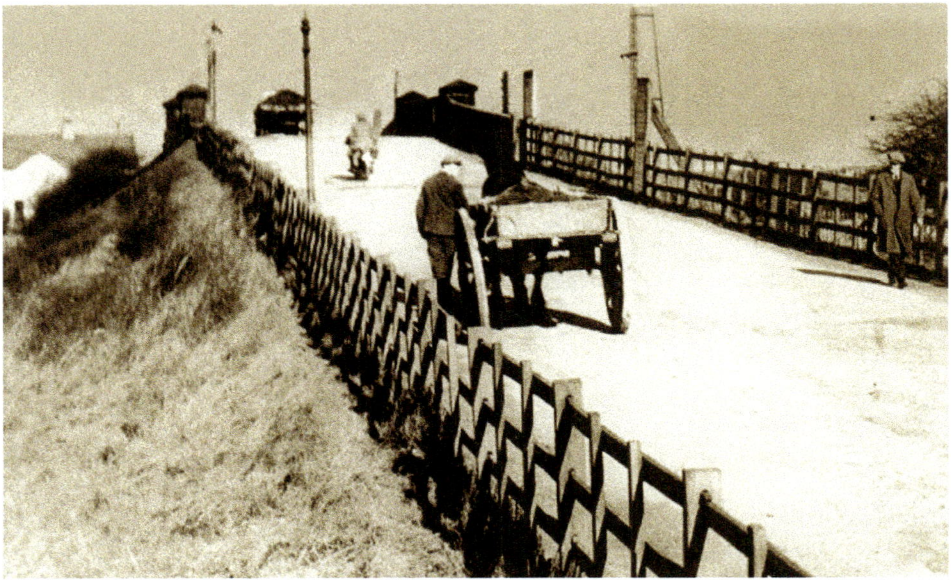

The bridge over the railway line at Moreton station. Pasture Road extended from Leasowe Common to Moreton station, and Station Road continued to Moreton Cross. However, when responsibility for Moreton was taken over by Wallasey Corporation there was also a Station Road in Wallasey, so the name Pasture Road was extended up to Moreton Cross.

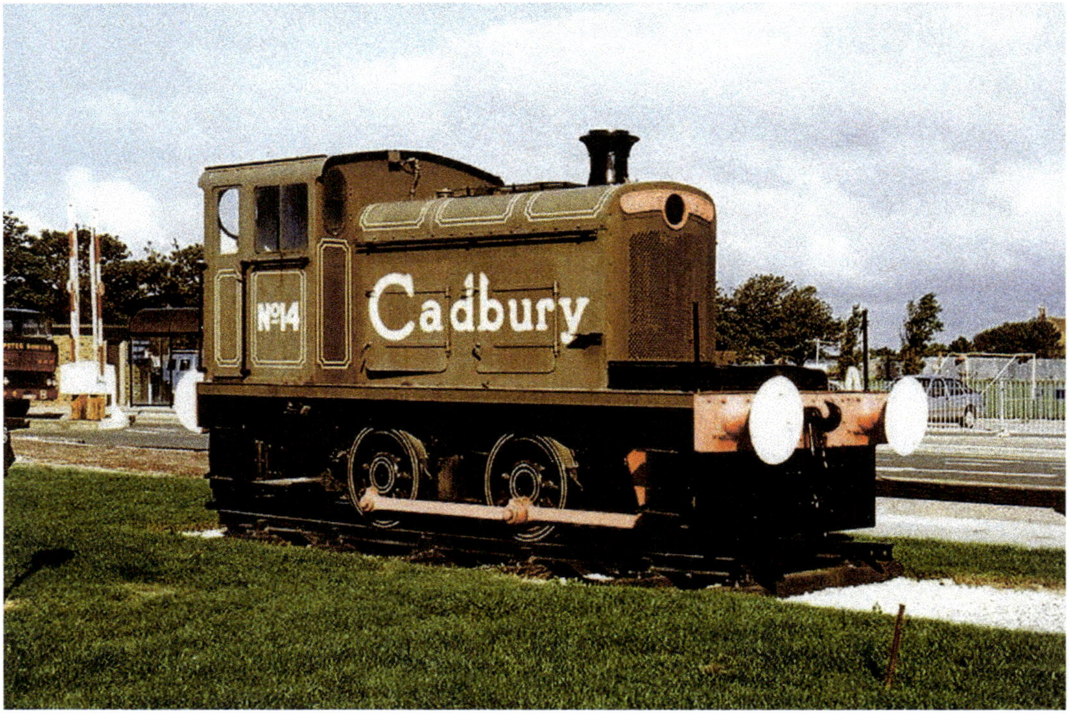

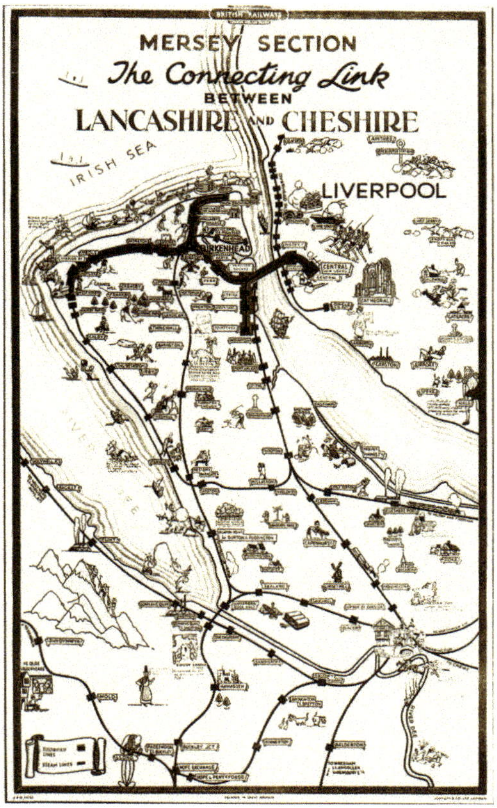

Above: Cadbury shunting engine No. 14 outside the Cadbury's factory at Moreton. No. 14 Hudswell Clarke D1012 of 1956 is now preserved in the car park at the Cadbury World, part of the Bournville factory. The locomotive arrived there from Premier Brands UK Ltd, Moreton, in February 2007.

Left: Mersey Section connecting Lancashire and Cheshire rail networks.

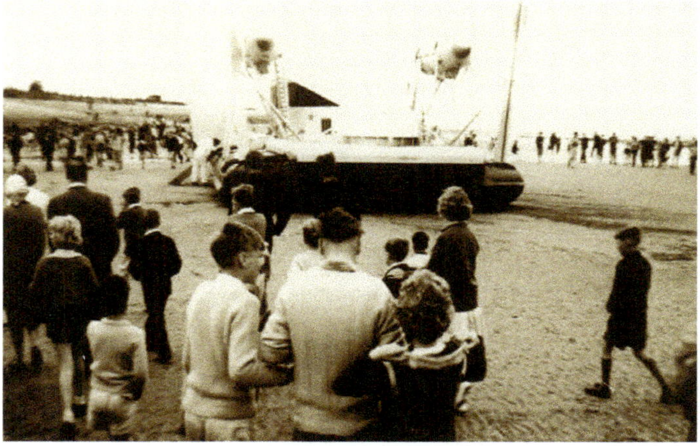

The hovercraft began operating between Moreton and Rhyl, North Wales, on 20 July 1962. It was a Vickers type VA3 craft and was the first mail and passenger hovercraft service in the world. It weighed around 10 tons and had a top speed of 60 knots. The service was operated by British United Airways, with Furness Withy as the local shipping agent. It was planned to operate twelve trips a day but this was only achieved on six days. The hovercraft operated its last trip from Moreton to Rhyl on 14 September 1962 when its engines failed. The craft broke from its moorings but the captain managed to start the engines. The following day the high winds and seas caused the craft to again break away from its moorings. It was eventually blown onto the sea wall and the crew were able to make it secure. It was later lifted out of the water on 17 September, and the service was terminated.

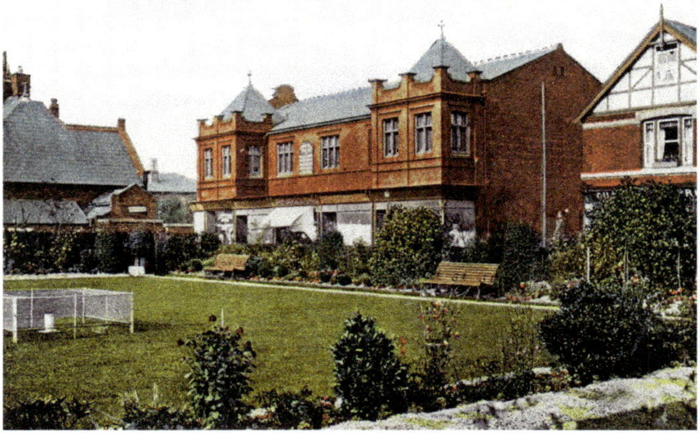

Hoylake Town Hall and Gardens in 1915. In 1690 William III set sail from Hoylake with a 10,000-strong army to Ireland, where they took part in the Battle of the Boyne. The departure point is known as King's Gap. The previous year a large force under Marshal Schomberg departed from Hoylake, and crossed the Irish Sea to Ireland and captured Carrickfergus. Up to the nineteenth century the small fishing village was known as Hoose, and the name Hoylake was derived from Hoyle Lake, which provided a safe anchorage for ships too large to sail up the River Dee to Chester. Parkgate and Hoylake were active fishing centres, with fleets of small trawlers and fishing boats working off the mouth of the River Dee, and in the deeper waters of the Irish Sea. Shrimps, cockles and mussels were important items of trade. Tranmere and Rock Ferry also had a number of fishing smacks working in the channels at the mouth of the estuary. Hoylake came under an urban district council until 1974, when it then became part of Wirral Borough Council.

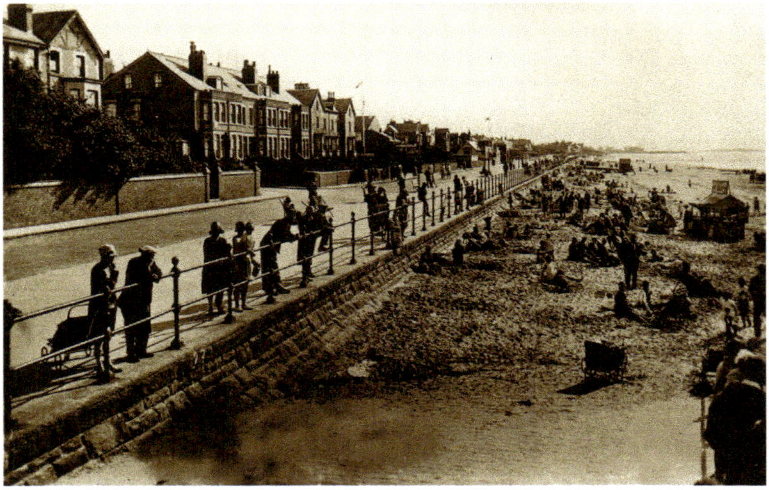

The promenade and sands at Hoylake in 1932.

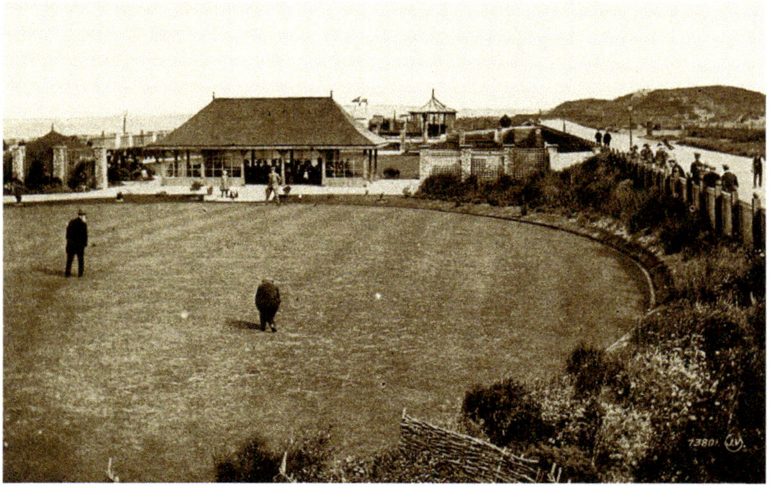

Promenade Gardens at Hoylake.

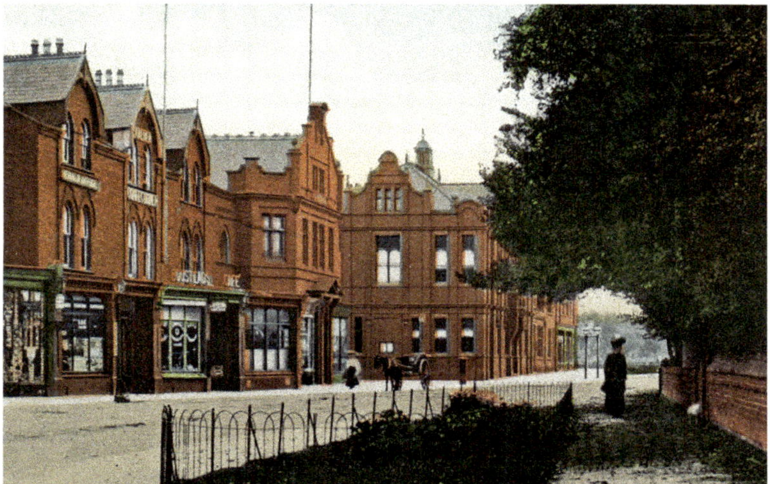

Market Street at Hoylake.

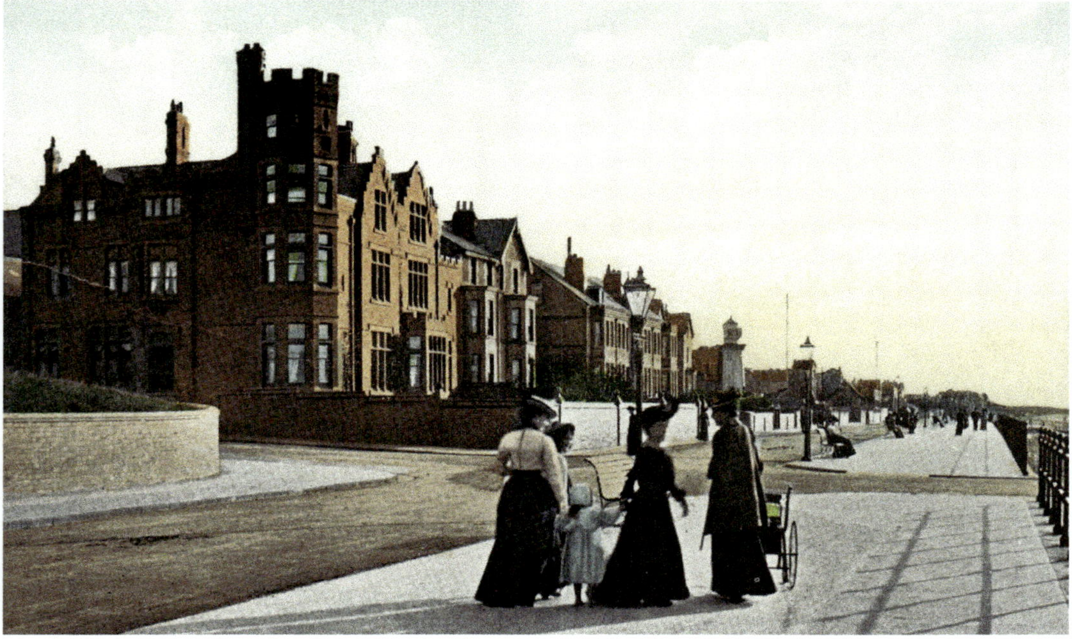

The Promenade, Hoylake.

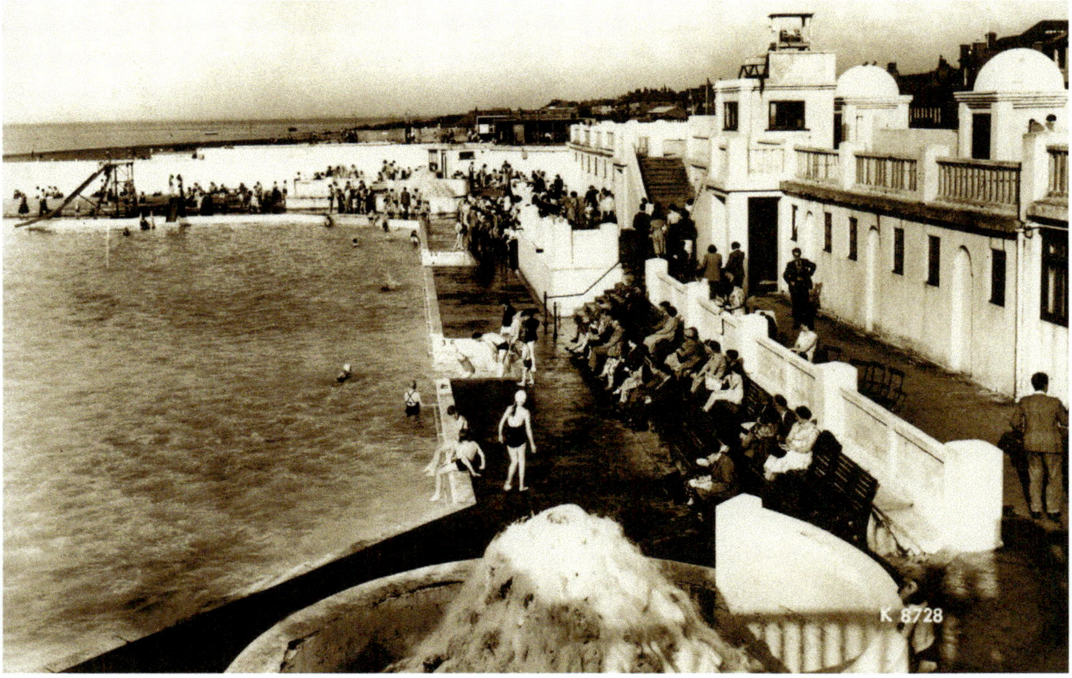

Hoylake Baths and Lido was opened in June 1913, rebuilt in the late 1920s and still very popular into the 1960s. When the new baths were opened at West Kirby in 1976 the Hoylake Outdoor Pool Trust took over the responsibility and management of the pool from Wirral Borough Council. However, the operation did not prove to be a success and the baths closed in 1981 and were demolished three years later.

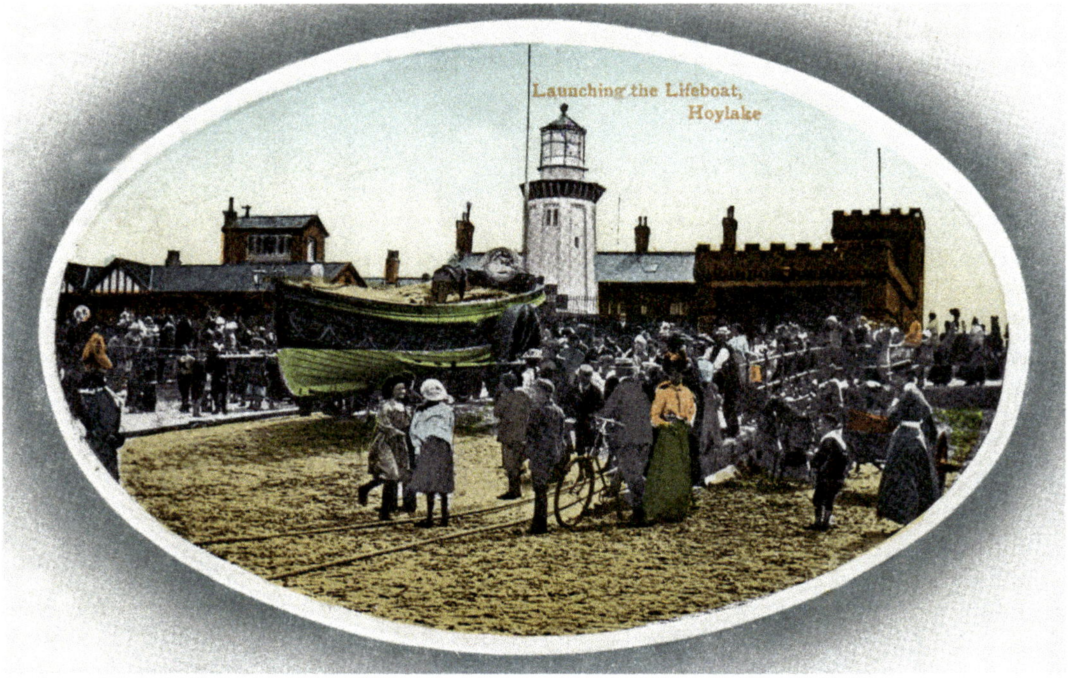

Hoylake lifeboat in 1910. The lifeboat station now has a Shannon class 13-06 RNIB lifeboat *Edmund Hawthorn Micklewood*.

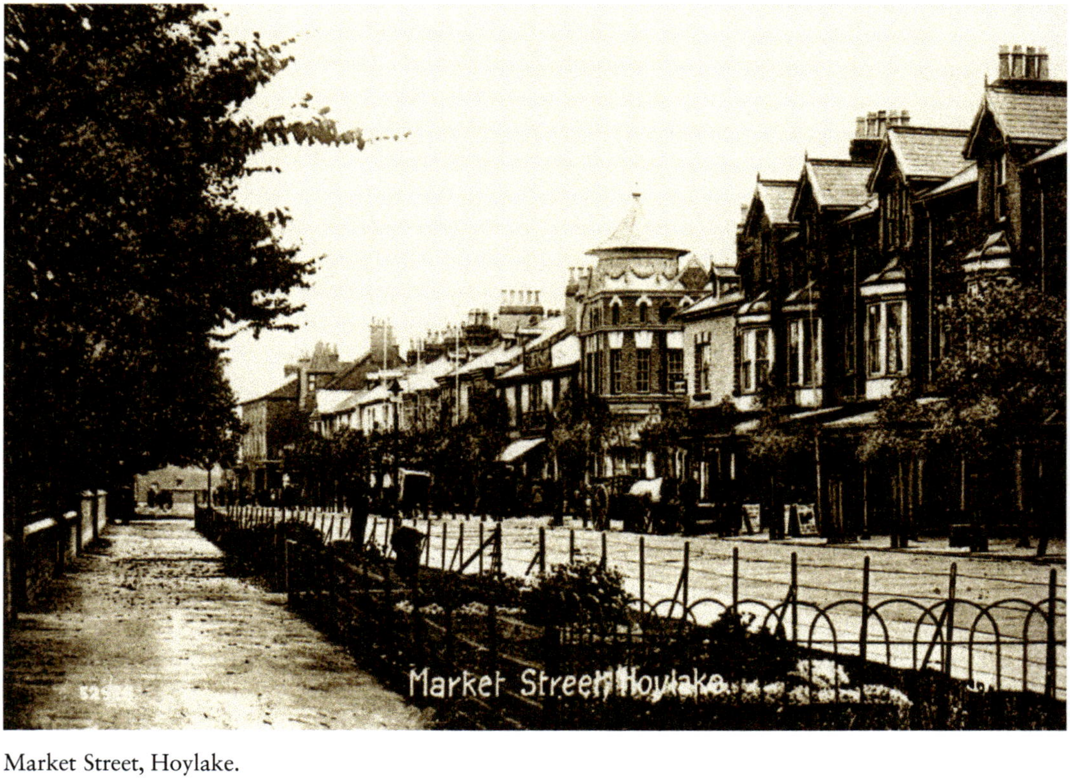

Market Street, Hoylake.

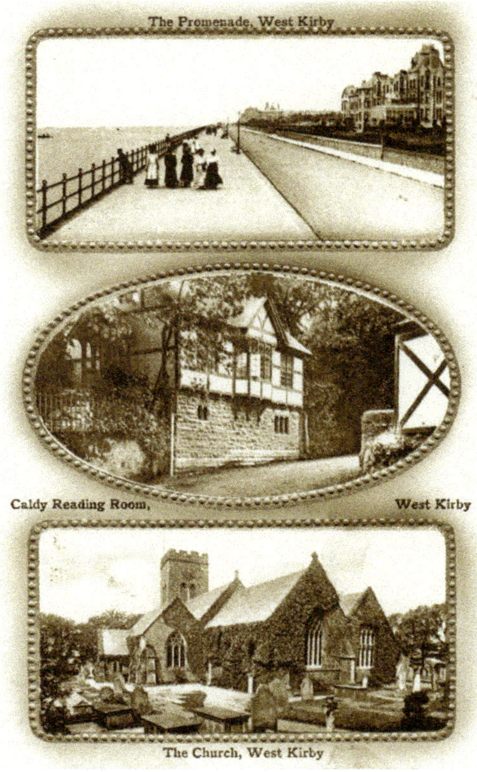

A postcard featuring West Kirby Promenade, Caldy Reading Room and West Kirby Church.

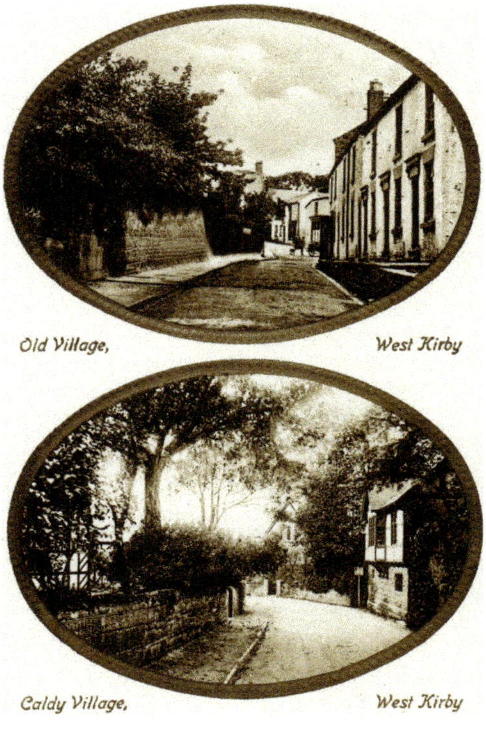

A postcard showing the Old Village, West Kirby and Caldy village.

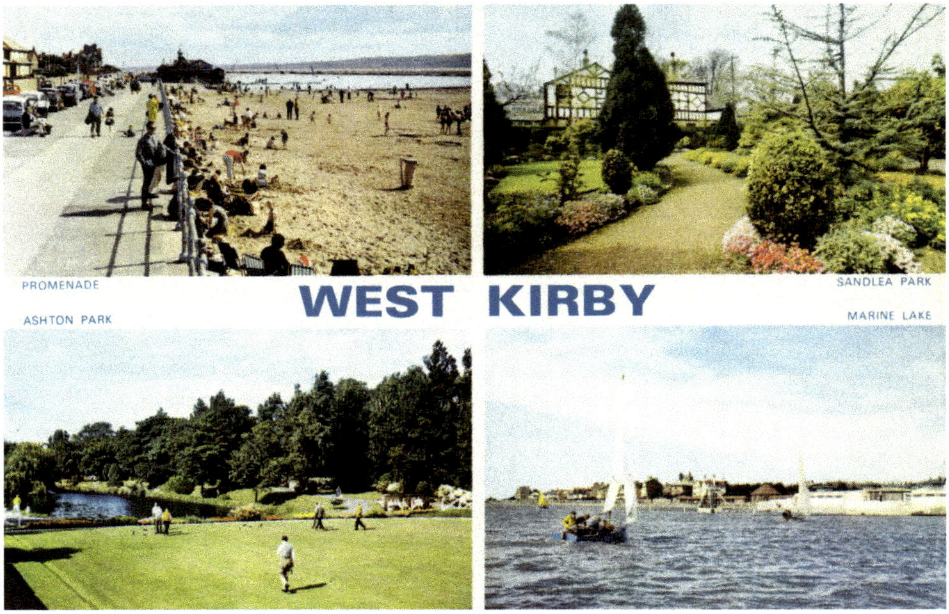

A postcard showing West Kirby Promenade, Sandlea Park, Ashton Park and the Marine Lake, West Kirby.

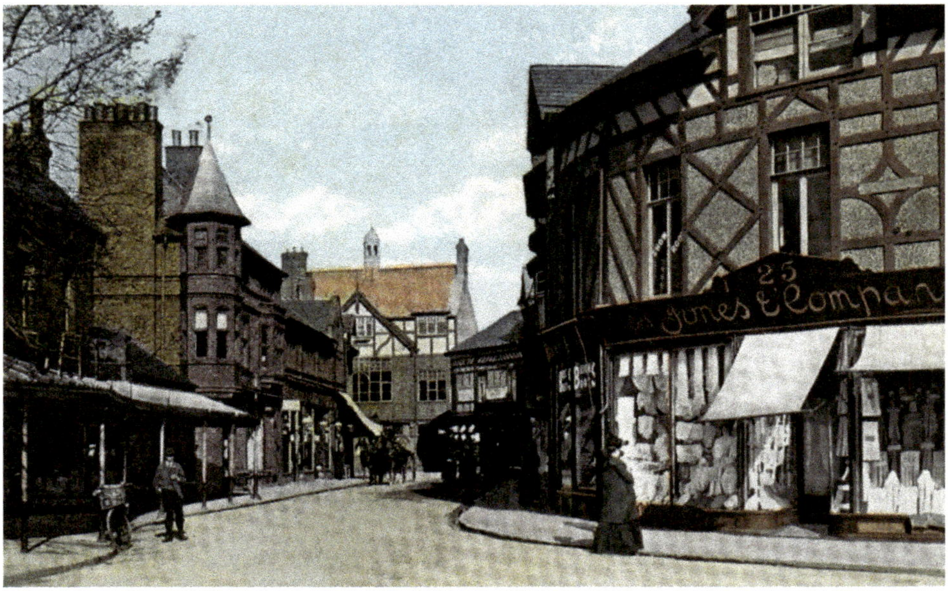

West Kirby town centre in 1912. The name West Kirby is of Viking origin – Kirkjubyr – meaning village with a church, and the 'west' distinguishes it from other towns in the area. The village was originally centred near St Bridget's Church but the main activity is now around the railway station. The original promenade wall was built in 1899 but suffered a leak in 1985. West Kirby was a township and parish within the Wirral Hundred and became part of Hoylake, West Kirby Civil Parish and Hoylake Urban District in 1894. The town contains Ashton Park, Sandlea Park and Coronation Gardens, which is located between the southern end of the promenade between South Parade and Banks Road.

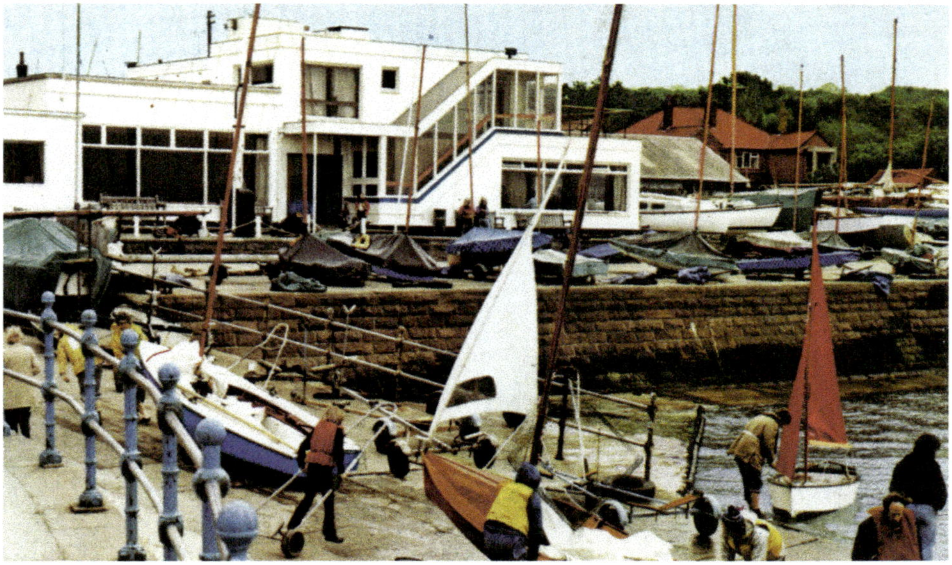

West Kirby Sailing Club. The first regatta was held on the lake in 1899 and a group of members of Hoylake Sailing Club agreed that a sailing club based in West Kirby would promote the sport of sailing and formed the West Kirby Sailing Club in 1901. The first clubhouse was at the Hydro Hotel, until a long-term lease was made on land on the foreshore near the lake in 1910. Plans for a new clubhouse were drawn up in 1952, and work began the following year. West Kirby Sailing Club now runs a number of championships and open meetings each year. The lake is now almost twice its original size and in 2015 the club held a weekend of sailing and social events to celebrate its 100th regatta.

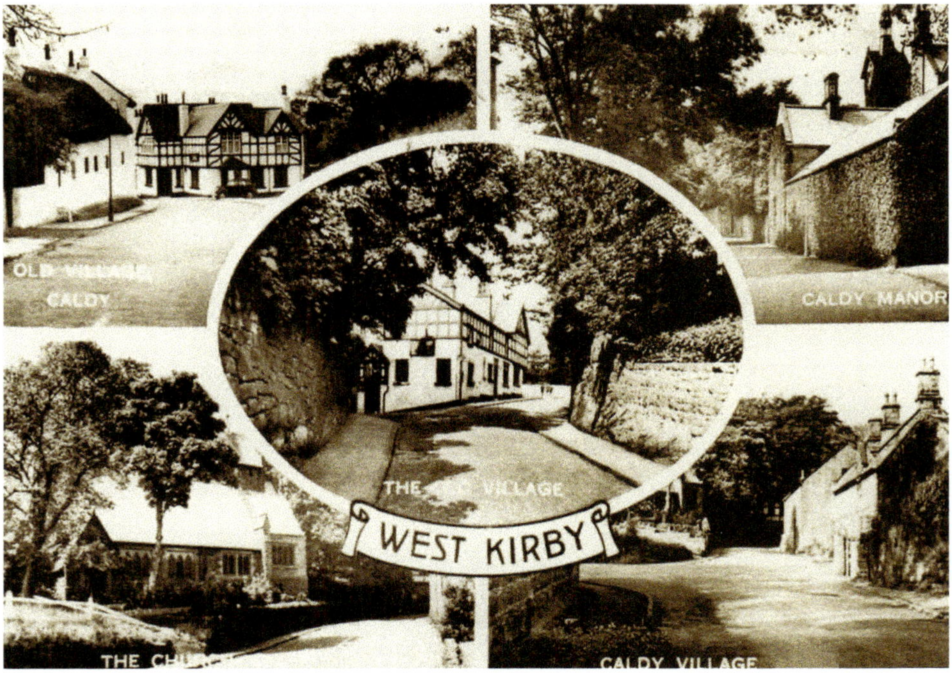

A postcard showing the Old Village, Caldy, Caldy Manor, the Church and Caldy village.

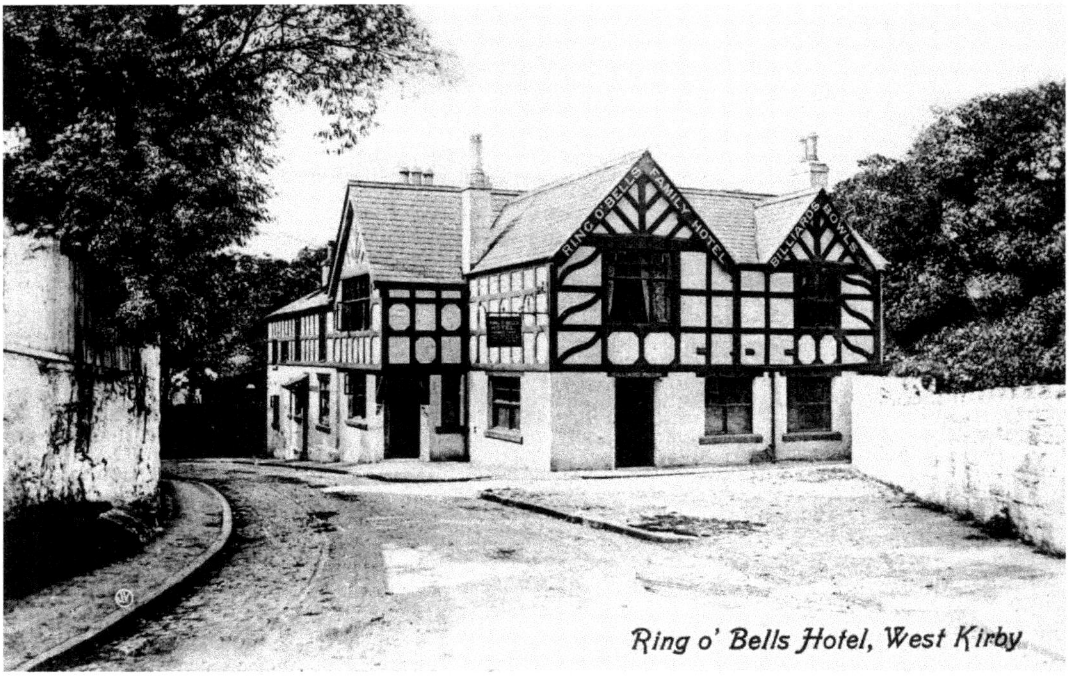

The Ring o' Bells in 1913.

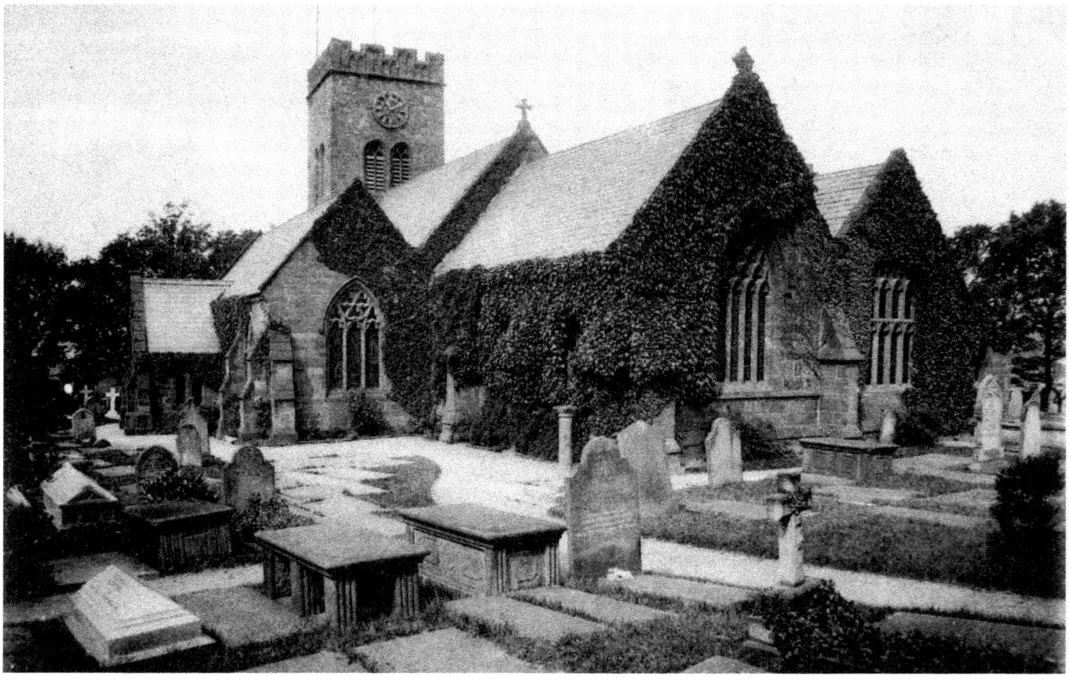

The parish church of West Kirby in 1903. St Bridget's is West Kirby's Church of England parish church, and the chancel of the present church dates back to around 1320. St Andrew's Church is West Kirby's second Church of England church, and was built as a chapel of ease for St Bridget's, gaining its own parish in 1920.

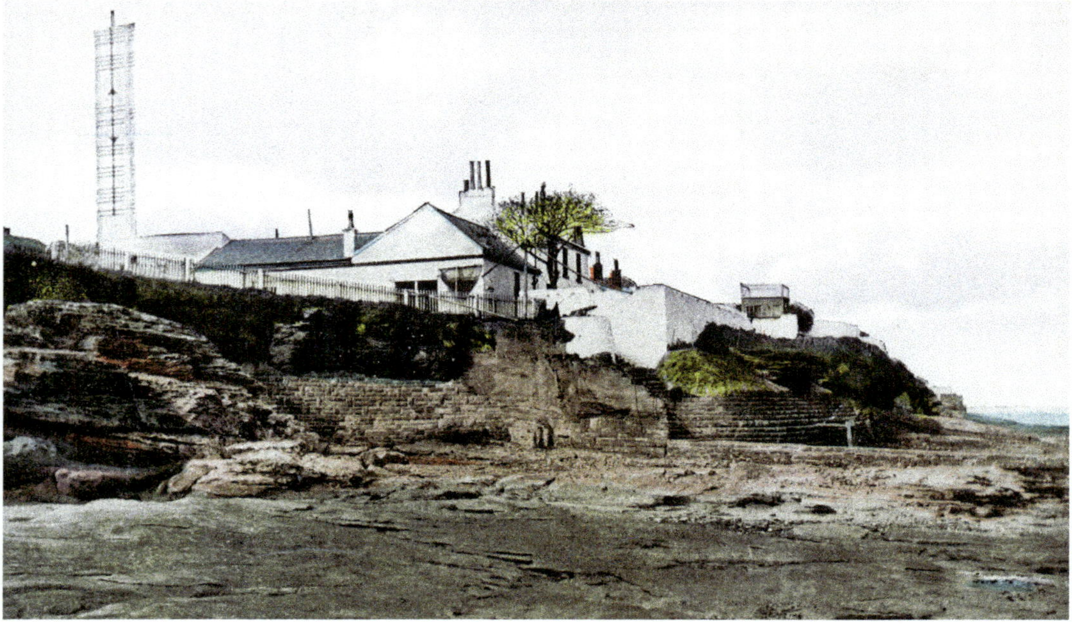

Hilbre Island, off West Kirby, originally belonged to the township of Little Meols, and has been included in the ecclesiastical parish of St Oswald's, Chester, since early times. The island formally belonged to the dean and chapter of Chester, who sold it around 1856 to the Mersey Docks and Harbour Board, who erected a telegraph station and tidal gauge. There was a cell of monks of Chester who undertook a pilgrimage to our Ladye of Hilbyri, and a charter of 1081 refers to a church on the island. A sculptured Saxon cross and other antiquities have been found. The records of the port of Chester show a number of trading vessels belonging to the island. Hilbre Island is composed of red sandstone rocks, with the existence of a bed of breccia around 1 feet thick.

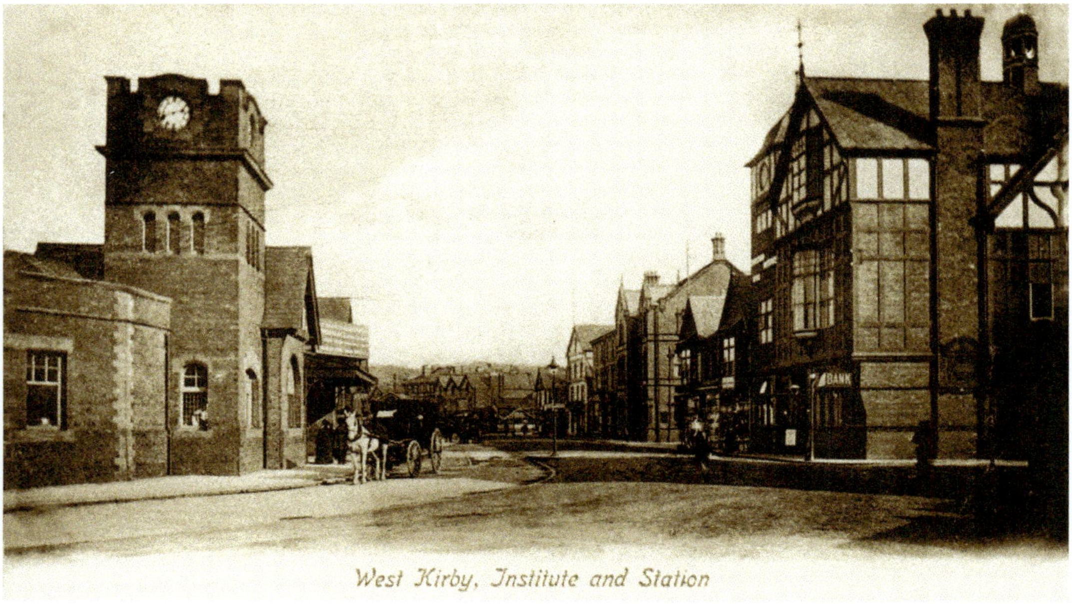

West Kirby Institute and station.

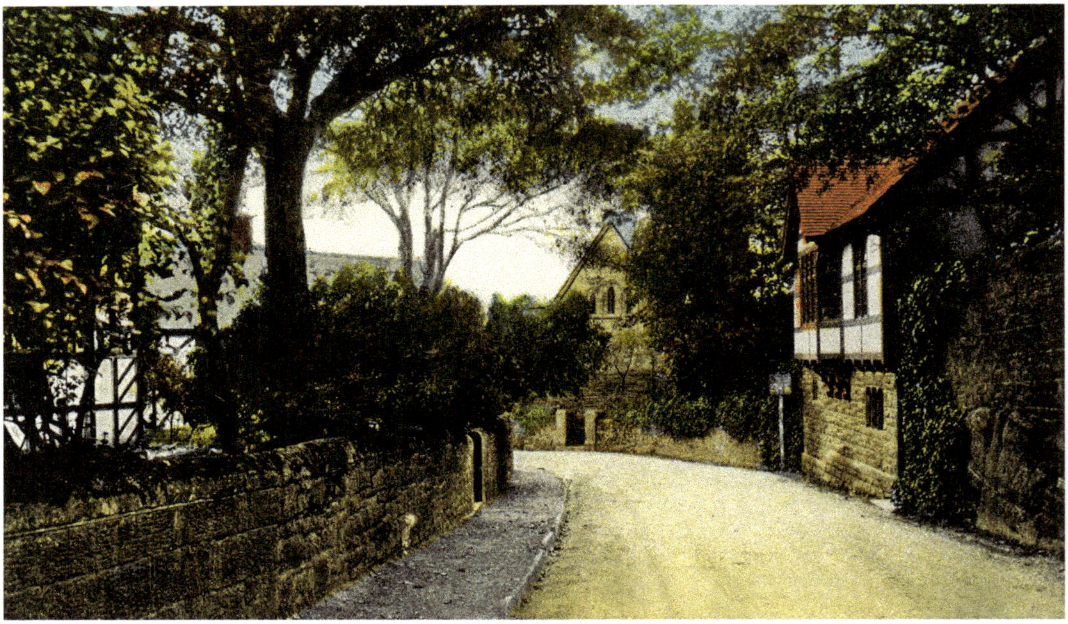

Caldy village was mentioned in the Domesday Book as owned by Hugh of Mere and is close to a large area of National Trust land. Caldy was a township in the West Kirby parish of the Wirral Hundred and was mainly a farming and agricultural village. Between 1894 and 1933 Caldy was part of Wirral Rural District, then Wirral Urban District. The Local Government Act of 1974 brought it under Wirral Borough Council.

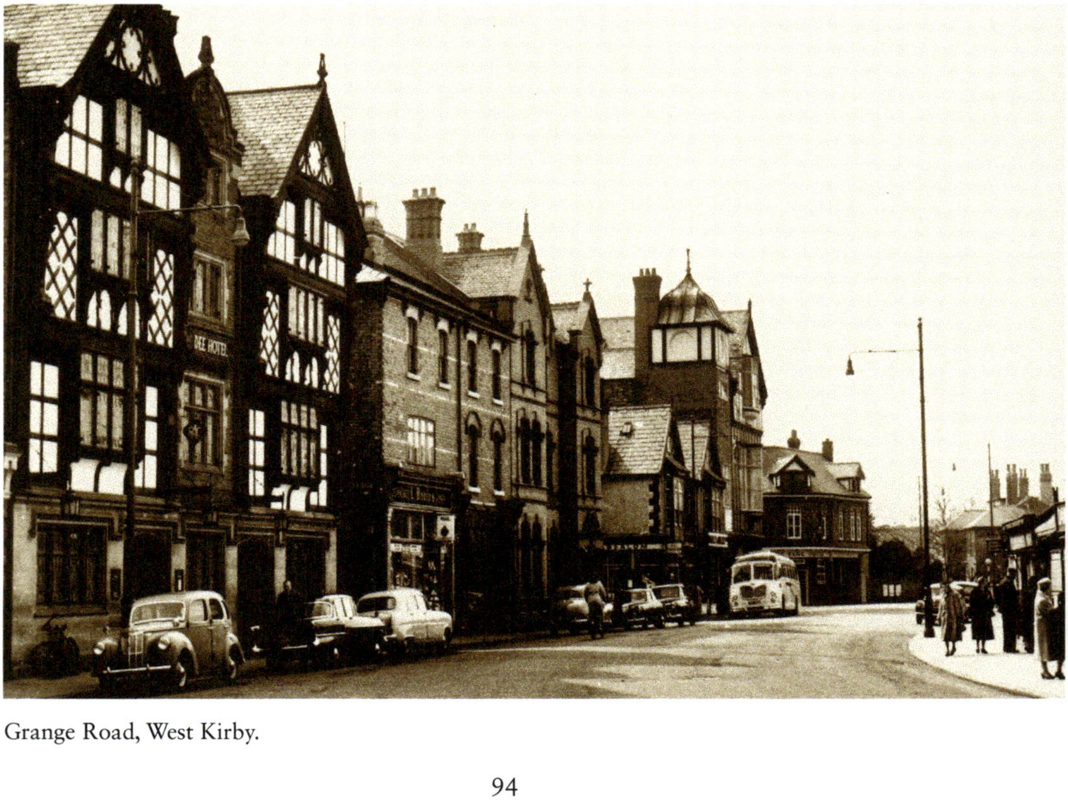

Grange Road, West Kirby.

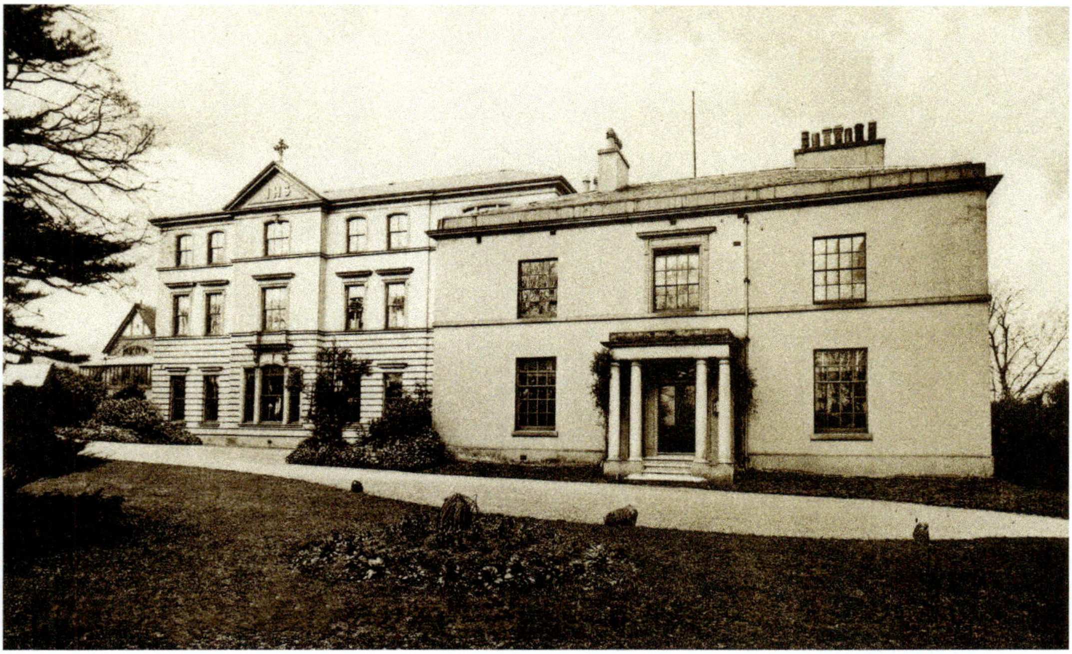

Upton Hall School was founded in 1849 as a girls' convent school by nuns of the Society of the Faithful Companions of Jesus (FCJ), a religious society founded in France by Marie Medeleine. The school was first situated in Lingdale House and moved to its present site in Upton Hall, which was then a small mansion. An extension was built, which is now known as the Upton Building, and a boarding school for girls was opened, known as Birkenhead Convent.

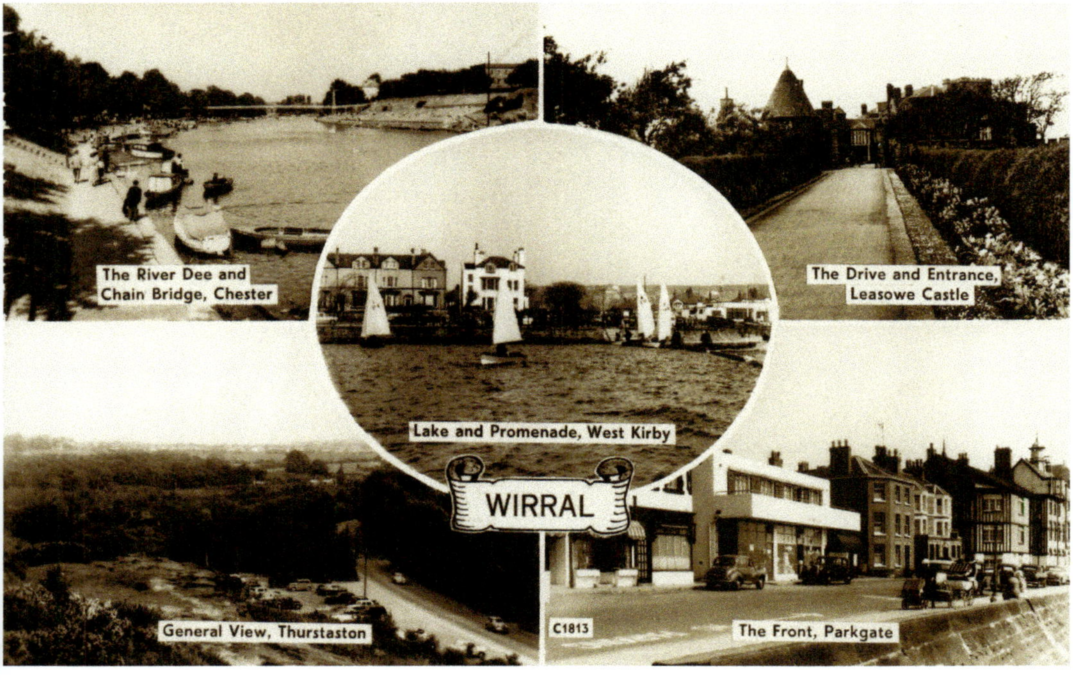

Postcard featuring Leasowe Castle, Thurstaston and Parkgate.

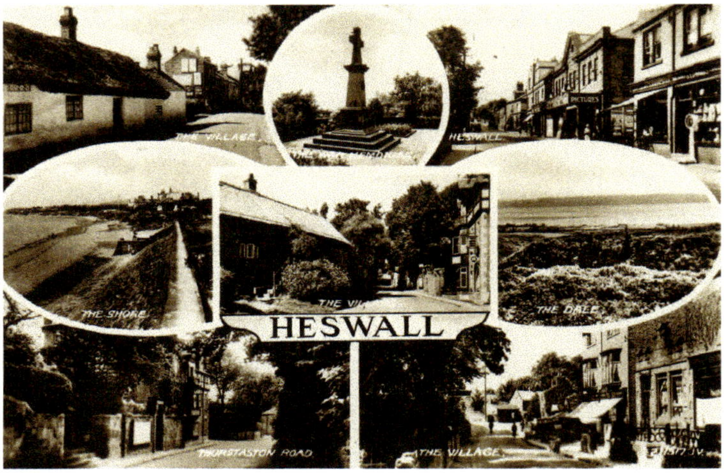

Heswall was recorded in the Domesday Book as Eswelle, owned by Robert de Rodelent, who acquired much of the land on the eastern side of the River Dee. The area became the property of Patrick de Haselwall, who was Sheriff of Cheshire. Before 1897 it was known as Hestlewelle or Hesselwelle, and the building of the railway enabled wealthy merchants from Liverpool to move to the town and commute to work at Liverpool. Gayton, Heswall, Pensby and Thingwall all became connected together by continuous housing. The Royal Liverpool Children's Hospital opened in Heswall as Liverpool County Hospital for Children in 1909, with extensive views over the River Dee. The hospital closed in 1980 and the site was developed by the building of a Tesco supermarket.

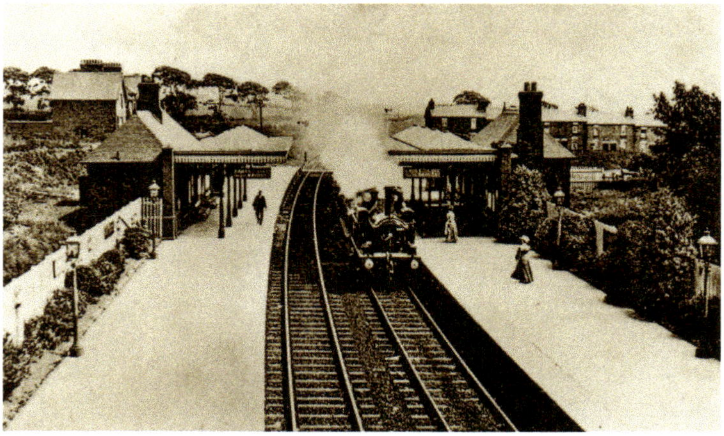

Heswall station was on the GW&LNW joint railway line, which opened in 1886 and ran from West Kirby to Hooton. The station closed to passengers in 1956 and to goods in 1962. Riverbank Close is now on the site of the old station. Rail services from Heswall are now provided from the station situated on the eastern edge of the town. The station was refurbished in 2008 and was previously known as Heswall Hills. It is on the line between Bidston and Hawarden Bridge, which was opened to goods and passengers in 1896. Heswall Hills station was opened two years later in 1 May 1898 and the line became part of the London & North Eastern Railway on 1 January 1923. Iron-ore trains operated from Bidston Dock to the John Summers Steelworks at Shotton until 1980 when the service finished. Proposals have been put forward to electrify the line, which would link with Merseyrail's electric service from Bidston station to Liverpool. From Monday to Saturday there is an hourly service between Bidston and Wrexham Central.